THE ECONOMY OF INDIA

THE INTERNATIONAL ECONOMIES SERIES

Already published:

The Japanese Economy by G. C. Allen
The Economies of West Africa by Douglas Rimmer

THE ECONOMY OF INDIA

V. N. Balasubramanyam

Senior Lecturer in Economics,
University of Lancaster

Routledge
Taylor & Francis Group

LONDON AND NEW YORK

To
Maya and Rajeev

First published 1984 by Westview Press

Published 2019 by Routledge
52 Vanderbilt Avenue, New York, NY 10017
2 Park Square, Milton Park, Abingdon, Oxon OX14 4RN

Routledge is an imprint of the Taylor & Francis Group, an informa business

LC 85–51220

Typeset by Deltatype, Ellesmere Port

ISBN 13: 978-0-367-29162-4 (hbk)
ISBN 13: 978-0-367-30708-0 (pbk)

Contents

List of Tables

List of Tables

Principal Dates

Five-Year Plans

Formation of the Planning Commission, March 1950
First Five-Year Plan (1951–6)
Second Five-Year Plan (1956–61)
Third Five-Year Plan (1961–6)
Interim Annual Plans (1966–9)
Fourth Five-Year Plan (1969–74)
Fifth Five-Year Plan (1974–9)
Sixth Five-Year Plan (1980–5)

Wars and Military Conflicts

Indo-Chinese conflict, 20 October 1962 – 21 November 1962
Indo-Pakistan conflict, 5 August 1965 – 23 September 1965
Indo-Pakistan War, 3 December 1971 – 17 December 1975

Foreword

Indian economic performance has attracted considerable commentary and controversy. Once, during the 1950s and early 1960s, the envy and role model for many developing countries, Indian developmental policies and methods have increasingly drawn critical attention as a number of other economies have registered dramatic gains in growth and in equity with different methods. An overall assessment is clearly necessary.

Dr Balasubramanyam has written a lucid and penetrating review of India's economic performance, which conveys a balanced picture while giving the reader an insight into the lively controversies that India's articulate and talented economists have continually engaged in.

Here the reader will find, for example, a detailed review of critical policy questions such as the pervasive nature of import and industrial controls and their effect on efficiency, growth and poverty, and the grand debate between the proponents of greater outward-orientation of the economy, and its opponents. In the end, Dr Balasubramanyam opts for a more open economy, with greatly reduced reliance on command instruments: but he does it fairly and judiciously, having given due consideration to the critics.

Dr Balasubramanyam's work deserves to be widely read. It will certainly be an invaluable asset to students of development economics who wish to study the Indian experience in depth. It will offer them illumination with pleasure.

Jagdish Bhagwati
New York

Preface

Books on India's economic performance and policy are not a rarity. The broad theme of much of the recent literature is India's relatively low-growth performance and the failure of her economic policy to relieve mass poverty and unemployment to any appreciable degree. A number of explanations and prescriptions for India's economic problem have been suggested. These range from critiques of the broad design of India's inward-looking development strategy to analyses of specific aspects of the economy such as the structure and performance of the agricultural sector, the size and course of public-sector investment, productive efficiency of public enterprises, and the impact of private foreign investment and foreign aid on the structure and performance of the economy. There has been an outpouring of books, monographs and articles on these and other aspects of the economy. There are, for instance, four full-length books on India's export performance and policies alone. Such is the immense volume and variety of the literature, that students of economic development attempting to gain a perspective on the Indian economy are likely to find the task forbidding.

This book is intended to help students who are trying to sift this vast literature with a view to gaining an understanding of India's economic problems and obtaining a perspective on the major policy debates. It is, therefore, in the nature of an introductory essay designed to provide a succinct non-technical exposition of India's economic performance and policies. In each of the chapters, an attempt has been made to ground the discussion in the relevant economic theory. The short annotated bibliography at the end of the book provides a guide to further reading.

In the course of writing this book I have incurred an immense intellectual debt to several people. My greatest debt is to my former teacher, Professor Jagdish Bhagwati. His incisive comments on an earlier draft have saved me from a number of conceptual and factual errors and improved the presentation of the book. I owe much to Professor Alasdair MacBean and Dr Peter McCawley for their detailed comments on an earlier draft; and to Dr D. P. Chaudhuri, Dr R. M. Sundrum and Professors Max Corden and Peter Bauer for their comments on parts of the book. I am also indebted to colleagues D. T. Nguyen and O. M. Westall for discussions on the chapters on agriculture and population. I should also thank the publisher's reader for his perceptive comments which have added to both the substance and the presentation of the book. I would also like to acknowledge my gratitude to Dr Robert Baldock, Academic Director of Weidenfeld and Nicolson, for his encouragement and patience in awaiting the completion of the book. I should add that none of these people are in any way responsible for either the errors or the views expressed in the book.

I am grateful to Miss Jane Peill for patiently typing the several drafts of the book.

V. N. Balasubramanyam
Lancaster

1 Introduction

India evokes many images. The familiar one is that of a big, poor democratic country. One in seven of the world's population lives in India, and with a total population of 690 million she ranks second only to China in absolute numbers. She is the seventh biggest country in the world with a total land area of 3.2 million square kilometres. The regions that compose India are extremely heterogenous in their resource endowments, climate, languages and infrastructure. India possesses a wide and varied resource base, including large reserves of iron ore and coal. Although domestic sources supply only a third of India's oil requirements at present, she is reported to possess considerable reserves of crude oil and natural gas. And she is endowed with an efficient Civil Service framework, an inheritance from the days of the British Raj, preserved and nurtured over the past three decades.

Another familiar image of India, somewhat tarnished by the emergency régime in the mid-seventies, is that of the world's most populous democracy; a constitutional democracy which incorporates both the Westminster-style parliamentary government and the US-style federalist structure. While the central parliament is supreme in the spheres of defence, foreign policy and general economic policy, there is also a devolution of certain powers to the states. These include the rights to levy taxes on land and agricultural income. The states are also entitled to grants-in-aid and developmental assistance from the central government, which has the sole right to levy taxes on income and foreign trade.

The triad of democracy, socialism and economic planning have been the declared cornerstones of India's economic and political philosophy ever since her inception in 1947 as an independent sovereign state. The principal architect of democratic socialism and economic planning in India was Jawaharlal Nehru, her first Prime

Minister. A product of Harrow, Cambridge and the Inner Temple, natural scientist by training, lawyer by profession and a historian and man of letters, Nehru's ideas on democracy and socialism were influenced by his Western education and his sense of history. To Nehru, socialism was the outcome of an ongoing historical process. And it meant the pursuit of egalitarian objectives in conjunction with political democracy. He saw socialism as interdependent with modernization and industrialization and equated with economic planning.

Since 1950, India's approach to economic development has been within a framework of planning. But centralized planning in India has not been equated with the suppression of private enterprise. Although there is a large and growing public sector, India's basic approach to economic organization has been that of a mixed economy. The State does own and manage several key industries including steel, coal and fertilizers; and banking and life insurance in the service sector are under State investment. But in several other sectors, State enterprises coexist with privately-owned enterprises; and a large chunk of economic activity, including agriculture, is not encroached upon by the State. This philosophy of a mixed economy has been the result of both pragmatic and political considerations. Jawaharlal Nehru's statement to the India Parliament in 1956 sums up admirably the pragmatic considerations underlying the mixed economy approach: 'I can understand "prevent that, control that, plan for that"; but where there is such a vast field to cover, it is foolish to take charge of the whole field when you are totally incapable of using the whole area yourself. Therefore, you must not only permit the private sector, but, I say, encourage it in its own field.'[1] It should, however, be noted that over the years, the State has sought increasingly to regulate the activities of the private sector through an extensive system of controls, including licensing and price controls.

India's sheer size and diversity, her commitment to democracy and the philosophy of a mixed economy have all exacted a price; relatively slow and chequered economic progress. Size, though it may confer advantages such as a large potential market, also makes policy formulation, coordination and implementation so much more difficult. The need to forge compromises, coalesce divergent interest groups and maintain parity between different sectors and regions of the economy is ever-present in all economies, irrespective of their economic and political ideologies. And in heeding them, economic efficiency may have to be sacrificed. But these problems pose a severe challenge to a nascent democracy with a federalist structure and a 'mixed' economy. The thought that India's commitment to democratic socialism, though laudable, may have exacted a price in the form of economic inefficiencies cannot be entirely dismissed.

The one compelling image of India, though, is that of an abysmally poor country. In terms of per capita income she ranks sixty-sixth among a group of seventy-seven developing countries. And with a per capita income of US $260 in 1981, she is classed among the low-income developing countries in the international league tables.[2] But it could be argued that per capita income expressed in dollars is a misleading indicator of levels of living. As often noted, the official exchange rates at which incomes in domestic currencies are converted into dollars may be overvalued and may not reflect the true purchasing power of the domestic currencies. Furthermore, per capita income figures say little about the distribution of income.

But several other socio-economic indicators of levels of living also point to a grim picture of widespread poverty. One such indicator of the extent of poverty relates to the nutritional norm of the minimum number of calories people need for a healthy existence. There is a great deal of controversy among Indian economists on the choice of this norm and the estimates of poverty based on it. But they are agreed that on a conservative estimate, more than 40 per cent of the Indian population – or a staggering 200 million people – live in absolute poverty. In other words, they cannot afford the incomes necessary to purchase the minimum calorie-equivalent amounts of food. The incidence of poverty is highest in rural India. More than 70 per cent of the population live in rural areas, and it is estimated than 40 to 50 per cent of the rural population can be designated as absolutely poor: those who cannot afford the nutritionally-determined minimum food requirements.[3]

Most other indicators paint an equally depressing picture. Although life expectancy at birth has gone up from thirty-three years in the early fifties to fifty-two years in 1983, it is still low relative to that of other Asian countries with per capita incomes comparable to that of India, such as Sri Lanka (Table 1.1). The infant mortality rate at 121 per thousand live births is also relatively

Table 1.1 Economic and Social Indicators: India and Selected Developing Countries

Country	Per capita GNP (US $) 1981	Average annual growth rate of per capital GNP (%) 1960–81	Adult literacy rate (%) 1980	Life expectancy at birth (years) 1981	Infant mortality rate 1981	Number enrolled in primary schools as percentage of age group 1980	Number enrolled in higher education as percentage of population aged 20–24 1979
India	260	1.4	36	52	121	76	9
China	300	5.0	69	67	71	117	1
Sri Lanka	300	2.5	85	69	43	100	3
Pakistan	350	2.8	24	50	123	57	2
Indonesia	530	4.1	62	54	105	98	—
South Korea	1,700	6.9	93	66	33	107	14
Malaysia	1,840	4.3	60	65	30	92	3
Thailand	770	4.6	86	63	53	96	13
Kenya	420	2.9	47	56	85	108	1
Mexico	2,250	3.8	83	66	54	120	15
Brazil	2,220	5.1	76	64	75	93	12
Colombia	1,380	3.2	81	63	55	128	11

Source: *World Development Report* (World Bank, 1983).

high. Again, the proportion of children in the relevant age groups enrolled in primary and secondary schools has increased appreciably over the years. Even so, India's record on elementary education is relatively poor. It is disconcerting too, to note that the adult literacy rate for the country as a whole is no more than 36 per cent; in other words, two-thirds of the population above the age of fifteen cannot read or write.

Another significant indicator of the level of living standards is the opportunities for employment. Unemployment as a percentage of the total labour force in 1980 is estimated at 8 per cent. This figure may be no higher than that for most other developing countries, but in absolute numbers it amounts to a staggering 12 million. Indeed, it is estimated that if account is also taken of the number underemployed, the rate of unemployment may be as high as 12 per cent of the total labour force of 268 million people, or a total number of 30 million.[4] As the Planning Commission notes, 'the absolute numbers unemployed is staggeringly large, and larger than any country in the world for which any statistics are available.'[5]

Another feature of the India social landscape is the wide disparity in incomes and standards of living between the various regions. Available estimates show that in the year 1978 in twelve states of the Indian Union, accounting for 65 per cent of the population, per capita national product was below the national average of Rs 1,005. On the basis of net domestic product figures, the states of Punjab, Harayana, Maharashtra and Gujarat are assigned to the high-income bracket, while the states of Bihar, Uttar Pradesh, Jammu and Kashmir, Assam and Orrissa belong to the low-income group.[6] The economic distance between the high-income and the low-incomes states is indicated by the fact that affluent Punjab at one extreme has a per capita net domestic product of Rs 1,688, whereas the abysmally poor state of Bihar at the other extreme has a per capita net domestic product of Rs 700. Regional economic imbalances are also indicated by the fact that Gujarat, Maharashtra, Tamil Nadu and West Bengal, with only 30 per cent of the total population, account for 60 per cent of the value added and 49 per cent of the total labour force in manufacturing. Again, in the agriculturally developed Punjab the value of agricultural output per head of rural population is as high as Rs 3,361, compared with a low of Rs 888 in Rajasthan.

One could argue that all this is a partial and woefully incomplete image of India; it hardly does justice to the real achievements of the country in the face of heavy odds and severe constraints. At the time of independence in 1947, India inherited an impoverished economy from the British. By most accounts it was not only poor, but also stagnant. Over the previous three decades of British rule, growth of output of food was negligible; output of food per head of population, in fact, declined despite the relatively low growth of population of 1 per cent per year. The rate of growth of national output during the three decades preceding independence was a mere 1 per cent, resulting in a complete absence of growth of per capita income. The incidence of communicable diseases such as smallpox and tuberculosis was widespread, and the expectation of life at birth was a mere thirty-three years. More than 80 per cent of the children in the age group 6–11 had no schooling. Although there did exist a modern industrial sector, it was mostly confined to agriculture-based industries such as jute textiles and cotton textiles, and accounted for a mere 9 per cent of the total labour force. Indeed, it has been argued that British economic policy paid little heed to the development of traditional industries and may have been responsible for their demise.[7]

It should also be noted that since independence, the country has had to cope with the aftermath of the two military conflicts with China in 1964 and Pakistan in 1966, the political disruption caused by the emergency régime of 1973–4, and the severe droughts in 1965 and 1966.

Judged against this background, India's economic performance during the past three decades (1950–80) appears remarkable. The average rate of growth of net national product per annum over this period was around 3.5 per cent, and was comfortably ahead of the population growth rate of around 2 per cent per annum. Again, the rate of growth of agricultural output of around 2.5 per cent per annum over the period 1950–80, though inadequate in many respects, is a remarkable achievement compared to the virtual stagnation experienced by the agricultural sector during the last three decades of the British Raj. Indeed more often than not in recent years India has been able to reduce her dependence on imports of food appreciably, and achieve near self-sufficiency.

The most impressive achievement of India, however, is in the field of industrialization. Perhaps the most arresting image of India since independence is that of a rapidly industrializing country. In the year 1979–80, industrial output accounted for 24 per cent of India's total net domestic product; the rate of growth of industrial output, though it has decelerated to around 3.5 per cent per annum since the mid-sixties, was as high as 7.4 per cent per annum during the period 1951–65. India is ranked fifteenth among the nations of the world in terms of industrial output, and her recent entry into the world markets as an exporter of non-traditional manufactures, notably engineering goods, has elevated her to the ranks of the developing countries collectively labelled as the Newly Industrializing Countries (NICs). Another feature of India's manufacturing sector is the wide range of goods it produces, from nuclear reactors to textiles and leather goods.

India also ranks high among the nations of the world in her endowments of technical and scientific personnel. As Amartya Sen remarks, 'in the number of students enrolled in higher education as a percentage of the population aged twenty to twenty-four, not only is India a considerable distance ahead of any other country of comparable income level, but there is in fact no country with even twice India's per capita income that comes anywhere close to its higher education ratio.'[8] In China, for example, as Sen points out, the number of students in institutions of higher education is about 1 per cent of the corresponding age group, whereas in India the ratio is 8 per cent.

The record of India's growth and industrialization in the post-independence period is no doubt impressive, but it is of little comfort to the millions of people who live in abject poverty, bereft of the basic necessities of life. The industrialization the country has achieved may be a source of national pride, but it offers little consolation to the millions of people who are unemployed; and the fact that nearly two-thirds of the adult population cannot read or write casts a dark shadow on India's achievements in the sphere of higher education.

It should also be noted that India is not the only developing country that has achieved a relatively high rate of growth of national output in the post-colonial period. Several others have not only achieved much higher rates of growth than India, but also a superior record in combating hunger, poverty and unemployment. As Jagdish Bhagwati, writing in the early seventies, remarked, 'It is now clear that the Indian economic performance, while a definite improvement over that of the pre-independence period, is less than satisfactory whether one takes the "capitalistic" index of growth rates of income or the "socialist" indices of eradication of poverty and reduction of income inequality. International comparisons show that our growth rate during the last two decades since planning began has been bettered by a number of other countries of different sizes, political persuasions and economic ideologies; Taiwan, South Korea, Brazil and Israel are only a few of the examples that may be mentioned."[9]

The central issue, then, is why has India not done better and where have her economic policies gone wrong? This is an issue which has aroused a great many controversies among Indian economists. These debates span a wide range, from issues relating to the role of the State in the development process and the basic strategy of development, to those concerning resource mobilization and allocation.

Prominent among these debates are those concerning the strategy of inward-looking development centred on industrialization which India has pursued, with its attendant implications for resource allocation. The strategy took shape with the inception of the Second Five-Year Plan (1956–61), and although there have been significant modifications in specific policies since then, the basic strategy has remained intact. As is well known, the strategy emphasized the role of investment in the development process, centring on the production of capital goods. Resource allocation and foreign trade policies were accordingly geared to the promotion of industrialization with emphasis on 'heavy industry'. During the fifties the debate centred on the economic rationale for the emphasis placed on investment and the production of investment goods. Significant in this context was the view that the Second Five-Year Plan had erred in over-emphasizing investments in heavy industry and capital goods, to the relative neglect of investments in agriculture and the production of consumer goods. According to this view, increased production and demand for consumer goods would have stimulated productive efficiency, employment and savings, and a capital goods sector would have emerged in due course as a response to the demands created by the consumer goods sector.[10]

A variant of this view, expressed in more recent writings, is that while the planners were justified in emphasizing the key role of investment goods in India's economic development, they have erred in paying too little attention to the wage goods constraint. According to this view, increased money incomes alone would not solve the problem of poverty. What is required is the production of wage goods – consumer goods, including food, which the poor buy with their wages. And the major shortcoming of India's economic strategy is 'the failure of economic policy to either identify the wage goods constraint or give adequate attention to the allocation of resources to increasing the production of wage goods . . .'[11]

There are several explanations for this failure to identify the wage goods constraint and increase the production of wage goods. Most of them centre on the insufficient recognition of problems of agricultural development, and the failure of the government to mobilize resources for development effectively. Admittedly, growth of agricultural output has been inadequate, and the balance between the growth of food production and the growth of population continues to be precarious. Even so, as widely noted, the problem of poverty and hunger arises not so much because there is a basic shortage of food as such, but because the poor lack the incomes to purchase it.[12] Indeed, it may not be far-fetched to argue that in a productive economy with increasing opportunities for employment and incomes, food can be imported if domestic agriculture is incapable of meeting the demand.

Again, the prevailing pattern of income distribution skewed in favour of the rich may be a factor of importance in the low growth in output of wage goods. In a mixed economy such as India, with a sizeable private sector, the government may not be able to exercise complete control over the pattern of production of consumer goods. The pattern of production would respond to the signals provided by the market, and the underlying pattern of income distribution would determine these market signals. If the income distribution is skewed in favour of the upper-income groups, demand and resources are likely to be diverted to the production of 'inessential' luxury consumer goods demanded by the rich, as opposed to the essential wage goods demanded by the poor. But why is it that the income distribution is skewed, and what are the factors responsible for the low growth in employment opportunities and incomes for the poor?

There is a substantial body of evidence in support of the proposition that the main reason (though not the only one) for the low growth in employment and incomes and the widening disparities in income between rich and poor is the inward-looking strategy of development pursued by India, centred on import-substituting industrialization. This is not to say that the country was wrong to pursue a policy of industrialization; nor that the adoption of a philosophy of import-substituting industrialization in itself was a folly. But it is the case that the policy-makers were over-zealous in pursuing the policy, in the course of which they paid scant attention to the role of the market and the price mechanism in the efficient allocation of resources. Instead they relied on an excessively detailed and cumbersome panoply of bureaucratic controls over foreign trade and resource allocation to promote the objective of industrialization. These controls have included not only quantitative restrictions on imports but also a detailed system of industrial licensing and price controls, designed to regulate the activities of the private sector. The social costs and economic inefficiencies perpetrated by these policies have been widely noted. The low growth in incomes and employment opportunities, increased concentration of incomes and economic power, and resultant failure of the economy to generate an increased demand for and production of wage goods are all largely to be traced to this *modus operandi* of import-substituting industrialization. In recent years, there has been a move towards a more liberal economic régime emphasizing economic efficiency in resource allocation; but it appears to have yielded few dividends, maybe because the economy has yet to recover from the strains imposed on it by earlier policies. This is a theme that is developed at greater length later in the book, especially in Chapters 4, 6 and 7.

All in all, India provides a rich tapestry of economic and social milieu. The fifteen officially recognized languages spoken by the population, with their many dialects; the caste system, in some respects peculiar to India; her hoary history with its rich culture and traditions; all have been of allure to the sociologist and the cultural anthropologist.

But it is India's economic problems, policies, performance and prospects that have dominated most discussions. Given the immense variety, not to speak of the magnitude of problems she poses, it is not surprising that every aspect of India's economy has been the subject of extensive research, and that she has been the test case for a variety of models and themes of development. India's teeming millions and the patterns of their livelihood have been the focus of demographers and economists alike. Their studies have provided rich insights into the inter-relationship between population growth and development, socio-economic causes of population growth, costs and benefits of family planning programmes and methods of evaluating them. An outstanding example of this genre of studies is Robert Cassen's admirable review of India's population problems, including projections of future population size, an evaluation of the thesis that children could be a good investment and an analysis of the effects of population growth on rate of growth of national product. Investigation into the livelihood patterns of India's population, besides providing a wealth of information, has brought into sharp focus the conceptual problems in measuring unemployment and poverty. Well known in this context are studies by Pranab Baradhan, B. S. Minhas, V. M. Dandekar and N. Rath, involving attempts at defining poverty norms.[13]

Much of the pioneering work on agriculture in developing countries pertains to India. Indian agriculture was the focus of the celebrated debates in the sixties on the doctrine of zero marginal productivity of labour, the supply response of farmers in poor countries to economic incentives and the hypothesis that farmers in traditional agriculture are efficient but poor.[14] Equally significant are the empirical studies on the relationship between size of farms and productivity, the terms of trade between agriculture and industry and their implications for sectoral resource transfers and inter-sectoral growth, and the effects of the Green Revolution on growth and welfare. Notable amongst these studies are those by A. M. Khusro on size of farms and productivity, work by Francine Frankel and Pranab Bardhan on the impact of the Green Revolution on income distribution and employment, and Ashok Mitra's analysis of the terms of trade and class conflict.[15]

It is, however, India's industrialization experience that has attracted most attention. Much of the debate in this area is concerned with India's strategy of import-substituting industrialization, with its attendant industrial licensing and resource allocation policies. Major spin-offs from this debate include insights into the impact of different sorts of foreign trade régimes on growth, employment and income distribution, and the conceptual and methodological problems involved in measuring the degree of protection afforded by tariff and quota régimes. Outstanding in this class of studies are the incisive analysis of the effects of India's system of economic controls on economic efficiency by Jagdish Bhagwati and Padma Desai, and the analysis of India's foreign trade régimes by Bhagwati and T. N. Srinivasan.[16] In addition, there are a number of studies assessing the performance of India's public enterprises and the role of small-scale industries in the Indian economy.

Export pessimism has for long pervaded Indian economic policy. That India's exports were faced with an external demand constraint was one of the professed reasons for the pursuit of an inward-looking strategy of development in the early years of planning. On a more general plane, it is often argued that India is a continental economy in the style of the United States and there is little reason for her to depend on foreign trade. These strictures and generalizations, however, have not precluded extensive investigations into India's export trade structure and performance. A number of studies have investigated the supply and demand constraints facing India's exports at the disaggregated commodity level. These also include analysis of the effects of the 1966 devaluation on India's exports, the economic costs and benefits of the complex system of export incentives provided by the government, and the bilateral trading arrangements of India with the countries of the Eastern Bloc.[17]

Self-reliance, often interpreted as self-sustained growth without foreign aid, has been a major objective of Indian economic policy. Nevertheless, India has received substantial amounts of foreign aid, although in per capita terms her aid receipts compare poorly with those of many other aid recipients in the developing world. The role of foreign aid in India's development effort has also been the subject of extensive investigation, including study of the impact of aid on domestic savings and investment, effects of tied aid on development, and the economics of P. L. 480 food aid, especially significant in the Indian context.[18]

Relative to some of the Latin American and East Asian developing countries, private foreign investment has not been of much significance to India; but what there is tends to be concentrated in the technologically intensive manufacturing industries. And India has been a significant importer of technology through technical collaboration agreements with foreign-owned firms. Once again, there is a sizeable body of literature on the role of foreign private capital and technology in India's development effort. The well-known debates on the appropriateness of imported developed-country technology for developing countries have been rehearsed in the Indian context too. Recently India has joined the ranks of technology exporters. Although mostly confined to the Middle East and other Asian countries, India's role as an exporter of technology has attracted the attention of researchers.[19]

Alongside this flurry of studies on various aspects of the Indian economy is the rich and controversial literature on Indian planning models and methodology. Indeed, India has been a pioneer in development planning among the developing countries. The renowned Mahalanobis model, which formed the basis for the Second Five-Year Plan of India, was one of the first attempts at providing a comprehensive methodological framework for planning development. A number of studies set in motion by the Mahalanobis model, criticizing its internal consistency and the validity of the premises on which it was based, have enriched the literature on economic planning.[20] Again, long before considerations of equity and poverty became major issues in development economics, Indian economists were thinking in terms of 'planning for a minimum level of living.'[21] In addition there are also a number of econometric studies and mathematical models on such aspects as savings behaviour in India, and the demand for money.

Given that India's development effort has not been a success story, has all this intellectual fervour been pointless? Do the Indian economists deserve the acerbic comment of a recent observer of the Indian scene, that 'Indian economists are a cheerful, convivial lot, who see much of each other, like to talk shop, and amuse themselves by playing what amount to economic war games, constructing and tearing down theoretical models. In this activity human problems tend to disappear.'[22] This, although it makes for attractive journalistic copy, is much too harsh a judgment on an effort which has put India at the forefront of intellectual work on development, with contributions from both Indian and Western economists. Indian economists, like their counterparts elsewhere, do play economic war-games: but this has generated as much light as heat. Moreover, an endeavour which has for the most part concerned itself with identifying the extent and causes of poverty could hardly be accused of losing sight of human problems. In any case, development effort is a learning process, with debate and discussion being an integral part of the process; given India's sheer size and diversity, there has been much to learn.

This book is a report on what we have learned about India's development problems over the past three decades. Drawing upon some of the rich and varied literature on the Indian economy, it describes and analyses India's economic policy and performance.

The scheme of the book is as follows: Chapter 2 reviews India's population structure, the pattern of livelihood of her teeming millions and the extent of poverty in the country. Chapter 3 analyses the growth performance and the structure of India's national product. This is followed in Chapter 4 by an analysis of the trends in savings and capital formation in the Indian economy. The structure and performance of India's agricultural sector, including a discussion of the Green Revolution, forms the subject of Chapter 5. Chapter 6 is devoted to a discussion of India's industrialization experience. It analyses India's industrial structure and growth performance, summarizes the recent literature on the costs of import-substituting industrialization and evaluates the policy debates on India's industrialization programme. Chapters 7, 8 and 9 are devoted to an analysis of India's external economic relations.

While Chapter 7 discusses the role of private foreign investment and technology imports in the Indian economy, Chapter 8 reviews the role of foreign aid in India's development process. Chapter 9 analyses India's foreign trade with special reference to the export sector, and Chapter 10 draws together the main conclusions of the book.

2

The Teeming Millions and their Livelihood

The one image of India that dwarfs all others is that of a seething mass of humanity living in abject poverty. The allegories often employed to portray the sheer size and the rate of growth of India's population are familiar: the land of every seventh person in the world; a country with more people than Africa and Latin America put together; thirteen million babies – or the size of Australia's population – added on each year. Equally staggering is the picture of India's poverty: of the total number of 800 million absolutely poor in the world (those receiving incomes less than US $150 per year), more than half are Indian.[1]

It is widely believed that there is a causal relationship between population growth and India's poverty, and that population control is central to the solution of the development problem. Admittedly, the sheer size of India's population and the relatively high growth-rate of her population in recent years have added to the complexity of the development problem. The interrelationship between population and development, however, is complex. It is a matter of dispute whether the growth of population is the cause or a consequence of under-development. Nor are there any settled conclusions on vital issues such as the effects of population growth on savings, capital formation and technical progress. Equally in dispute are the factors that contribute to a decline in fertility rates. This chapter reviews the debate on the interrelationship between population and development in the context of India.

Size and structure of India's population

The first Indian census was taken in 1871. It is estimated that at that time the population of India's present boundaries was around 209 million. The 1981 census put India's total population at 684 million.

While the period between 1871 and 1941 was marked by unsteady growth, there has occurred a remarkable acceleration in the growth of population since 1941, especially over the last twenty years (Table 2.1).

Table 2.1 India's Population

Year	Millions	Decennial Growth Rate
1871	209.1	
1881	210.9	8.6
1891	231.4	9.7
1901	238.4	3.0
1911	252.1	5.8
1921	251.3	−3.1
1931	279.0	11.0
1941	318.7	14.2
1951	361.7	13.5
1961	439.2	21.4
1971	547.8	24.7
1981	683.8	24.8

Source: R. Cassen, *India: Population, Economy, Society* (Macmillan, 1978), p. 7 and *Census Report* (1981).

As Robert Cassen remarks, India's population growth prior to 1941 was nothing unusual compared with what was happening simultaneously elsewhere. But since then there appears to have occurred a parting of ways, with the rate of growth of population decelerating in most developed countries, and accelerating in India and most developing countries. Since 1921 the annual average rate of growth of India's population increased by about one quarter of 1 per cent every decade, from 1.25 per cent for the decade 1931–41, to around 2.25 per cent over the last two decades.[2] This rate of growth, though, is not exceptionally high. Several Latin American and African countries have experienced rates of growth of population in excess of 3 per cent per annum; but given the relatively large base of India's population, a rate of growth of 2.25 per cent has resulted in an impressive increase in total numbers. Over the decade 1971–81 alone, India added 135.6 million people to her population. Moreover, there appears to have been no appreciable decline in the rate of growth of population over the past two decades.

The Demographic Transition model

The growth rate of the population of a country, ignoring the effects of international migration, is given by the difference between the crude birth-rate and the crude death-rate, which measure the annual number of births and deaths per thousand of the population, respectively. In most developing countries, the death-rate has declined substantially over the last five decades – in some of the Asian countries, almost to the levels prevailing in the developed countries. Unfortunately there has been no comparable reduction in the birth-rates. It is this decline in the death-rate relative to the birth-rate that accounts for the relatively high rates of growth of population in most developing countries. In India, the death-rate by the end of 1978 is estimated to have been around 14.2, and the birth-rate is put at 33.3. This compares with the average figures of 31.2 for the death-rate and 45.2 for the birth-rate during the period 1931–41.[3]

It is often argued that this particular configuration of death-rates and birth-rates which the developing countries such as India are experiencing is but a passing phase in their development process, to be followed by a phase in which both the birth-rate and the death-rate decline. According to the demographic transition model, modernization results in a sharp decline in the death-rate at first, to be followed by a comparable fall in the birth-rate. In the intervening years there will be a large increase in population. This, in fact, has been the experience of the present-day developed countries. During the late eighteenth and early nineteenth century, most European countries experienced a sharp decline in the death-rate but a stable birth-rate. Since the mid-nineteenth century, however, they have experienced a fall in the birth-rate comparable to that of the death-rate. Most developing countries of the present day, it is argued, are in the low death-rate but relatively high birth-rate phase of the demographic transition.

But the reasons for the dramatic decline in death-rates in the developing countries during the twentieth century appear to be entirely different from those that brought about a decline in mortality rates during the nineteenth century. Although the interpretation of nineteenth-century demographic history is fraught with dispute, it is widely believed that the decline in mortality during the period was primarily due to improvements in living standards, including public hygiene, rather than advances in medical science. In contrast, the decline in death-rates in the developing countries in this century appear to have been a result of advances in modern medicine and the eradication of epidemic diseases rather than improved living standards.[4] This is plausible, especially so in the case of India where improvements in general living standards have been marginal. The appreciable decline in the death-rate which the country experienced, from 36.3 during the decade 1921–30 to 17.0 in 1961–70, appears to have been primarily due to the control of malaria and cholera and the eradication of smallpox. Since then the decline in mortality rates appears to have slowed down, from 17.0 in 1961–70 to around 15.0 during 1971–81.[5] In the absence of substantial improvements in living standards, especially in that of the 30 to 40 per cent of the population classified as absolutely poor, further reductions in the mortality rate may be difficult to attain. Admittedly, the birth-rate has declined from around 44 per thousand during the fifties to the present level of around 33 per thousand. But the rate of decline in the birth-rate at about two to three points per decade has been slow, and the second phase of the demographic transition model appears to be prolonged in the case of India.

The factors which influence the birth-rate are much more difficult to identify than those which influence the death-rate. Indeed, the relative importance of the factors which contributed to the decline in fertility in the developed countries during the course of their demographic transition is a matter of continuing debate among economic historians. A bewildering variety of reasons have been suggested, for instance, to explain the decline in fertility in the late nineteenth century in England. These include increased social and geographical mobility, improved living standards, widely diffused knowledge of contraceptives, decline in infant mortality, emancipation of women and the decline of religion.[6] Altogether this amounts to saying that it was economic and social development which brought about a decline in birth-rates. It is of little help to the development economist, however, to be told that economic development ultimately results in a falling birth-rate. His or her concern is with identifying a set of factors that would fairly swiftly promote attitudes and values conducive to low fertility. Development itself, after all, involves not only growth in incomes but also changes in attitudes and values.

Children as an investment good

Explanations for the relatively high birth-rates in developing countries frequently include the prevalent social attitudes and values that are conducive to high fertility. While some of these are conditioned by religious beliefs, many are the result of economic perceptions. Foremost amongst these is the supposed belief amongst the poor that children are an economic asset. In the jargon of the economist, children are regarded as an investment good: their contribution to the family income tends to be substantial; they are a form of insurance for one's old age; and the inter-generational flow of income in traditional societies is from the children to the parents.[7] Such attitudes and values obviously promote fertility. But are such perceptions valid? Are children a good investment? What are the economic costs and benefits of investment in children?

Robert Cassen's statistical simulation exercises, utilizing data for India, show that a child could be a good investment only on the basis of certain implausible assumptions regarding the costs and benefits of rearing a child.[8] The method employed to assess the returns to investment in a child is the familiar one of assessing the present value of the future net earnings stream of an investment. Net earnings are estimated by making assumptions regarding the direct and indirect income contribution of the child above the costs of maintaining it, from age 0–40, and these earnings are discounted back to the present at an appropriate discount rate. If the present value of the net earnings of the child calculated thus turns out to be positive, the child is regarded as a good investment. This procedure is similar to comparing the net earnings of the child with the income that would accrue if, instead of maintaining the child, the money required to maintain it were to be invested at the going rate of interest compounded up to the age at which the earnings of the child start. Obviously the estimates would be sensitive to the assumptions made regarding the costs of maintaining the child, its earnings and the discount rate. Cassen's exercise shows that on the assumptions that the child begins earning at the early age of five, that the costs of maintaining it are a bare minimum (or what Cassen terms 'malnutrition' costs), that the child's earnings exceed costs by 20 per cent, and that the rate of discount is 10 per cent, the child begins to pay off as an investment at age fifteen. If it is assumed that the child starts earning at the age of seven instead of five and the earnings exceed costs by 40 per cent, the investment pays off only after thirty years. It could, however, be argued that net earnings are likely to increase with the age of the child, and the figure of 20 to 40 per cent net earnings assumed in these calculations may be an underestimate. In fact, Cassen cites studies which estimate earnings to exceed costs by 65 per cent from age fifteen to nineteen and by 120 per cent from age twenty to fifty-four. This may be so for some groups of children whose parents can afford better schooling and education for them, but it is doubtful for the vast number of poor families living on the edge of subsistence.

Moreover, as Cassen argues, the earnings figures that are relevant in calculating the returns to investment in children are not the actual percentages earned above consumption costs, but the percentage above costs which the parents may actually receive from their children. It is likely that such returns to the parents would decline once the child starts a family of its own and has to shoulder additional financial burdens. Further, more often than not it is the sons rather than the daughters who are likely to make a contribution to the family income. In most Indian families, once the daughter is married, her economic contribution accrues to her husband's family. Incidentally, this may be an explanation for the widely noted preference for sons on the part of Indian parents.

In sum, a child is a good investment only on very restrictive assumptions. Indeed, the assumption concerning the costs of maintaining a child appears to be implausible. As Cassen remarks, if we assume that the costs of maintaining a child approximate the 'malnutrition' costs (the child receiving in its sixth year only 35 per cent of the calories required by an adult), it is doubtful whether the child would live, let alone earn 20 per cent or more above costs.

Many may find the notion of regarding children as an investment good distasteful. But such a perception may underlie the social attitudes favouring large families in countries such as India – a perception that may not have been entirely unreasonable in the past, when land was plentiful, and when the orbit of one's life was the family and the village. In the altered conditions of the present day, however, when the pressure of labour on land and the costs of maintaining a child have both increased considerably, no such rationale for large families may exist. What the economic analysis of the costs and benefits of children outlined above shows is that the perception that children are a good investment is based on false premises. As Cassen remarks, the expectations of parents may favour large families, but many parents are bound to find their expectations defeated.

Each generation of parents, however, may persist with such expectations and false perceptions because of their limited horizons. In the absence of alternative solutions, or because of a lack of awareness of alternative solutions to their problem of poverty and long-term security, they opt for a 'second-best solution' – the perceived security of a large family. The search of the development economist is for the means and methods by which the horizons of the poor can be altered and their attitudes changed.

Fortunately, recent demographic experience of several developing countries shows that the problem is not intractable. Countries with widely differing economic and social structures and differing rates of income growth, such as Sri Lanka, Hong Kong, Malaysia and Mauritius in the Asian region and Costa Rica, Chile, Jamaica and Puerto Rico in the western hemisphere, have achieved a dramatic reduction in birth-rates over a fairly short span of time. Their success is generally attributed to the spread of literacy and education, and the efforts many of them have made to provide the basic necessities of life for the population. These include health, nutrition and employment opportunities; in fact, they are the prerequisites for the success of a programme of birth control.

It is worth noting in this context that the controversy surrounding Stephen Enke's well-known thesis – that the rate of return to a unit of investment in programmes designed to prevent a birth in developing countries such as India far exceeds the rate of return to a unit of investment in capital formation – also revolves around the issue of the prerequisites for the success of birth-control programmes.[9] Enke's thesis is based on reasoning similar to that employed in estimating the rate of return to investment in children, outlined above. In essence, his thesis is that the net present value of the benefits to society (net earnings stream of a child over its lifetime discounted back to the present) of an additional birth tends to be negative; the cost of preventing a birth through contraceptive methods is fairly low; hence, compared to the rate of return to investment in physical capital formation, most of which exhibits a relatively low output-capital ratio, the rate of return to unit investment in birth-control measures tends to be high.

The thesis has been challenged on several grounds.[10] Much of the criticism is directed not so much at Enke's assumption that the net benefits to society of an additional birth are negative, but at the assumption that the costs of preventing a birth are low. It is argued that Enke confines himself to consideration of the costs of providing the contraceptives, ignoring the substantial costs of administration that birth-control programmes entail. Further, there is no guarantee that such programmes meet with complete success, and if the success rate is low, the costs of the programme would turn out to be high. And such programmes are unlikely to have a high degree of success in the absence of the prerequisites for their success. These prerequisites are education, health facilities, decline in infant mortality and employment opportunities. This, in fact, may be the reason for the limited success achieved by birth-control programmes in India.

Population policy

India's Sixth Five-Year Plan (1980–5) rightly emphasizes that population policy should be a multi-pronged but integrated approach, comprising education and employment (particularly of women), eradication of poverty, maternal and child care services including immunization, prophylaxis and nutrition, and the development of health-care facilities in rural areas.[11]

Although India's policy-makers have long acknowledged the need for a population policy, this recent statement – enlightened, perhaps, by the limited success of the massive campaigns for birth control in the years past – clearly spells out the need for a multifaceted and integrated approach. The lessons learnt from the well-intentioned but misguided campaign of compulsory and coercive sterilization programmes of 1976–7 appear to be especially significant in the context. Most commentators are of the opinion that the anxiety, tensions and distrust caused by the programmes – dubbed by Indian demographers as the 'Sanjay Effect', after the late Sanjay Gandhi who spear-headed the campaign – have seriously set back India's birth-control programmes. This episode illustrates not only the limitations of a coercive campaign for birth control, but also the need for an integrated population policy.

The long term goals of population policy set out in the Sixth Five-Year Plan are to reduce the birth-rate from the level of 33 per thousand in 1980 to 25 per thousand by 1996 and the death-rate from 13.2 per thousand to 9.4 per thousand, resulting in a total population of 864 million by 1996. The attainment of the objective, however, is heavily contingent upon an effective strategy of birth-control programmes. Because of India's demographic history, a relatively high proportion of the country's total female population is in the reproductive age group of 15–44 years. This figure, put at 45 per cent in 1980, is estimated to increase to 49.2 per cent by the year 1996. Given this demographic profile, the Indian Planning Commission estimates that a total of 15.5 million sterilizations would be required over the Sixth Five-Year Plan period (1980–5) for maintaining the birth-rate at the existing level. In order to reduce the birth-rate to 21 per thousand by the end of the century, the proportion of eligible couples to be protected with birth control must increase from the present level of 22 per cent to 60 per cent; a formidable task, compounded by the excesses of the 1976–7 compulsory sterilization campaign. Indeed, some would argue that the task is impossible and India may have to accept the fact of a relatively high rate of population growth for the foreseeable future. But this counsel of despair may be unfounded, for there is evidence to show that population growth is amenable to control provided the government delivers the correlates of declining fertility – education, minimum levels of income, health facilities and employment opportunities. Of these, education appears to be of prime importance.

Education and fertility

While there are very few irrefutable propositions in demographic history, the one that appears to have survived unscathed is the causal relationship between education and declining birth-rates. The most impressive recent illustration of this relationship is provided by the experience of Costa Rica, a middle-income developing county in the international per capita income league tables. Between 1955 and 1960 Costa Rica's population is reported to have increased at an annual rate of 4 per cent, but by 1971 the growth rate had dropped to 3 per cent. The birth-rate is reported to have declined from a peak of 47 per thousand in 1961 to 28 per thousand by 1973. Demographers attribute this dramatic decline in birth-rates to the pervasive spread of literacy and the rapid acceleration of upper-level primary school education, especially among women. By 1973, two-thirds of the country's youngest women had completed primary school education, a factor which is reported to have influenced the birth-rate significantly. The decline in fertility is stated to have begun after two or three years of schooling, gathering momentum with five years of schooling.[12] It should be added that although education may have had a significant impact on fertility in Costa Rica, it was not the only factor. Costa Rica's economic policy during this period also gave high priority to public-health measures, investment in infra-structure, land redistribution, agricultural extension programmes and job creation in the modern sector, all of which appear to have reduced absolute poverty in Costa Rica with their attendant effects on the birth-rate.[13] Education, however, appears to have played a significant role in changing social attitudes towards fertility.

Although sketchy, there is some evidence from India also in support of this suggested relationship between education and fertility. Birth-rates are found to be relatively low and family planning programmes more successful in Kerala, Gujarat, Maharashtra, Punjab, Tamil Nadu and West Bengal, where literacy rates are substantially above the national average. Especially noteworthy in this context is the experience of the state of Kerala. The state has a literacy rate of 63 per cent as opposed to the national average of 36 per cent, a birth-rate of 26.4 compared to the national average of 33 and an infant mortality rate of 55 as opposed to the national average of 132.[14] The striking feature of Kerala's experience is that, apart from her high literacy rate, she displays none of the other features that are characteristic of Costa Rica. The per capita income of Kerala, for instance, is below the average figure for India as a whole, and unemployment is relatively high; yet education appears to have influenced fertility rates in the region.

One explanation for this apparent paradox is that education creates a demand for birth-control programmes; for education results in the realization that one's family size could be one of deliberate choice. Beyond that, education heightens one's hopes and aspirations for one's progeny; especially in an environment which sets store on formal education. In countries such as India a formal degree or diploma has a relatively high rate of return on the job market. Literate parents with five or six years of schooling often strive hard to provide a relatively high level of education for their children. They limit their family size not because it affords them a better standard of living, but because it enables them to provide for the education of their children. Primary education endows parents with this degree of rationality in decision-making. In addition, education liberates women in traditional societies from their perceived role as mere procreators, and endows them with aspirations for a better life not only for themselves, but also for their children.

Education, though, is but a means to an end. The end is a better standard of living. An educated population whose aspirations were not realized in some measure could only mean a disgruntled population, with adverse consequences for the political and social stability of the country. It is thus that family planning programmes should include not only education but also the assurance of at least a minimum level of incomes, health, housing and nutrition.

In sum, there is reason to be optimistic about the prospects for a decline in the rate of growth of India's population. If birth-control programmes have failed to arrest the growth of population in the past, it is because they were narrowly construed and often misguided. But the fact that there are regions in India, such as Kerala, which have experienced a decline in birth-rates despite their relatively low level of incomes suggests that literacy and education could be a major factor in bringing down birth-rates. Education in combination with the assurance of a minimum level of incomes and public goods could go a long way in arresting the rate of growth of population.

The macroeconomics of population growth

Ever since the publication of Thomas Malthus's celebrated *Essay on the Principle of Population* in 1798, the relationship between population and economic growth has been an enduring theme in development literature. Malthus's message was that increases in per capita income would only result in a larger population, putting pressure on limited land, with the law of diminishing returns then dictating a fall in labour productivity, thereby forcing per capita consumption below subsistence level. It is also frequently argued that population growth depresses savings, and forces a change in the composition of investment away from physical capital formation in favour of health, education and social welfare. Such a change in the composition of investment would adversely affect the growth rate of national product. All this has not gone unchallenged, however.

Though not a critique of the internal consistency of Malthus's thesis, it is now received wisdom that he failed to foresee the dramatic increases in agricultural productivity due to the application of modern science and technology. But could growth of population itself stimulate agricultural output? It has been argued that population growth was indeed a factor of importance in the increases in agricultural output experienced by eighteenth-century England.[15] Perhaps much more relevant to the present-day developing countries is Esther Boserup's thesis that in primitive societies, increasing density of population on land induces development.[16] She argues that it jolts primitive communities out of their leisurely ways of life and work and spurs agricultural innovations. This sort of challenge and response mechanism, however, is unlikely to be of significance in countries with a relatively high density of population to begin with. Given the technology at hand, agriculture is likely to have reached the limits of its productivity in such communities, and further increases in productivity may have to await the application of the fruits of modern science and technology.

India's experience suggests as much. Her density of population at 221 persons per square kilometre is high compared to the levels of less than 15 in most African and Latin American countries. Whatever population growth could contribute to agricultural production appears to have been achieved during the fifties. The output of food grains over the period 1949–50 to 1960–1 increased at about the rate of 2.8 per cent per annum, exceeding the rate of growth of population, estimated at 1.9 per cent, over this period. A substantial part of this growth in food grains output has been attributed to the utilization of previously uncultivated land, and labour-intensive processes.[17] It is conceivable that during this period, population growth provided both the impetus for extending the area under cultivation and the labour force required to do so.

The experience during the sixties and seventies, however, is in stark contrast to that of the fifties. This was a period of relatively rapid population growth (estimated at around 2.2 per cent per annum). The economy appears to have sustained the momentum in the growth of food grains output which was experienced during the fifties. It is, however, of significance that a substantial proportion of the growth in output during the late sixties and seventies is attributed to increases in yield per acre rather than extension of the area under cultivation. This increase in productivity was almost entirely due to the increased application of fertilizers, improved seeds and irrigation. Indeed, according to one estimate, more than 50 per cent of the increase in output over the period 1964–5 to 1970–1 could be attributed to the increased application of fertilizers and other inputs.[18] These, though, could hardly be regarded as population-induced agricultural innovations of the sort suggested by Boesrup, especially in view of the considerable amounts of under-utilized labour reported to be prevalent in rural India. In view of all this, the conclusion that population growth has had very little positive impact on the growth of agricultural output appears to be inescapable.

The composition of investment

It is frequently argued that population growth depresses the growth rate by diverting resources from physical capital formation into welfare expenditures such as education and health. This, though, is the old orthodoxy; the new conventional wisdom is that such expenditure is a form of investment. Education and health not only provide consumer satisfaction, but also enhance the skills and productive capabilities of the workforce and contribute to the growth of output. Expenditures on education and health, therefore, are to be treated as a form of investment and included in the estimates of capital formation.

This, in fact, is the view expressed by Rati Ram and T. W. Schultz in the context of their discussion on population and schooling in India.[19] They argue that investments in schooling have been a factor of significance in the growth of total capital formation in India. Reported conventional estimates of capital formation show that it increased from 15 per cent of NNP in 1950–1 to 19 per cent in 1967–8. Rati Ram and Schultz estimate that over this period, investments in schooling increased from 5 per cent of NNP to 11 per cent. Inclusive of these investments, gross capital formation is shown to have increased from 20 per cent of NNP in 1950–1 to 30 per cent by 1967–8. Furthermore, they estimate that schooling contributed 2.7 per cent to the recorded increase in the total agricultural output of 28.7 per cent over the period 1951–61, and 1.5 per cent to the increase in agricultural output of 21.1 per cent over the 1961–71 period. They suggest in addition that the improved health of the agricutural workforce also contributed significantly to the increase in agricultural productivity.

Official statistics also show impressive strides made in schooling: In the late seventies, 90 per cent of children aged 6–11 were enrolled in primary schools; 40 per cent of children aged 11–14 were enrolled in secondary schools.[20] These figures are a substantial improvement over those of the fifties. Expenditure on education as a proportion of NNP also increased, from 1.2 per cent in 1950–1 to 3.2 per cent by the late seventies.

This is an impressive record, though hardly an adequate one given the vast increase in the absolute size of her population which India has experienced over the years. It should be noted here that the relatively high figures for investment in schooling that Rati Ram and Schultz report include both expenditure on education by the State and the income foregone by the students during their period of schooling. The latter represents the opportunity costs of education to the students and their parents. This is the income they could have consumed or saved if they had not opted for education. It would not be far-fetched to argue that in a poor country such as India, most of this income would have been consumed rather than saved – in other words, very little of it would have been available for physical capital formation. And parents were willing to sacrifice their current consumption because of the prospect of increased future rates of return that education offers. These costs borne by the parents present a demand for education; a demand which the State in India has attempted to meet, but not by an amount that would suggest that there has occurred as significant change in the composition of capital formation.

It should also be noted that despite the impressive school enrollment figures cited above, the literacy rate for the country as a whole was no more than 36 per cent in 1981, an improvement of seven percentage points over the 1971 figure. Obviously, expenditure on education has been spread too thinly to have an impact on literacy. It is also widely noted that primary school enrollment figures tend to be inflated, the quality of education provided is relatively poor, and the drop-out rate is fairly high in primary education. Furthermore, a large proportion of education expenditure (nearly 30 per cent) is spent on higher education. It is an acknowledged fact that the social rate of return to higher education tends to be relatively low, and high levels of unemployment amongst the educated groups of the population is a major problem facing the country. This is partly a result of the misallocation of resources in the education sector and partly a result of the lamentably poor quality of higher education. It is conceivable that if population were growing more slowly, the resources devoted to education could have been put to better use, with a significant improvement in the performance of the education sector.

Population growth, however, may have altered the composition of investment within the category of produtive investment. One such major shift that has occurred since the sixties is the increase in expenditure of foreign exchange and capital on the importation and domestic production of fertilizers. Because of the need to feed a rapidly-growing population in an agricultural environment which had reached the limits of increasing output by labour-intensive means, the government may have been compelled to expend substantial amounts of capital and foreign exchange on fertilizers. Arguably, a slower rate of growth of population would have released these resources for productive investment elsewhere in the economy.

Effects on savings

It is a familiar theme in the literature on demography that the combination of increasing fertility among the young and falling death-rates among the old results in an increased burden of dependency. In other words, the ratio of people in the non-working age groups of 0–15 and 64 years and above to the people in the working age group 15–64 goes up. This results in a fall in the savings per head of population, because the ratio of the total number of net consuming units to net producing units in the economy has increased. The proportion of people in the non-working age groups in India's total population is estimated to be around 45 per cent. The dependency ratio could in fact be higher than that represented by this figure because of the substantial numbers of unemployed in the working age group.

It is, however, debatable whether a high dependency ratio necessarily depresses the savings rate. Those living below the poverty line or just above the subsistence level can hardly afford to save. For this group, which constitutes around 40 per cent of the population in India, the question of reducing savings to support additional dependents hardly arises. To them, additional dependents merely mean a reduction in their already low living standards. Much of the saving within the household sector in Indian is done by a small proportion of the population in the middle and upper-income groups, and even these groups may support additional dependants at the expense of consumption rather than savings. There is also some empirical evidence in support of the thesis that size of families in developing countries has little effect on the savings rate.[21] Moreover, India has experienced a sustained upward trend in the savings rate of households over the past three decades.

In sum, there is little evidence in support of the thesis that rapid population growth has had a substantially adverse effect on either the savings rate or the composition of investment. However, it may have altered the composition of 'productive' investment in favour of fertilizers and other agricultural inputs and against capital formation, but it is possible that the government would have undertaken such investments in agriculture even if the country had experienced a relatively slow rate of growth of population. After all, even during the sixties the per capita availability of food was inadequate by nutritional standards; and as Cassen states, the agricultural output of 1970 would not have been greatly excessive for the population of 1960. It would have meant about 2,600 calories per head as opposed to the then prevalent level of 2,000 calories.[22]

For all these reasons, it may not be far-fetched to argue that population growth in India has neither promoted nor depressed the growth of total output. But it has undoubtedly held down the rate of growth of per capita incomes. It is a matter of simple arithmetic to demonstrate that if population growth matches or exceeds output growth, the growth of per capita incomes is depressed. In the equation $y=O/P$, where y is per capita income, O stands for output and P for population, if the growth of P exceeds that of O, y will decline. In India, total output over the past three decades has increased at an annual average rate of 3.5 per cent and the growth of population has been around 2.2 per cent. These figures indicate that the annual average growth in per capita incomes over these three decades was around 1.3 per cent. There is little doubt that Indians have been eating into their prosperity by producing too many children. These figures on average incomes, however, say little about the distribution of the income, the extent of poverty in India and the state of the poor.

The state of the poor

There is an extensive and controversial literature on poverty in India, including studies on personal income distribution. A number of such studies relating to the early and mid-sixties show that the poorest 20 per cent of the population received only 7 to 8 per cent of total income, whereas the richest 20 per cent received more than 46 per cent of the income. These studies also show that while income disparities are large in both urban and rural areas, they are somewhat smaller in the rural areas compared with the urban areas, and that income disparities in the rural areas may have declined over time.[23] But these estimates tell us little about the extent and nature of absolute poverty; indeed, it is conceivable that the degree of concentration in incomes may have declined in the rural areas because of increasing equality of incomes among the upper- and middle-income groups, with very little change in the share of the lower-income groups. Hence the concern of Indian economists with the measurement of absolute poverty rather than relative income distribution.

Who are the poor and how should absolute poverty be defined? The absolutely poor in India are identified as those whose consumer expenditure falls below a predetermined minimum – the poverty line. The minimum level of expenditure is defined, in turn, on the basis of a predetermined nutritional norm – the minimum number of calories required for subsistence. The quantities of foodstuffs usually consumed which would yield the required minimum of calories is then estimated. Money needed to purchase these quantities of food at the current, or a base year, price level then defines the minimum level of expenditure. The proportion of the population who cannot afford this estimated minimum level of expenditure constitutes the absolutely poor.

There are a number of estimates of absolute poverty in India based on this approach, but these estimates differ from one another because of differences in assumptions regarding the nutritional norm, the income and expenditure levels on which they are based, and the price indices chosen to arrive at the level of expenditure required to buy the minimum quantities of food.

One of the frequently cited estimates of absolute poverty in India during the sixties, by P. K. Bardhan, specified Rs 15 per capita per month in the rural areas, and Rs 18 per capita per month in the urban areas as the minimum level of expenditure required for subsistence. On this basis he found that in 1960–1, 38 per cent of the rural population and 32 per cent of the urban population were living below the poverty line. Even more disconcerting is Bardhan's finding that the proportion living below the poverty line increased from 38 per cent in 1960–1 to 54 per cent in 1968–9 in the rural areas, and from 32 per cent to 41 per cent in the urban areas.[24] Another estimate by B. S. Minhas, however, suggests that between 1960–1 and 1967–8, the proportion of population in the rural area living below the poverty line declined from 46 per cent to 37 per cent. Minhas uses a per capita annual income level of Rs 200 at 1960–1 prices as the minimum necessary for subsistence. The principal reason for the difference in these two estimates is that Bardhan employs the agricultural labour consumer price index to estimate the real income required in 1968–9 to buy the minimum level of food for subsistence, whereas Minhas uses the national income price deflator. The agricultural labour consumer price index doubled over the period 1960–1 to 1968–9, whereas the national income price deflator increased by 70 per cent. It could be argued that the agricultural labour consumer price index is the appropriate index to use in estimating the required minimum level of expenditure in rural areas, as a large proportion of the rural poor are agricultural labourers. It is shown that when this index is used instead of the national income deflator, even Minhas's estimates of distribution of income show increasing absolute poverty.[25]

Another estimate of poverty which has attracted wide attention is that by Dandekar and Rath.[26] On the basis of a nutritional norm of 2,250 calories per day per adult male, they estimate that in 1960–1 rural consumers would have required a per capita income of Rs 171 per annum, and urban consumers Rs 271 per annum for bare subsistence. On this basis it is estimated that 40 per cent of the rural population and a little under 50 per cent of the urban population were absolutely poor in 1960–1, and there was little change in these proportions by 1967–8. A recent estimate by the Planning Commission for the year 1977–8 puts the proportion of population below the poverty line in rural areas at 51 per cent, and in urban areas at 38 per cent. These estimates are based on a poverty line of Rs 65 per capita per month (1977–8 prices) for the rural areas, corresponding to a minimum daily calorie requirement of 2,400 per person, and Rs 75 per capita per month for urban areas, corresponding to a calorie requirement of 2,100 per day. According to the Planning Commission, there has been no marked change in the extent of absolute poverty in India in recent years.[27]

While these various estimates of absolute poverty based on nutrition norms differ from one another because of differences in the data and assumptions on which they are based, the validity of the nutrition-based norms approach to the estimation of poverty has been disputed.[28] The minimum number of calories required for subsistence may vary, not only between individuals, but also within individuals at different points of time. Different individuals with identical body weight and similar occupations may vary in their calorie intake. Sukhatme, for instance, argues that the recommended nutritional requirement (2,200 or 2,400 calories per day) is a recommended average and not a minimum. To say that anyone eating below the average is undernourished amounts to considering anyone eating above the average as overnourished. It is argued that a proper estimate of poverty has to be arrived at by comparing the range of distribution of calorie requirements with the actual intake of calories. On Sukhatme's adjustment of the distribution of requirements against the distribution of intake, the estimated population below the poverty line is reduced to 25 per cent in urban and 15 per cent in rural areas.[29] This is substantially lower than the estimates cited above.

It is possible, therefore, that the estimates based on the norm of minimum calories required for subsistence may have overstated the extent of absolute poverty in India, and that the task of alleviating poverty may not be as hopeless as it seems. This, though, should not detract from the magnitude of the problem, for even a relatively conservative figure of 30 per cent of the total population living below the poverty line would mean a total number of 200 million people on the edge of bare subsistence. Moreover, the poorest among the poor may be living in 'infernal destitution', as B. S. Minhas puts it. It should also be noted that these estimates of poverty are based on requirements of food only, to the exclusion of other basic necessities of life such as clothing, access to safe drinking water, sanitation and health facilities.

This picture of malnutrition and poverty is rendered even more poignant by the fact that the basic problem may not be one of an absolute shortage of food, but one of a lack of command over the purchasing power to buy food on the part of the poor.[30] The rate of growth of output of food grains, at around 2.7 per cent per annum over the period 1949–50 to 1978–9, has just about kept pace with the rate of growth of population. Total output of food grains in 1980–1 reached a record level of 133 million tonnes, exceeding the previous level of output of 132 million tonnes in 1978–9. The virtual cessation of food imports and the sizable buffer stocks of food which the country has built up in recent years lend credence to official claims that India has achieved 'self sufficiency' in food. Yet the number of people living below the 'poverty line' has increased.

All this is not to say that there is an abundance of food in the country or that supplies are adequately matched to needs. With growth in incomes, the demand for food is likely to increase rapidly. In low-income countries, such as India, not only is a high proportion of income spent on food, but a substantial proportion of any increase in that income is also spent on food. In other words, at low levels of income the income elasticity of demand for food tends to be relatively high. In general in the rural areas in India, expenditure on food constitutes three-quarters of total consumer expenditure, while in urban areas it is around 62 per cent. Available estimates put the income elasticity of demand for food in India in the region of 0.4 to 0.5. It is also of significance that of every increase in the income of the rural poor, 97 per cent is estimated to go on consumption expenditure compared with only 56 per cent for the rural rich. Food purchases take 89 per cent, and food grains alone 41 per cent, of the increase in consumption of the rural poor.[31] In the absence of a growth in supplies to meet the growth in demand for food, there would be a sharp increase in food prices, the brunt of which would fall on the poor. The long-run trend in the growth of food output is discussed in greater detail in Chapter 5; suffice it to note here that the present level of food output could go a long way towards improving the lot of the poor and malnourished. The basic problem, however, is one of providing them with the incomes to purchase the food.

Unemployment

How best to put purchasing power into the hands of the poor? The poor in India possess few tangible earning assets. As the Planning Commission reports, the poorest 30 per cent of the rural population have a bare 2 per cent share in total assets. The bulk of the assets the poor possess are the huts they live in, some household goods and livestock.[32] Land reform and asset redistribution have figured prominently in the Indian policy framework for the alleviation of poverty, but these policies have met with limited success, and their net impact on poverty is debatable.[33]

It could, therefore, be argued that the only direct and immediately effective method of putting purchasing power into the hands of the poor is through providing opportunities for the exploitation of the one asset they possess – their labour. This, however, raises the issue of whether poverty should be equated with unemployment, and what the criteria for identifying and measuring unemployment should be.

Relevant in this context is the illuminating distinction between 'time criteria' and 'income criteria' for identifying the unemployed and underemployed, suggested by Raj Krishna.[34] According to the time criteria, a person is unemployed or underemployed if he is gainfully occupied during the year for less than some optimum number of days or hours defined as full employment. According to the income criteria, a person is unemployed or underemployed if he earns an income per year less than that required for a desirable minimum level of living. Dandekar and Rath, in the study cited earlier, in essence adopt the income criteria when they argue that 'an adequate level of employment must be defined in terms of its capacity to provide a minimum level of living.' On this basis 30 per cent of the rural population in India in 1969 (128 million people) would be classified as unemployed, as their incomes fell below the level required for a minimum level of living. Raj Krishna, however, takes issue with this and argues that Dandekar and Rath 'abandon the time criterion altogether for measuring unemployment and, in effect, reject the distinction between poverty, considered as consumption below a certain minimum, and unemployment, considered as an involuntary failure to get income yielding work for the normal number of working days in a year.'[35]

The import of this statement is that not all of the poor may be unemployed. Many amongst the poor may be working for the number of hours or days prescribed by the time criteria to be adjudged fully employed, but the remuneration they receive for the work they do may be inadequate for a desired minimum standard of living. In fact, Raj Krishna's estimates, based on National Sample Survey data, show that in the early seventies the poor in India (30 per cent of the population with incomes below the desired minimum) were more numerous than the 'idle' (17.7 per cent of the labour force unemployed or under employed according to the time criteria).

Admittedly, identifying the unemployed with the absolutely poor overstates the magnitude of the unemployment problem. Furthermore, alleviating the poverty of the unemployable as opposed to that of the unemployed and the underemployed requires different sets of policies. In the one case it requires income transfers, and in the other, policies directed at promoting gainful employment opportunities. Even so, it is of little solace to the poor who are working to be told that they are employed according to the time criteria. What they require is adequate remuneration for their work. To put it in another way, not only the act of working but also the remuneration it yields should be taken into consideration in estimating unemployment. Those employed according to the time criteria may be getting inadequate remuneration for several reasons including low wage bargaining power, low productivity due to lack of skills, and a lack of correspondence between the kind of labour they can offer and the type of work that is available. Although it may not be strictly correct to identify poverty with unemployment, most of the policies required to alleviate poverty involve improving opportunities for employment in one way or another, especially when policies involving redistribution of assets such as land reform, though desirable in principle, may be difficult to implement in practice.

India's record on the creation of employment opportunities, however, is woefully poor. Raj Krishna's estimates for the year 1971 suggest that 9 per cent of the labour force, or a staggering 21.5 million people, were unemployed – 19 million in the rural areas where the incidence of poverty is highest, and 2 million in the urban areas. This estimate of Raj Krishna is based on the application of the time criteria coupled with the 'willingness criteria'. The latter identifies unemployed or underemployed as those who are willing to do more work than they are doing at present. The estimate, therefore, includes only those who are wholly unemployed and the severely underemployed who are obviously willing to work more. If account is taken of those underemployed in addition to the severely underemployed and the unemployed, the unemployment figure for 1971 reaches 29 million people.

More recent estimates reported by the Planning Commission for the year 1980 puts the total number of workers seeking work and unable to find it at 21 million people,[36] which constitutes around 9 per cent of the labour force. This estimate is based on the so called 'daily status' concept of unemployment. It identifies the number of people unemployed on any given day in a reference week. High as it is, this figure cannot possibly capture the full extent of unemployment in India, as it does not take account of the substantial numbers who are underemployed in the country.

There is no dearth of diagnoses and prescriptions for the solution of the unemployment problem in India. The frequently suggested reasons for the worsening unemployment situation over the years include growth of population, slow growth in investment, factor price distortions and the adoption of inappropriate technologies in the modern manufacturing sector. Many of these factors may be interrelated and may have reinforced one another, resulting in low growth in employment opportunities. While we discuss these issues in detail in later chapters, it is sufficient to note here that a large part of the blame for the low growth in employment opportunities must ultimately lie with the inward-looking economic strategy, centred on the policy of import-substituting industrialization, which India has pursued. As will be argued in Chapters 6 and 7, it is this strategy that has provided the incentives not only for the establishment of relatively capital-intensive industries but also for the adoption of 'inappropriate' capital-intensive technologies.

The conclusions of this chapter can be briefly summarized. Population growth may not have had a sizable impact on the growth of total output one way or the other, but it has limited the growth of per capita incomes. To the extent that the poor have larger families they have been forced to bear a greater degree of hardship and deprivation, but a relatively large family size may be a consequence rather than a cause of poverty. Low levels of education, the perception that a large family is an economic asset, and high rates of infant mortality may all be conducive to high fertility. As Robert Cassen remarks, the growth in population is due to the failure of the economy to deliver 'the correlates of declining fertility' to the mass of people – better health, education and employment opportunities. Indeed, tautologous as it may seem, it is the failure of the economy to deliver health, education and employment opportunities to the mass of the people that may lie at the root of the problem of overpopulation and poverty.

3 Growth Performance

Economic growth is usually defined as a sustained increase in the aggregate national product, or per capita product. Gross Domestic Product (GDP), defined as the total volume of final goods and services produced within a country's territory, is the conventional indicator of growth. Statisticians have for long bemoaned the problems associated with measuring GDP. How to distinguish final goods, the production of which contributes to GDP, from intermediate goods which merely sustain their production? What weights should be attached to goods and services which do not enter the nexus of the market? How to isolate real changes in the magnitude of goods and services produced from changes arising from associated price levels?

The woes of the statistician, however, appear to be trivial compared to those of the economist attempting to measure social welfare in terms of GDP indices. It is obvious that although GDP and per capita income figures may measure overall growth performance of the economy, they indicate little or nothing about the distribution of the product within the community. It is not only the size of the cake that matters, but also the manner in which it is shared. It is, of course, true that the larger the cake the more there is of it to share: hence the presumption that growth and economic well-being go together.

This, though, is of little solace to the development economist. In most developing countries, growth has resulted in some improvement in the economic well-being of their citizens in general. And in the case of some relatively high growth performers like Thailand, Yugoslavia, South Korea and Taiwan there has also been a dramatic reduction in absolute poverty and income inequalities. But in several others – fast and slow growth performers alike – personal and regional income disparities have increased and growth has had a negligible impact on development.

Yet growth cannot be dismissed out-of-hand as an objective of development. While growth may not be a sufficient condition for development, it is nevertheless a necessary condition; and although it may not be an indicator of social welfare it does indicate the productive capacity and potential of the economy. On that basis this chapter briefly reviews the growth performance of the Indian economy.

The record in brief

It is almost banal to say that developing countries lack a reliable and cohesive set of national income statistics. Lack of the necessary administrative machinery for collection and processing the data is not the only problem. In most developing countries, a sizeable portion of the product is either consumed within the producing unit or bartered for other goods and services; their value has to be indirectly estimated and the resulting figure may be subject to a high degree of error. But India has an efficient corps of administrators, and over the years has achieved considerable refinement in the methods employed in collecting and processing national income data. Well known are the successive rounds of the National Sample Survey which have generated valuable data on consumption patterns, land holdings, agricultural output and agricultural employment, among other things. There is also an extensive system of reporting on the pattern of land use which covers almost 93 per cent of India's geographical area. Over the years, data collection on agricultural production, which accounts for nearly 45 per cent of the national product, has been improved. Although nearly 40 per cent of the national product – mostly pertaining to agriculture, small industries and the services sector – are based on indirect estimation procedures, these are continuously refined. And the concepts and methods employed in estimating the national product of the country have been the subject of intense research and debate among the Indian economists.[1] It would be fair to say that although India's national income estimates are far from the ideal, she is one of the few developing countries which provides a set of comprehensive data based on extensive surveys.

The Central Statistical Organisation (CSO) provides an array of data on Gross National Product (GNP), Net National Product

Table 3.1 Net National Product, Total and Per Capita, 1950–1 to 1980–1

Year	Net National Product (Rs billion)		Per Capita Net National Product (Rs)		Growth Rate (%)		
	Current Prices	1970–1 Prices	Current Prices	1970–1 Prices	Net National Product (1970–1 Prices)		Per Capita Product
1950–1	83.33	167.31	246.0	468.1	Actual	Target	
I Five-Year Plan							
1951–2	91.56	170.86	250.8	468.1			
1952–3	89.35	176.99	240.2	475.8			
1953–4	96.01	188.54	253.3	497.5	3.6	2.1	1.8
1954–5	87.45	193.28	226.6	500.7			
1955–6	92.72	199.53	235.9	507.7			
II Five-Year Plan							
1956–7	107.23	210.46	267.4	524.8			
1957–8	107.01	205.87	261.6	503.3			
1958–9	120.23	223.29	287.6	534.2	4.0	4.5	2.0
1959–60	124.29	226.76	291.8	532.3			
1960–1	132.63	242.50	305.6	558.8			
III Five-Year Plan							
1961–2	139.87	250.39	315.0	563.9			
1962–3	147.95	254.14	325.9	559.8			
1963–4	169.80	267.46	365.9	576.4	2.2	5.6	0.4
1964–5	200.00	288.08	422.0	607.8			
1965–6	206.37	271.03	425.5	558.8			
Three Annual Plans							
1966–7	238.48	272.98	481.8	551.5			
1967–8	280.54	297.15	554.4	587.3	4.0		1.8
1968–9	286.10	305.13	552.3	589.1			
IV Five-Year Plan							
1969–70	316.10	324.08	597.5	612.6			
1970–1	342.35	342.35	632.8	632.8			
1971–2	365.73	347.15	660.2	626.6	3.4	5.7	1.1
1972–3	402.70	341.91	711.5	604.1			
1973–4	504.24	359.67	870.9	621.2			
V Five-Year Plan							
1974–5	594.46	365.02	1005.9	617.6			
1975–6	620.69	400.64	1024.2	661.1			
1976–7	670.83	404.51	1082.0	652.9	5.4	4.4	3.4
1977–8	759.35	448.62	1197.7	695.0			
1978–9	809.92	463.06	1249.9	714.6			
1979–80	872.53	438.22	1316.0	661.0	−5.4		−7.5
1980–1	1042.01	472.11	1556.9	696.3	7.7		5.3

Source: *Annual Economic Survey 1981–2* (Government of India).

(NNP) – which is equal to GNP net of depreciation – and per capita product (Table 3.1). The series referred to as data on 'real' national product nets out the effects of changes in the price level relative to 1970–1, and expresses the value of national product in terms of rupees of unchanged 1970–1 purchasing power.

An examination of the series in current prices shows that, save for fluctuations during the First Five-Year Plan period, NNP has steadily increased. These fluctuations, as well as the relatively low growth in national output during the first half-decade of the sixties, is to be attributed to fluctuations in agricultural output. Especially significant in this context is the negligible increase in national product during 1965 and 1966. There are also marked divergences between the two series, with the series in constant 1970–1 prices being substantially higher than that in current prices during the period 1950–5 and the converse being the case since 1971–2. What these divergences indicate is that the price level during the earlier period was appreciably low relative to 1970–1. In addition, Table 3.2 shows that there has been a substantial increase in the price level in the decade of the seventies. Indeed, the economy enjoyed a remarkable degree of price stability during the period 1950–66; the price level increased by only 3 per cent per annum over this period.[2] The rapid increase in the price level since then, especially over the decade of the seventies, has largely been a consequence of shortfalls in agricultural output, growth in defence expenditure due to the military conflicts with China and Pakistan in the sixties and the Bangladesh War in the early seventies, the oil crises, and increases in money supply.

The series on real per capita product also shows a steady increase,

Table 3.2 Index Numbers of Wholesale Prices for Major Groups of Commodities (1970–1 = 100)

	1971–2	1973–4	1975–6	1976–7	1977–8	1978–9	1979–80	1980–1
All commodities	105.6	139.7	173.0	176.6	185.8	185.8	217.6	257.3
Primary articles	100.9	141.8	165.8	167.2	183.8	181.5	207.0	238.0
Manufactured products	109.5	139.5	171.2	175.2	179.2	179.5	216.0	257.0
Implicit NDP deflator	105.2	140.2	154.4	165.2	170.7	175.4	199.1	220.7

Source: *Annual Economic Survey, 1981–82* (Government of India).

save for the year 1965–6, until the seventies. It is, however, less robust than the aggregate product series, and during the eight-year period between 1970–1 and 1978–9 it shows a fall in four years. This lacklustre performance of the per capita product series is mainly to be attributed to the growth in population at around an average rate of 2.5 per cent per annum.

The growth rate

National product figures in absolute terms, though, say little about the performance of the economy over time. The conventional yardstick of economic performance is the annual average rate of growth of national product, but whether a particular rate of growth is high or low can only be adjudged with reference to an assumed 'norm'. But what is this norm to be? For instance, India's growth rate of around 3.5 per cent per annum over the past three decades is decidedly high compared to that achieved in the days of the British administration (estimated at no more than 1 per cent per annum for the first half of the twentieth century). This is an impressive record, but it is not unique. Several other newly independent countries such as Pakistan, Kenya, Sri Lanka, Egypt and Indonesia have also achieved growth rates in excess of 3 per cent. In fact, in several of these countries the rate of growth has been appreciably higher than that of India, ranging from 4.5 per cent to 6 per cent.[3]

India's growth performance compares even more unfavourably with that of star performers like South Korea, Taiwan, Brazil, Mexico, Hong Kong and Singapore, all of which have registered average growth rates in excess of 5 per cent. It is now trite to remark that international comparisons of growth rates which ignore differences between countries in economic structure, resource endowments and socio-political characteristics are of limited usefulness. Indeed, it can be argued that India, because of her size and diversity, is in a class by herself among the developing countries, and that her record bears no comparison with that of others. Admittedly, her socio-political characteristics and size do pose problems for economic management, and these have been factors in her relatively slow economic growth. But her very size and diversity have also endowed India with considerable, if not bountiful, amounts of labour and natural resources. Her endowment of natural resources, though inferior to that of many Latin American and African countries, is superior to that of many Asian countries, and the fair supply of educated élite and the trained corps of administrators which India possesses puts her at a decided advantage over most other developing countries.

Yet South Korea and Taiwan, with a relatively inferior resource endowment and high density of population, have out-performed India in terms of growth rates. So too have Brazil and Mexico among the Latin American countries. Much more apt, perhaps, is a comparison of the growth performance of India with that of China. Apart from being the two most populous countries in the world, they both began their development effort in the early fifties with roughly similar levels of per capita income ($50–60, at 1952 US prices); and in both countries, agriculture accounted for a preponderant share of national product and employment. The one major feature that sets China apart from India is that she has followed a Soviet-type command system of economic organization, whereas India has adopted a system of economic planning within the framework of a mixed economy. Recent estimates show that over the period 1950–80, the annual average rate of growth of GNP for China was around 6.7 per cent and GNP per capita increased at an annual average rate of 4.5 per cent. This contrasts with the growth rate of 3.6 per cent for total GNP and 1.5 per cent for per capita GNP that India achieved over the same period.[4] There appears to be no escaping the conclusion that several others have achieved higher growth rates than India, with different sizes, resource endownments, economic ideologies and political persuasion.

International comparisons apart, what can we say about India's growth performance over the past three decades? It is a legitimate source of national pride that India was able to achieve a growth rate of 3.5 per cent per annum in the face of heavy odds: the military confrontations with China and Pakistan in 1962 and 1965 and the severe droughts of 1965 and 1966. Surprisingly enough, India's growth performance over the fifteen years ending in 1965, which was marked by the two wars and droughts, appears to have been much more stable than her achievement since then.

At 1970–1 prices, net national product grew at an annual rate of 3.6 per cent over the First Five-Year Plan period (1951–6), at 4.0 per cent per annum during the Second Five-Year Plan Period (1956–61) and at 2.2 per cent per annum during the Third Five-Year

Plan Period (1961–6). Excluding the last year of the Third Five-Year Plan, which witnessed an unprecedented drought and the war with Pakistan, the rate of growth for the Third Five-Year Plan period is around 4.4 per cent. For the entire first fifteen years of economic planning, from 1950–1 to 1964–5, the economy registered a compound rate of growth of 3.7 per cent per annum. Excluding the two drought years of 1965–6 and 1966–7, the compound rate of growth per annum for the thirteen-year period from 1966–7 to 1979–80 works out at 3 per cent per annum.

It is disconcerting that the growth rate over the latter period was no different from that achieved during the relatively turbulent first fifteen years of planning. Moreover, the growth rate over the second period was subject to wide year-to-year fluctuations compared with that of the first period. The coefficient of variation, a statistical measure of the fluctuations in annual growth rates around the trend rate, is estimated at 0.64 for the first period and 0.84 for the period 1965–6 to 1976–7.[5] The high growth rates for individual years in the 1970s were mostly due to favourable weather conditions which resulted in appreciable increases in agricultural output. It should also be noted that save for the First and Fifth Five-Year Plans the growth rate has fallen far short of the successive Five-Year Plan targets of a 5 per cent growth per annum. The growth rate over the Fifth Plan, though it matched the target, was subject to wide year-to-year fluctuations, with the years of high growth rates coinciding with the years of good harvests. Furthermore, industrial production fell far short of the rates targeted in the plan.

Sectoral composition of national product

Simon Kuznets' pioneering statistical study of the growth experience of thirteen developed countries over several decades suggests that growth is likely to be accompanied by a decline in the share of agriculture in total output and an increase in the share of the manufacturing and service sectors.[6] Such changes in the sectoral composition of national product reflect the changes in technology, input combinations and demand patterns that accompany growth. Agriculture is likely to experience a declining trend in its share of national output, because of both the relatively low income elasticity of demand for its products, and the shifts in demand towards the products of other sectors which are induced by the changes in technology and patterns of life and work experienced by a growing economy. Accompanying these changes in output structure would be a decline in the share of agriculture in the total labour and capital employed in the economy, brought about mainly by a growth in agricultural productivity. Indeed, the growth in agricultural productivity may be a precondition for industrialization and growth.

The reasons for the key role of agriculture in the process of industrialization and growth are not hard to find. As often noted, agricultural growth contributes to the process of industrialization through (i) supplying food, the principal wage good, and agricultural raw materials; (ii) providing a demand for inputs, such as fertilizers, produced by the industrial sector; (iii) providing a demand for consumer goods produced by the industrial sector, and (iv) providing a source of supply of savings and labour. Indeed, few countries have experienced sustained growth and industrialization without developing the agricultural sector. In most of the present-day developed countries, agricultural growth accompanied and in some cases preceded the process of industrialization. This has also been the experience of the relatively high growth performers amongst the present-day developing countries such as South Korea and Taiwan.

The changes that have occurred in the sectoral composition of India's national product over the past three decades broadly conform to the observed historical patterns. The share of agriculture in NNP has declined from more than 50 per cent in the 1950s to around 37 per cent in recent years. The share of the manufacturing and services sectors has increased from around 10 per cent and 26 per cent respectively to 16 per cent and 40 per cent (Table 3.3).

These trends however, are not robust enough to support the argument that the economy has experienced a major structural transformation. The changes that have occurred in the composition of output were mostly confined to the period 1950–65, and have not been sustained over time. In fact, the share of the manufacturing sector in total national product has remained stable at around 16 per cent since the mid-sixties. While the share of the tertiary sector in national output has registered an upward trend, much of this increase appears to have been on account of public administration and defence, trade, storage, and hotels and restaurants. There appears to have been no significant increase in categories, such as transportation and communication, vital to the infrastructure of the economy.

Table 3.3 Sectoral Composition of Net Domestic Product (percentage shares at 1970–1 prices)

	1950–1[a]	1965–6	1970–1	1975–6	1978–9	1979–80
Agriculture and allied activities	59.00	47.73	49.20	44.00	40.25	37.00
Manufacturing	9.93	15.73	13.30	13.80	15.80	16.20
Total secondary sector	14.40	22.00	19.70	19.73	22.16	22.68
Trade, transport and communications	11.82	15.88	15.80	17.20	18.40	19.33
Banking and insurance	0.91	1.68	1.86	2.05	2.76	2.90
Public administration and defence	2.70	4.37	4.74	5.57	5.90	6.74
Total tertiary sector	26.60	30.57	31.10	36.27	37.59	40.32
Total Net Domestic Product	100.00	100.00	100.00	100.00	100.00	100.00

[a] = Sectoral shares in total GDP

Source: Estimated from data in *Estimates of National Income* (Central Statistical Organisation February 1964) and *Report on Currency and Finance* vol. II, 1980–1 (Reserve Bank of India, Bombay).

Nor have there been any significant changes in the sectoral composition of the labour force. The primary sector including agriculture, forestry, mining and quarrying – accounting for 71 per cent of the labour force in 1979 – continues to be the major source of employment. While there was a marginal decline in the proportion of the total labour force accounted for by agriculture, from around 72 per cent in 1951 to 69.6 per cent in 1961, it remained constant at that figure over the census period 1961–71. The recently published census data for 1981 shows that the share of agriculture in the total labour force had declined to 66.7 per cent, and the share of the category of 'other workers' had increased from 30.3 per cent in 1971 to 33.3 per cent in 1981. It has, however, been shown that the 1981 census under-enumerated the number of workers; when adjustments are made for the under-enumeration there appears to be little change in the structure of the labour force over the period 1961–81.[7] Further, the proportion of agricultural *labourers* as opposed to *cultivators* increased from 17.2 per cent of the labour force in 1961 to 26.9 per cent in 1971, and continued to account for 25 per cent of the labour force according to the latest census data.

The share of industry in the total labour force has remained unchanged at around 11 per cent since 1960. While the share of the tertiary sector in the total labour force has increased over the years, reaching 18 per cent in 1979, much of it appears to have been on account of increases in employment in the category of community, social and personal services, mostly in the public sector. This category, which includes public administration, accounts for 48 per cent of the total employment generated by the public sector, while manufacturing accounts for less than 10 per cent of public sector employment.[8]

A key factor in the low degree of structural transformation and growth which India has experienced appears to be the low growth performance of the agricultural sector. As stated earlier, agricultural growth has been a factor of importance in modern economic growth.

In the case of India, the growth performance of the agricultural sector has particular significance for several reasons. First, as stated earlier, the agricultural sector accounts for a substantial proportion of both national ouput and labour force. Given its sheer size, it is obvious that the growth performance of the sector would have a significant impact on the overall growth rate of the economy. Second, agro-based industries account for a substantial proportion of total industrial ouput. In the year 1950 they accounted for 60 per cent of total industrial production. Although this proportion has declined over the years, agro-based industries have continued to account for a substantial proportion of 33 per cent in the total industrial production index in recent years. The growth performance of these industries would obviously be affected by a low growth in the supply of agricultural raw materials. Third, it is reported that rural consumption of manufactured consumer goods such as clothing, footwear, sugar and edible oils is nearly two and a half times that of urban consumption.[9] This should be of little surprise, as nearly 80 per cent of the population in India lives in rural areas, and 70 per cent of the labour force depend on agriculture for their livelihood. Again, it is obvious that if demand for manufactured goods were to grow, there would have to be a sustained and substantial increase in agricultural output and agricultural incomes.

Of significance in this context is the finding of several statistical studies based on analysis of the input-output matrices for the economy, that while the secondary sector uses the inputs produced by the primary sector and the trend in this direction has been upward since 1965, the primary sector's demand for the products produced by the manufacturing sector is relatively low.[10] This observed relatively low level of dependence of agriculture on industry may be due to the low level of technology in use in agriculture, and the low growth in agricultural incomes. These findings, too, serve to underscore the importance of growth in agricultural output for industrial development in India.

The growth performance of the agricultural sector over the past three decades, though, appears to have left much to be desired. While the structure and performance of the agricultural sector are discussed in detail in Chapter 5, a few salient points are noted here. As is to be expected, the growth rate of the economy has been susceptible to fluctuations in agricultural output, its dominant sector. The long-term growth rate of agricultural output over the period 1949–50 to 1979–80 has been in the region of 2.5 per cent per year; food grains production increased by 2.5 per cent per year and non-food grains production by 2.6 per cent. Such rates of growth are not low by historical standards, and compare favourably with those of most other South-east Asian countries. These long-term growth rates, however, conceal the vicissitudes in agricultural performance over the period, especially the loss of momentum in the growth of output since the mid-sixties. This has been a period of mixed fortunes, with agricultural output being smitten by the successive droughts in 1965-6 and 1966–7 and boosted by the exceptionally favourable weather conditions in 1977–8.

But even with the exclusion of the two drought years of 1965–6 and 1966–7, the rate of growth of total agricultural output over the period 1967–80 turns out to be lower than that achieved over the period 1960–5. While we discuss the growth performance of agriculture in detail in Chapter 5, it is sufficient to note here that the growth rate of output for the period 1967–80 was 2.5 per cent per annum, compared with the rate of growth of 3 per cent per annum achieved over the period 1950–65. Much of the growth in output over the period 1967–80 was on account of increases in yield per acre, particularly in the case of wheat.[11] Admittedly, other crops such as rice and jowar have also exhibited an upward trend in productivity. But these increases in yields have not been large enough to compensate for slow growth in the area under cultivation with regard to most crops.

Furthermore, there are wide regional variations in the growth of agricultural output, especially between the regions in the North-west of India and those in the North-east. While yields per acre in rice, for instance, have registered dramatic increases in the former region, they have stagnated in the latter. As the Sixth Five-Year Plan document notes, much of the increases in the disparities in per capita incomes between the various states of the Union in recent years is to be attributed to differential progress in the agricultural sector. States which experienced an increase in agricultural income also gained in terms of per capita incomes relative to the others.

Although the evidence is not conclusive, it has been noted that in the past, states which experienced a relatively high growth rate of agricultural output also showed a decline in the share of agriculture in their total labour force, and states with a relatively low growth of agricultural output experienced an increase in agricultural population.[12] However, as stated earlier, for the country as a whole, there appears to have been little change in the proportion of the labour force dependent on agriculture.

Although inconclusive, the available evidence appears to lend support to the presumption that the growth performance of the agricultural sector has been a factor of significance in the growth performance of India's industrial sector. We discuss the structure and performance of the industrial sector in detail in Chapter 6. It is sufficient to note here that while there was a remarkable acceleration in the rate of growth of industrial output at around 7.4 per cent per annum over the period 1951–65, it dwindled to 3.8 per cent over the period 1965–80. While there are several explanations for the deceleration in the growth of industrial output over the second period, including organizational inefficiencies, power shortages, shrinking demand for consumer goods, poor labour relations and low growth in public sector investment, the low-growth performance of agriculture appears to be one of the proximate causes.

Statistical exercises based on a macro model of the economy, in fact, show that agricultural output is positively related to the demand for industrial consumption goods. In addition, an increase in agricultural output is shown to have a positive impact on savings and investment of the household, government and corporate sectors.[13] This, in turn, would facilitate the growth in output of basic and capital goods industries. Further, it is reported that simulation exercises performed on the model indicate that a 1 per cent increase in the growth rate of agricultural output results in close to 1 per cent increase in the growth of industrial output. As stated earlier, even though the late sixties witnessed dramatic increases in the productivity of wheat, the rate of growth of agricultural output as a whole (including non-food grains) was no higher than that during the period 1950–65; in fact, the rate of growth of non-food grains output over the second period was markedly lower than that in the first period. And as stated earlier, it is since the mid-sixties that the dependence of the secondary sector on the inputs provided by the primary sector appears to have increased. Yet another factor of significance in the relatively low growth of industrial output since the mid-sixties is the existence of high level of under-utilized capacity. This aspect is discussed in greater detail in Chapter 6; suffice it to note here that the low levels of average income in the agricultural sector could be one of the reasons for the deficiency in demand.

While the performance of the agricultural sector has been a factor of importance in the low degree of structural transformation which the economy has experienced, the industrial structure that has evolved and the economic climate that has prevailed have also been none too conducive to a major structural transformation. The panoply of bureaucratic controls over economic activity in general and foreign trade in particular have not only given rise to a high-cost industrial structure, but also depressed enterprise and productive investment. Half-hearted attempts at institutional reform, and politically motivated fiscal and pricing policies have also been factors in the low growth performance of the agricultural sector. The loss of momentum in the growth process observed since the mid-sixties may be largely a consequence of these interventionist policies of the government. These aspects are discussed in later chapters.

It is frequently argued that the relatively low growth performance of the economy since the mid-sixties is due to an inadequacy of resources. Admittedly, savings and investment rates stagnated over the period 1966–73; but this deceleration in savings and investment was mainly due to the poor savings performance of the public sector, a consequence of both increases in government consumption and inefficiences in resource mobilization. In any case, the economy has achieved unprecedently high recorded savings and investment rates since 1973. Yet the growth rate achieved by the economy has fallen far short of that to be expected from such high savings and investment rates. This is an episode which amply illustrates the proposition that high rates of savings and investment alone are not the recipe for growth. Equally important are the manner in which investment is allocated between different sectors and branches of the economy activity, and the efficiency with which it is utilized. Chapter 4 discusses these issues.

The main conclusions of this chapter can be briefly summarized. The growth performance of the economy, though notable, has been disappointing in contrast with many other countries. The agricultural sector has been characterized by a modest and somewhat lacklustre performance. There has occurred very little change in the occupational structure, and agriculture continued to be the mainstay of employment. The low growth performance of the agricultural sector has been a factor of significance in both the low degree of structural transformation experienced by the economy, and the loss of momentum in the growth of industrial production and the growth rate since the mid-sixties.

4

Savings and Investment in the Indian Economy

For long, it was the conventional wisdom that poor countries are poor mainly because of their inability to save and invest. Moulded in this wisdom were the 'vicious circle' and the 'low-level equilibrium trap' explanations of underdevelopment. Low income levels result in low savings and hence low levels of investment and incomes. Beyond that, growth of population ensures that per capita incomes stay depressed. A 5 per cent rate of savings and investment would only result in a 1 to 2 per cent increase in national income, and if population was also growing at 1 to 2 per cent per annum, there would be no growth in per capita incomes. The only avenue of escape from this 'low-level equilibrium trap' is to engineer a 'big push' – a greatly increased savings and investment effort.

Recent experience, however, shows that most developing countries, including India, have achieved high rates of savings and investment despite their low levels of per capita income. They have been able to do this because of changes in income distribution in favour of income groups with a relatively high propensity to save, and the development of institutions and instruments for the mobilization of savings. But high rates of savings and investment have not always resulted in high rates of growth. This suggests that high rates of savings and investment are not an unerring recipe for growth: equally important is the efficiency with which they are utilized, or the investment absorptive capacity of the economy. This in turn is a function of the nature and composition of investment, the availability of complementary factors such as human skills, and the presence of institutions and attitudes conducive to growth. India's development experience amply illustrates these propositions. This chapter analyses the trends in savings and investment in India, and discusses the relationship between savings and investment and the growth performance of the economy sketched in Chapter 3.

The strategy

Savings and investment have been central to India's economic strategy. Indeed, an arresting feature of India's Five-Year Plans is their optimism concerning the ability of the economy to mobilize domestic savings. A clear expression of this optimism is to be found in the First Five-Year Plan document, which enunciated the long-run objectives of planning. The savings-centred Harrod-Domar growth model provided the theoretical underpinnings for the plan. The plan, however, departed from the model in distinguishing between the average propensity to save and the marginal propensity to save. While the Harrod-Dormar model assumes savings to be a constant proportion of income, with the average propensity to save being equal to the marginal propensity to save, the First Five-Year Plan projected the marginal propensity to save to increase over time from around 0.20 in the initial years to 0.50 over the longer run.

The Mahalanobis growth model, which provided the intellectual underpinnings for the Second Five-Year Plan, gave a further thrust to this optimism concerning savings.[1] Indeed, the model dispensed with an explicit savings function and postulated both savings and investment to be a function of certain structural features of the model. The initial version of the model identified two broad sectors – the capital goods sector and the consumer goods sector. The basic assumptions of the model were that the productivity of investment (the output-capital ratio) in the consumer goods sector was higher than that in the capital goods sector, and that capital goods, once installed, could not be shifted from one production sector to another.

The logical conclusion following from these assumptions of the model is that the supply of capital goods is essentially a function of the manner in which the resources initially available for investment are allocated between the two sectors. The higher the proportion of initial investment allocated to the capital goods sector, the higher the flow of capital goods and investment in the subsequent periods. The strategy would no doubt result in a smaller volume of consumption goods in the short run, but it would result in a higher growth rate, and in the longer run in an increased rate of growth of consumption.

It was also the implicit assumption of the model that because the volume of output of consumption goods would be lower in the short run, savings would be higher at the margin. As Bhagwati and Desai put it, the basic premise of the model was 'that if you produced capital goods and steel, thus increasing the share of investment in GNP, that would automatically mean a higher rate of savings since one cannot eat steel'.[2]

The non-availability of consumer goods, though, may not deter consumers from demanding them. In a market economy, such excess demand for consumer goods and services could result in inflationary pressures and balance of payments problems. In fact, the capital-goods-oriented investment strategy of the Second Five-Year Plan did result in a severe balance-of-payments crisis. Increased inflows of foreign aid, however, enabled the country to bridge the balance-of-payments gap and contain inflationary pressures.

The point to note, however, is that the Mahalanobis strategy was based on confidence about the ability of the economy to generate the required savings. The emphasis of the model was on structural bottlenecks, including the limited scope for generating additional foreign-exchange earnings through growth in exports, and the imperative need for a growing supply of domestically-produced capital goods to sustain investment and growth.

The Mahalanobis model has left a strong imprint on India's economic philosophy. Successive Five-Year Plans have reaffirmed their faith in the ability of the economy to generate savings. 'Self-reliance', meaning a speedy elimination of the dependence on foreign aid, has been a basic objective of Indian planning. Enunciated for the first time in the Third Five-Year Plan, the objective has been reaffirmed in the later plans, although the terminal date for the elimination of aid inflows has been postponed time and again. Implicit behind this objective is the ability of the economy to generate the required savings from domestic sources, including the government and the household sectors. In sum, a sense of optimism concerning savings, and a faith in the ability of the economy to sustain a high investment rate have been central to India's economic philosophy. India's record on savings and investment over the past three decades, though it may not have matched the planners' expectations, appears to vindicate their belief that a low level of per capita income need not be a deterrent to an increased savings and investment effort.

The record

India's savings and investment record over the past three decades has been impressive: save for the seven-year period 1966–73, when both the savings and investment rates were stagnant, there has been an upward trend in both magnitudes. Further, with the exception of the three annual plans during the mid-sixties, the realized rates of savings and investment appear to have approached and in some cases exceeded the rates targeted under the Five-Year Plans. Admittedly, much of the savings of the household sector, the principal contributor to savings, has been in the form of physical assets; and inventory accumulation has accounted for a substantial proportion of capital formation in recent years: a pattern of savings and investment which is not conducive to the growth of output. This pattern of savings and investment, however, appears to be no more than a rational economic response of economic agents to the prevailing economic stimuli. The point to note, though, is that the economy has exhibited a basic impetus to save and invest; much more so than most other developing countries subscribing to a democratic political framework.

As Bhagwati and Desai writing in 1968 remarked, 'India's performance in raising her average rate of domestic savings appears to have been perhaps the most impressive aspect of her economic growth.'[3] Indeed, the rates of savings and investment which the economy has achieved during the latter half of the decade of the seventies could be called dramatic (Table 4.1). As the Planning Commission notes with pride, 'it is apparent that the country has achieved a high savings rate despite its low per capita income. In fact, our saving rate is comparable to that of middle-income and even some high-income industrialised countries.'[4]

Composition of savings

Households, the private corporate sector and the government are the main sources of domestic savings. It is a frequently observed phenomenon that in most developing countries, it is the household sector which accounts for a relatively high proportion of domestic savings, whereas in the developed countries, it is the undistributed

Table 4.1 Savings and Investment in the Five-Year Plans

	Pre-Plan Year 1950–1	End of I Five-Year Plan 1955–6		End of II Five-Year Plan 1960–1		End of III Five-Year Plan 1965–6		End of 1968–9		End of IV Five-Year Plan 1973–4		End of V Five-Year Plan 1978–9		VI Five-Year Plan 1984–5
		T	A	T	A	T	A	T	A	T	A	T	A	T
Net Domestic Savings (% of NNP)	6.6	7.0	8.83	9.7	9.34	11.5	11.28		9.6	12.2	15.0	15.7	19.3	
Net Capital Formation (% of NNP)	6.38	7.0	9.36	10.7	12.72	13.1	13.91		10.9	14.5	15.7		19.4	
Gross Domestic Savings (% of GDP)	10.2		13.91		13.5		15.6		14.1		19.3		23.9	24.48
Gross Capital Formation (% of GDP)	10.0		14.3		16.9		18.2		15.4		20.0		23.9	25.11

T = Targeted rate
A = Actual rate

Sources: S. L. Shetty, 'Structural Retrogression in the Indian Economy since the Mid-Sixties', *Economic and Political Weekly* (February 1978).
Basic Statistics Relating to the Indian Economy, 1950–1 to 1978–9 (Central Statistical Organisation, New Delhi).
Sixth Five Year Plan (1980–85) (Planning Commission, Government of India).

profits of the corporate sector and the budgetary surpluses of the government which constitute a major source of savings. These differences in the composition of savings reflect the differences in the level of economic organization between these groups of countries. The household sector in developing countries tends to be large, including not only the consuming units but also the large number of unincorporated business enterprises and proprietory concerns – the so-called self-employed. It is the savings of these enterprises which accounts in part for the relatively high share of households in total domestic savings.

It is, however, a dictum of most texts on economic development that in developing countries, it is the government sector which should shoulder the burden of mobilizing savings. The amount of savings required to meet growth objectives of such countries tends to be large, and the savings rate may have to be raised from 4 to 5 per cent of national income to 12 to 15 per cent in a short span of time. This would imply a steep increase in the marginal propensity to save: a tall order for most poor countries, where increased consumption expenditure is likely to make a heavy toll on additional income. Hence the need for the government to mobilize savings.

India's policy-makers also have assigned a major role to the government in mobilizing resources for development. Yet it is the

Table 4.2 Sectoral Composition of Savings

	Total Domestic Savings (Rs billion)	Household Sector (Percentage of total)	Government Sector (Percentage of total)	Corporate Sector (Percentage of total)
1970–1	45.66	77.5	17.6	4.9
1973–4	83.69	81.3	13.0	5.7
1974–5	96.40	66.7	25.3	8.0
1975–6	111.63	71.5	25.4	3.1
1976–7	138.86	73.0	25.0	2.0
1977–8	153.91	76.0	22.0	2.0
1978–9	175.02	79.4	19.0	1.6
1979–80	173.60	76.4	18.8	4.8

Sources: *Basic Statistics Relating to the Indian Economy: 1950–51 to 1978–79* (Central Statistical Organisation, Government of India), and *Report on Currency and Finance* vol. I, 1980–1 (Reserve Bank of India).

household sector which accounts for a preponderant share of total savings in India (Table 4.2). In fact, while the share of the household sector has rarely been lower than 70 per cent of total savings, that of the government sector has fluctuated over the years from a high of 30 per cent in 1964–5 to as low as 13 per cent in 1967–8.[5]

The household sector

The household sector accounts on average for more than three-quarters of total domestic savings in India. The ratio of household savings to disposable income rose steadily from around 4 per cent in 1950–2 to 16 per cent during 1976–8 (Table 4.3). Indeed, the savings ratio of the sector exhibited an upward trend even during the years 1966–73, the period of economic stagnation; and the contribution of the sector has been a significant factor in the dramatic increase in the country's savings rate since the early seventies.

Table 4.3 Ratio of Savings to Disposable Income

1950–2	1962–4	1965–7	1968–70	1971–3	1974–6	1976–8	1978–80
4.05	6.99	9.85	10.32	11.50	13.80	16.00	15.0

Source: V. K. R. V. Rao, 'Savings, Capital Formation and National Income', *Economic and Political Weekly* 31 May 1980.

The preponderance of the household sector's share in total savings is admittedly a feature that India shares with most other developing countries. The savings of the unincorporated business enterprises, included in the household sector, are a factor in explaining the high proportion of household savings in total domestic savings. Even so, a 75 per cent share, which has stayed more or less constant for three decades, is much too large a figure to be accounted for by the contribution of unincorporated business enterprises alone. There are no data on the relative contributions of consuming units and unincorporated business enterprises to total household savings, but available data on income shares show that the share of the self-employed in NNP has stayed constant around 45 per cent since 1970–1. This suggests that individual consuming units have also played a significant role in the savings performance of the household sector.

It seems paradoxical that the voluntary savings of the household sector should be so buoyant in a poor country with a very low level of per capita income. The resolution of the paradox appears to lie in the changes in income distribution which have occurred over time. As V. K. R. V. Rao, commenting on the recent upsurge in savings, puts it, 'it is possible that the period has seen a redistribution of money income in favour of the savers as against the poor; and among the savers, in favour of those who respond less quickly in increasing their consumer expenditures than those who due to the different ways in which they look at incremental income as permanent or transitory; and in favour of the high-income groups whose marginal propensity to save is much higher irrespective of whether they regard the income as permanent or transitory.'[6]

This explanation draws upon well-known theoretical postulates concerning the relationship between income and savings. According to the Keynesian analysis of savings behaviour, the marginal propensity to save of the upper income groups tends to be higher than that of the lower income groups. A redistribution of income in favour of the upper income groups, therefore, would increase total savings. According to the permanent income hypothesis of consumption, enunciated by Milton Friedman, observed or measured income at any point of time consists of two components: a permanent income component and a transitory income component. The former refers to the income streams which income earning units expect to maintain with a fair degree of certainty over a period of time. The latter refers to unexpected windfall income gains or losses. Thus measured income of income recipients at any point of time could be higher or lower than their permanent income, depending upon whether they experience transitory income gains or losses. One of the major assumptions of the permanent income hypothesis is that income units save all of their unexpected transitory income gains.

If income is redistributed in favour of those who regard such increases in income as transitory, they are likely to increase their total savings. This, in fact, appears to be one of the explanations offered by V. K. R. V. Rao for the growth in household savings in recent years. In sum, his explanation amounts to saying that household savings have increased because income has been redistributed in favour of the high savers. Admittedly, this is not an illuminating explanation, for we know very little about the socio-economic characteristics of the high savers.

One aspect of savings behaviour in India which has attracted wide attention is the propensity to save of the rural households. Economic studies pertaining to the fifties and the early sixties have suggested that the propensity to save of the rural households tends to be substantically lower than that of the urban households.[7] It is also a much-lamented fact that the average savings rate of the rural sector, which accounts for a substantial proportion of the national product, should be depressingly low at around 4 per cent. This, though, should be of little surprise, for the 40 per cent of the total population living below the 'poverty line' could hardly afford to save. And the savings of the millions of people living just above the poverty line could only be negligible. A recent study by Raj Krishna and Ray Chaudhuri puts the critical minimum level of income at which positive savings in rural India are possible at Rs 201 per capita.[8]

The pertinent issue, therefore, is the propensity to save of the middle- and upper-income rural households, especially in view of the widespread suggestion that both the Green Revolution and the shift in the inter-sectoral terms of trade in favour of agriculture since the sixties have tilted income distribution heavily in favour of upper-income groups in the rural areas.[9] While there are no estimates of the savings propensities of income groups, it is reported in the study by Raj Krishna and Ray Chaudhuri (cited above) that the marginal propensity to save for rural incomes as a whole escalated from 1.33 per cent during the period 1950–1 to 1962–3 to 11.79 per cent during the period 1960–1 to 1973–4. It is also of significance that sample surveys of farms in areas such as Ludhiana in the Punjab, where irrigation and the new agricultural technology are widespread, show the average savings rate to be as high as 22 per cent.[10] It is apparent that the high savers suggested by V. K. R. V. Rao are not confined to the urban areas, but are also to be found within the high-income groups in the rural areas.

Yet another factor that has contributed to the dramatic increase in the savings rate since the mid-seventies is the increased inflow of workers' remittances from abroad. These are reported to have averaged around Rs 4 billion per annum over the period 1973–8. While there are no precise estimates of the impact of such migrants' remittances on savings propensities, it is widely believed that they have contributed to increased household savings in the form of financial assets.

It is frequently observed that a substantial proportion of household savings in developing countries is held in the form of physical assets such as land, and currency. Some physical assets – such as investment in bunding and irrigation, designed to improve agricultural productivity, and fixed investments undertaken by the self-employed – do constitute socially productive investment. But savings held in the form of gold, land and currency may not be socially productive, for those who sell the land and gold to the savers in the community may indulge in wasteful consumption expenditures. Investment in residential property may provide a hedge against inflation, but it may be socially unproductive, especially when it is not accompanied by new construction.

On average, 55 to 60 per cent of household savings in India are held in the form of physical assets (Table 4.4).[11] While there are no detailed data on the composition of these assets, it is widely believed that many of them are in the form of stocks of commodities and residential property, especially since the seventies. A large proportion of the financial assets held by households – nearly 40 per cent – is accounted for by contractual savings in the form of life insurance, provident and pension funds. Another 40 per cent is accounted for by deposits with banks, while shares and debentures account for a marginal 6 to 7 per cent of total financial assets. This

Table 4.4 Pattern of Household Savings (Rs billion)

	1970–1	1973–4	1974–5	1975–6	1976–7	1977–8	1978–9	1979–80
Total	35.4	68.07	64.30	79.80	101.12	117.12	133.82	132.68
Physical assets	21.7	32.00	40.65	40.60	52.27	64.78	66.36	63.92
	(61.0)	(47.0)	(63.0)	(51.0)	(52.0)	(55.0)	(47.4)	(48.0)
Financial assets of which:	13.7	36.1	23.7	39.2	48.9	52.3	67.50	68.76
Currency	3.5	8.1	0.20	3.2	11.41	7.3		
Net deposits with banks	2.7	12.6	10.1	11.3	17.6	24.0		
Net claims on government	−0.12	4.3	−1.0	7.2	−0.7	−3.1		
Life insurance, provident and pension funds	6.8	10.6	13.1	16.3	18.3	20.8		

(Figures in parenthesis refer to percentages of total savings)

Sources: *National Accounts Statistics*, 1970–71 to 1977–78 (Central Statistical Organisation, Government of India), and *Report on Currency and Finance* vol. I (Reserve Bank of India).

pattern of savings, which is heavily weighted towards physical assets, appears to be a factor in the phenomenon of savings without growth experienced by the economy in recent years.

The observed asset preferences of the households, however, may be a rational economic choice determined by the relative rates of return and security of investment which various assets offer. This proposition finds some support in a study of the asset preferences of the middle class in India, i.e. those with annual incomes in the range of Rs 5,000–15,000 – the dominant saving class.[12] The study, covering the period 1960–7, found that the preferred assets of the middle class were real estate, gold and silver. Over this period, the cost of living for the middle class is reported to have increased by 50 per cent. As the study argues, this loss in real income could have been compensated for only if the middle class held assets of an appreciating nature. The assets that appreciated over this period were land and buildings, whose prices increased up to three times, and silver and gold, whose prices increased by 85 per cent and 25 per cent respectively. These were the assets the middle class preferred, as opposed to government securities and corporate shares which registered a capital loss of 6 to 15 per cent over the years 1960–7.

The scenario appears to have changed very little during the decade of the seventies. The rate of inflation accelerated, with the general price index for urban non-manual employees doubling from 174 in 1970–1 to 343 in 1979–80. Although detailed data are not available, it is generally known that real estate prices increased steeply over the period; and the available data show that with the exception of variable dividend industrial securities, the prices of all other financial assets – including government securities – either stayed constant or declined over the decade of the seventies.[13] All this is consistent with the hypothesis that the savings preferences of households are economically rational and that they have responded to the prevailing rates of return on various assets in the economy.

The corporate sector

The corporate sector is not a significant contributor to savings in India. In fact, its share in total savings declined over the years (Table 4.2). Business savings are obviously a function of business profits and the propensity to save out of profits. Available evidence suggests that the corporate sector's propensity to save out of profits after tax is relatively high; it is estimated to range from 0.74 in the case of jute manufactures to 0.94 in the case of the aluminium industry.[14] The sector's declining share in total savings could only be attributed to declining profits.

Several factors appear to have contributed to the erosion of profits in the private sector. The primary causes, however, are the increased prices for inputs and wage costs confronting the sector. Both of these, to a large extent, are to be attributed to the shift in the terms of trade in favour of the agricultural sector, referred to earlier; for it increased not only the prices of agriculture-based inputs but also the price of food, the main wage good.[15] In addition, declining demand for final goods and steeply progressive rates of corporation tax may also have contributed to the deterioration in the savings performance of the corporate sector.

The government sector

The government sector accounts for more than 40 per cent of the gross fixed capital formation in the Indian economy, and its share in GDP has increased steadily over time to around 19 per cent in recent years. This, however, has not been matched by its savings performance, and the contribution of the government sector to total savings has been relatively low. After reaching a peak of 30 per cent in 1964–5, its share in total savings declined to around 12 to 17 per cent in the late sixties and has been in the region of around 22 per cent in recent years (Table 4.2).

Budgetary surpluses and the surpluses of the state-owned enterprises constitute the main sources of government savings. The government's ability to generate revenues – mainly through its tax effort – and to contain its current expenditures determine the size of the budgetary surplus. Although taxation has played a significant role in the government's savings performance, it is found to be deficient in several respects. Total government revenues increased from Rs 7.86 billion in 1950–1 to Rs 205 billion in 1979–80, with tax revenues accounting for more than 75 per cent of the total (Table 4.5). Tax revenues as a proportion of NNP increased from 9 per cent in 1950–1 to 21 per cent by 1978–9, approaching the levels found in some developed countries; but unlike the developed countries, India relies heavily on indirect taxes for its tax revenues. More than 70 per cent of tax revenues are accounted for by indirect taxes – mostly taxes on basic consumer goods – and their contribution has increased over the years. Admittedly, this is a trait which India

Table 4.5 Government Current Revenues (Rs billion)

	1950–1	1955–6	1960–1	1965–6	1970–1	1973–4	1976–7	1977–8	1978–9	1979–80
I Total revenues	7.86	10.27	17.72	37.04	58.63	87.89	152.58	164.35	183.65	205.30
(a) Tax revenues	6.27	7.68	13.50	29.21	47.52	73.89	123.32	132.37	149.91	167.76
% tax revenues to total	(79.80)	(74.80)	(76.18)	(78.86)	(81.05)	(84.07)	(75.06)	(80.54)	(81.63)	(81.70)
(i) Direct taxes	2.31	2.59	4.02	7.34	10.09	15.52	25.85	27.28	18.40	19.50
(ii) Indirect taxes	3.96	5.09	9.48	21.88	37.43	58.36	97.47	105.14	131.51	144.26
% indirect taxes to total	(63.16)	(66.30)	(70.22)	(75.00)	(78.80)	(79.00)	(79.03)	(79.42)	(87.80)	(86.00)
(b) Non-tax revenues	1.55	2.41	3.74	6.88	11.06	13.96	27.60	30.33	32.94	36.48
(i) Surpluses from State-owned enterprises							9.40	11.60	16.21	19.36

Sources: *Report on Currency and Finance* (Reserve Bank of India, various issues), and *Basic Statistics Relating to the Indian Economy: 1950–51 to 1978–79* (Central Statistical Organisation, Government of India, New Delhi, 1980).

shares with other developing countries, but it is one which she could have avoided. India has in operation a highly progressive system of income taxation, and income disparities have widened over the years, yet the contribution of direct taxes to total revenues has declined over the years. The widespread evasion of income tax, perhaps partly induced by the steep progressive structure, is much noted. If India could have controlled the evasion, her tax structure would have been much more equitable and productive.[16] Thus, while taxation has been a significant source of government revenues, India may not have fully exploited this source. The surpluses generated by state-owned enterprises, though they have increased over time, do not form a significant proportion of total government revenues.

Government current expenditure, including both developmental and non-developmental expenditure, increased from Rs 7 billion in 1950–1 to Rs 192 billion in 1979–80 (Table 4.6). Although the specific composition of development expenditure on items such as health and education may be questioned, few would dispute the need for increased government spending in these areas. Admittedly, there were extenuating circumstances dictating an increase in non-developmental expenditure as well. Defence expenditure, which doubled from Rs 7.6 billion in the mid-sixties to Rs 15 billion in 1973–4, may have been unavoidable because of the military conflicts with China and Pakistan and the Bangladesh War. However, defence expenditure accounted for 38 per cent of the total non-development expenditures in 1964–5, and has declined to around 16 per cent in recent years. The category labelled 'others' constitutes the biggest item under non-developmental expenditures. Included in this category is expenditure on administration, including tax collection and various forms of subsidies. Some part of this expenditure, such as the financing of famine relief in the mid-sixties and the upkeep of refugees from Bangladesh in the early seventies, may have been unavoidable. However, the bulk of the expenditure in this category is on account of administration and food subsidies. It should also be noted that it is public administration and not manufacturing which accounts for much of the employment generated in the public sector.[17]

Many of these factors which have contributed to the relatively low level of public-sector savings appear to be ingrained in the structure of the Indian political economy. In the urban sector, the

Table 4.6 Government Current Expenditure (Rs billion)

	1950–1	1955–6	1960–1	1965–6	1970–1	1973–4	1976–7	1977–8	1978–9	1979–80
I Total expenditure	7.3	10.0	16.4	33.1	57.2	86.7	135.0	146.9	174.4	192.1
II Developmental expenditure	2.1	3.9	6.9	13.4	33.0	35.4	60.2	69.3	84.4	95.1
III Non-developmental expenditure	5.2	6.1	9.5	19.7	33.5	51.3	75.8	77.6	90.0	97.0
of which:										
(i) defence	1.6	1.7	2.5	7.6	10.5	14.8	23.5	24.9	26.5	–
(ii) other, including administration	2.8	2.5	4.8	7.8	15.5	26.4	34.9	33.8	41.3	–
IV Non-developmental expenditures as % of total expenditures	71.2	61.0	58.0	60.0	58.6	59.1	56.1	52.8	51.6	50.5

Sources: *Report on Currency and Finance* (Reserve Bank of India, various issues), and *Basic Statistics Relating to the Indian Economy: 1950–51 to 1978–79* (Government of India, New Delhi, 1980).

panoply of government restrictions on prices and output have given rise to extensive black markets and black earnings which are untaxable. Available estimates of the size of unreported incomes as a proportion of GNP during the sixties range from 6 to 10 per cent, and a recent study estimates this percentage to have increased to an incredible 49 per cent by 1978–9.[18] While the precise extent of the black economy in India is a matter of dispute, it is generally agreed that it amounts to at least 15 per cent of the reported GNP; and the rate of growth of the 'unreported' economy may have also been higher than that of the reported economy in recent years.[19] The black economy, however, is not unique to India. Its growth in developed economies such as the UK has been noted in recent years. While steeply progressive rates of taxation and the incentives they provide for evasion have been factors in the growth of the black economy in the UK and India alike, the extensive system of controls on prices, output and imports has compounded the problem in India. The premiums obtained on the sale of import licences, for instance, have been reported to range from 50 per cent to 300 per cent. It is estimated that the sale of import licences at such inflated premiums was responsible for the generation of Rs 7,500 million in black money in 1970, or about half of the black money generated in that year.[20]

In the rural sector, the upper-income groups are lightly taxed or not taxed at all because of the reluctance of the state governments to lose the political support of the rural oligarchy. In India's federal set-up, taxation of agricultural incomes is a preserve of the state governments. Most of the states, including those in which agricultural incomes have risen sharply due to the introduction of new technology and irrigation, are reported to tax agricultural incomes sparingly or not at all. In fact, it is estimated that the incidence of agricultural income tax in general has always been less than a rupee per hectare.[21]

Again, it is the government's agricultural pricing policy which appears to have been a factor in the sharply increasing burden of government expenditure. One facet of this policy which is of significance in this context is the procurement price paid by the government to farmers for the purchase of food grains with which to operate the buffer stocks and the public distribution system. It is reported that despite the increasing trend in food grains production in recent years, the procurement prices paid for wheat and other

Table 4.7 Five-Year Plan Outlays and Their Financing (Rs billion and percentage shares)

	I Five-Year Plan (1951–6)	II Five-Year Plan (1956–61)	III Five-Year Plan (1961–6)	Annual Plans (1966–9)	IV Five-Year Plan (1969–74)	V Five-Year Plan (1974–9)	1979–80 (Annual Plan estimates)	1981–2	VI Five-Year Plan (1980–5) estimates
Total plan outlay (Rs billion)	19.60	46.77	85.77	67.56	161.60	393.03	126.01	174.17	975.00
Budgetary surpluses and surpluses of public enterprises	38.5	26.3	33.9	24.0	33.9	52.0	47.8	41.1	46.3
Domestic borrowing	34.9	30.7	24.6	30.0	40.5	29.8	32.8	42.2	38.4
Deficit finance	17.0	20.4	13.2	10.1	12.7	3.4	10.8	8.8	5.1
External aid	9.6	22.5	28.2	35.9	12.9	14.8	8.6	7.9	10.2
Total	100.0	100.0	100.0	100.0	100.0	100.0	100.0	100.0	100.0

Source: *Report on Currency on Finance* vol. II (Reserve Bank of India, 1982).

food grains have steadily increased. There could be no explanation for this increase save the political power of the agricultural lobby. The increase in procurement prices has in turn necessitated increased subsidies on the food sold through the public distribution system. Such subsidies are reported to have amounted to Rs 7 billion per annum in recent years, accounting for nearly half of the uncovered deficit of the central government's budget and mostly met by deficit financing.[22] In addition, there are the increased salaries and allowances paid to government employees necessitated by the rising trend in consumer prices outside the public distribution system.

Public borrowing: aid and deficit financing

Given the low level of budgetary surpluses, the government has had to resort increasingly to public borrowing, deficit financing or money creation, and external aid to finance the plan outlays. In general, current government revenues have financed less than 50 per cent of the various Five-Year Plan outlays; while external aid accounted for nearly a third of the outlay during the Third Five-year Plan and the three annual plans, deficit financing, and public borrowing have accounted for a proportion of the outlays in the various Five-Year Plans, varying from 40 to 50 per cent (Table 4.7).

These methods of financing development are neither novel nor specific to India. Several developing countries have resorted to similar tactics. But such methods have their limitations. We discuss the role of aid in India's development process in detail in Chapter 8; suffice it to note here that it may be an uncertain and fluctuating source of finance. Public borrowing, by providing acceptable government securities, may reduce consumption and promote savings. But if the purchase of securities is financed out of idle balance it may prove inflationary. Deficit financing or money creation through the sale of government stock to the central bank, in fact, is a method of imposing forced savings on the community, for the inflation it engenders is a form of indirect taxation on the holders of money balances in the community. Inflation reduces the real value of purchasing power of money balances, and the attempt on the part of money holders to restore their real value by increasing savings results in their relinquishing command over real resources. These accrue to the government which issues the money; but there are collection costs attached to this form of taxation. These consist of the waste of real resources and reductions in real income, which result from the attempt on the part of money holders to evade the tax by substituting real goods for cash. There are thus limits to the extent to which governments can rely on this method of financing development. Furthermore, the burden of inflation is not borne by the money holders alone. It falls on the entire population, hitting hard those whose money incomes do not keep pace with inflation.

Several developing countries, principally the Latin American countries, have in the past adopted inflationary financing as a creed.[23] In India, though, the government appears to have been forced to resort to money creation in the face of the political constraints on its tax effort. As Harry Johnson put it, 'inflationary financing may represent the only way of bridging deep political divisions. In the absence of agreement on taxation required to finance development and on the division of national income among claimants to it, countries may resort to inflationary financing'.[24]

This is an explanation which may have some validity in the case of India. Although the actual amount of money created for purposes of financing development expenditure has exceeded the amounts originally envisaged in the various plans, its share in total development expenditure has been relatively low, save in the Second Five-Year Plan (Table 4.7). Thus, in the Third Five-Year Plan, while the amount of deficit financing envisaged was Rs 5.5 billion, the actual amount turned out to be almost twice that figure at Rs 11.5 billion. Again, in the Fourth Five-Year Plan, the amount envisaged was Rs 8.5 billion, whereas the actual amount turned out to be Rs 10.7 billion. Even so, the share of deficit financing in total plan outlays was relatively low, at around 13 per cent (Table 4.7).

But coming on top of the rising budgetary deficits due to the Bangladesh War, growth in food subsidies, and increased administrative expenditures, deficit financing has been a factor in the relatively high growth of money supply during the decade of the seventies. During the period 1971–4, the annual average growth in money supply was around 15 per cent. While this growth was contained to less than 10 per cent during the years 1974 to 1976, it climbed back up again to around 18 per cent per annum during the years 1976–9. The growth in money supply has been one of the factors contributing to the relatively high rates of inflation experienced by the economy during the decade of the seventies, referred to in Chapter 3. The burden of the inflation appears to have been borne mainly by those without any sort of assets, and the agricultural labourers.

Savings and investment without growth

It is conceivable that India could have achieved much higher rates of savings and investment but for the lacklustre savings performance of the public sector. It is also possible that the low growth in public-sector investment was one of the principal reasons for the low growth performance of the economy during the period 1965–73. But this should not detract from what *has* been achieved, which is impressive in many respects. Apart from the recessionary years of the sixties, the savings rate has exhibited an upward trend. In fact, the domestic savings rate was in excess of the investment rate during the mid-seventies; and as the Planning Commission notes, 'total investment targets have, by and large, been met or exceeded in recent plans.'[25] Yet the realized growth rates, with rare exceptions, have been well below the rates targeted in the various Five-Year Plans.

It may not, therefore, be far-fetched to argue that low rates of savings and investment *per se* are not the basic reasons for the low growth performance of the economy. The proximate reason for the low growth performance is to be sought in the low productive efficiency of investment. Several studies, including the Sixth Five-Year Plan, have commented on the secular decline in the productivity of capital in the Indian economy.

The statistical measures of the productivity of investment usually employed are the marginal and average capital-output ratios. The marginal capital-output ratio measures the ratio of total investment to changes in national product, while the average capital-output ratio is the ratio of the capital stock of the economy to the total output. A more pertinent indicator of the productive efficiency of investment is the ratio of fixed investment net of inventories to the change of national product. Several sets of estimates of capital-output ratios for the Indian economy are available. Most of these estimates point to a secular decline in the productivity of investment. V. K. R. V. Rao's statistical analysis of the long-term trends in the incremental capital-output ratio – of total net investment to changes in GNP – at constant 1960–1 prices, shows that it increased from 2.39 for the decade of the fifties to 4.63 during the decade of the seventies. His estimates show that the average capital output ratio also increased from 2.7 during the decade of the fifties to 2.9 during the decade of the sixties and further to 3.33 during the decade of the seventies.[26]

More detailed and up-to-date estimates of the capital-output ratios, including the ratio of net fixed investment to increase in Net Domestic Product, (NDP) reported by R. M. Sundrum, also point to a rising trend over time (Table 4.8). Several points of interest emerge from this table. Both the incremental net capital-output ratio and the incremental net fixed capital-output ratio show a rising trend over the past three decades, save for a decline during the period 1965–6 to 1970–1. This decline is to be attributed to the recovery of output growth in the late sixties after the decline experienced during the mid-sixties due to the disastrous fall in agricultural output. Sundrum's estimates also show a relatively slow but rising trend in the average capital-output ratio.

Table 4.8 Annual Average Capital-Output Ratios

Period	Net Incremental Capital-Output Ratio	Net Incremental Fixed Capital-Output	Average Capital-Output Ratio
1950/51 – 1955/56	2.04	1.72	2.03
1955/56 – 1960/61	3.01	2.41	2.03
1960/61 – 1965/66	4.06	3.10	2.05
1965/66 – 1970/71	2.82	2.30	2.27
1970/71 – 1975/76	4.53	3.22	2.36
1975/76 – 1979/80	5.63	4.19	2.38

Source: R. M. Sundrum, *Savings, Investment and Economic Growth* (Working Paper No. 165, Centre for Development Studies, Trivandrum, March 1983).

It is possible for the average capital-output ratio to stay constant even though the incremental capital-output ratio is increasing. This would be so if the economy were experiencing improvements in methods of organization and utilization of inputs contributing to the productivity of the existing capital stock. This, in fact, appears to have been the experience of most developed countries where the average capital-output ratio has been observed to have stayed constant. But in the case of India the estimates reported above show a rising trend in both the incremental and average capital-output ratios, indicating relatively low technical progress.[27]

There are a number of explanations for the increasing trend observed in the capital-output ratios. The change in the composition of investment in favour of industry since the mid-fifties, and the increasing weight of technologically intensive industries in the manufacturing sector go some way in explaining the growth in the incremental capital-output ratio. Industry in general, and technologically intensive industry in particular, tends not only to be more intensive in the use of capital than agriculture but also to exhibit long gestation lags between the creation of capacity and output generation. But changes in the sectoral allocation of investment alone cannot account for the rising trend in both the incremental and average capital-output ratios. Equally important is the investment absorptive capacity of the economy, which is a function of the availability of human skills and institutions for the effective utilization of investment. In the absence of such skills, increased investment may only result in a wasteful use of resources, with little growth in productivity. While we discuss this issue at greater length in Chapter 6, it is sufficient to note here that the relatively low investment absorptive capacity of the economy may be a significant factor in the rising trend observed in the capital-output ratio.

Yet another reason for the observed increase in the measured capital-output ratios may be the growth in idle capacity in the manufacturing sector. Although there are no detailed estimates, available evidence points to substantial amounts of under-utilized capacity in various branches of Indian industry. Thus, a recent study notes that in the case of twenty-three out of a total number of forty-three industries for which data are available, capacity utilization during the latter half of the sixties and the seventies was lower than that during the period 1959–65. The study also reports data to show that for important industries such as steel, aluminium, fertilizers and cement, capacity utilization has not only been low but declined over the period 1976–7 to 1979–80.[28] Reasons frequently cited for the high levels of under-utilized capacity include shortage of raw materials, managerial inefficiencies, lack of coordination in industrial planning and deficiencies in demand for final goods.

While the relative weights of these factors in explaining the low levels of capacity utilization are not known, it is significant that deficiencies in demand for final products should be one of them, for lack of demand for goods and services is not a characteristic commonly associated with developing countries – at any rate not with a large and populous country such as India. Whether or not the demand for consumer goods produced by the manufacturing sector has actually declined in recent years in India is a matter of controversy. The hypothesis that the demand for industrial consumer goods has been a constraint on the utilization of capacity and growth of output is based on National Sample Survey data on the distribution and growth of consumer expenditure among different groups of income recipients in the population. It is estimated that in 1964–5, the richest 10 per cent of the population in the rural areas accounted for 32 per cent of the total consumption of industrial goods, whereas the poorest 50 per cent accounted for only 22 per cent of the total. In the urban areas, the top 10 per cent of income earners purchased 39 per cent of the industrial goods, whereas the bottom 50 per cent accounted for only 20 per cent of the total. It is argued that the poorer sections of the population who account for a relatively low proportion of the total consumption expenditure on industrial goods are being priced out of the market because of the increases in the price of food. A high proportion of the incomes of the poorer groups are spent on food, and with the increase in the price of food they have little left to spend on other consumer goods. One study estimates that while the lowest six deciles of income earners spent around two-fifths of their consumption expenditure on industrial goods in 1952–3, twelve years later the ratio was around three-tenths.[29]

Ranga Rajan, however, argues that if the data are extended beyond 1964–5 to 1973–4 there is only a small decline in the percentage of consumer expenditure on industrial goods, and the trend does not appear to be strong. He further argues that in absolute terms, total consumption expenditure on industrial goods of even the poorest deciles of the population increased from Rs 777 million to 981 million over the period 1960–1 to 1973–4, although the percentage share of total income spent on such goods may have declined. He also notes that the consumption expenditure of the upper-income groups is far from reaching saturation point, as the per capita consumption expenditure of the top 5 per cent of the rural population in 1973–4 was still less than Rs 75 per month.[30] On these grounds, Ranga Rajan argues that the hypothesis of a demand constraint on the growth of industrial production is hard to sustain.

Even so, it must be conceded that the absolute levels of consumer expenditure on industrial goods by the poorer groups are low. And while such expenditure may not have declined, there is little evidence to show that there has been a substantial increase in recent years. Further, as Ranga Rajan notes, organized industry at present is catering for only a limited section of the population: the upper-income groups whose pattern of consumption expenditure is oriented heavily towards luxury goods. For these reasons, the hypothesis that slow growth in demand for mass-produced consumer goods has been a factor in the low levels of capacity utilization and growth of industrial output cannot be entirely dismissed.

The central issue, however, is: why the stagnation in demand for consumer goods in such a large and populous country as India? A large and growing population cannot automatically lead to a growth in demand unless there is also a growth in the purchasing power of the population. As Sukhomoy Chakravarthy puts it, paupers cannot be consumers in a market economy unless special transfers are made.[31] In the Indian economy such transfers have scarcely occurred, and as detailed in Chapter 2 there has been no diminution in the proportion of the population designated as absolutely poor.

Sukhomoy Chakravarthy, in the study cited above, has argued that the demand problem in the Indian economy, far from being a transitional phenomenon of the seventies, is an important tendency which has become built into the system. According to him, the factors that have produced the demand problem have a lot to do with 'a growing rigidity in the structure of prices throughout the economy, both agricultural and industrial, with an upward trend imparted through a highly permissive monetary policy, insufficient generation of employment opportunities, absence of bargaining power on the part of the rural poor and the myopic character of private investment.' This is a formidable list of factors, most of which appear to be ingrained in the chosen strategy of development which the country has pursued; a strategy that has centred on import-substituting industrialization, with the public sector being regarded as the *primum mobile* of development.

The permissive monetary policy, as argued earlier, has been a consequence of the public sector's inability to finance its increasing share in capital formation through increased savings. The low level of public-sector savings is in turn a consequence of the government's unwillingness to tax the rural oligarchy for political reasons, the low productive efficiency of public enterprises, and the increasing burden of non-developmental expenditure. In the event, the government's recourse to money creation and indirect taxes, falling heavily on the poor, has contributed to the upward trend in prices, reduction in real income of the poor, and slow growth in demand.

There is a substantial body of evidence to suggest that the insufficient generation of employment opportunities has been largely a consequence of the import-substituting industrialization strategy. This aspect is discussed in greater detail in later chapters; it is sufficient to note here that the strategy has provided incentives for investment in inherently capital-intensive industries, and for the substitution of capital for labour in various lines of manufacturing. The myopic character of private investment which Chakravarthy cites, presumably referring to investment in the production of luxury goods in recent years, is also to be attributed to the chosen strategy of development. Atop all this are the black markets and black money which the government's extensive system of licencing and controls have stimulated; factors which could be significant in explaining the rising trend in prices and the concentration of economic power.

The conclusions of this chapter can be briefly summed up. The relatively low growth performance of the economy cannot be entirely attributed to low growth in savings and investment. Savings and investment rates have risen over the years, especially during the decade of the seventies, but due to a combination of supply and demand factors, the ability of the economy to absorb the investment has been low. Many of the reasons for this are to be sought in India's chosen strategy of development. V. K. R. V. Rao's summing-up of the situation as savings without justice and investment without growth appears to be apt.

5
The Agricultural Sector

No survey of the Indian economy can afford to neglect the agricultural sector. Agriculture is the dominant sector in the Indian economy; as stated in Chapter 2, although its share in the national product has declined from over 50 per cent during the decade of the fifties to around 35 per cent in recent years, it continues to be more than twice as important as the manufacturing sector, as a proportion of the national product. It harbours more than two-thirds of the labour force; it has also vital supply and demand links with the manufacturing sector. On the supply side, it is the source not only of food, the principal wage good, but also of raw materials to the manufacturing sector. On the demand side, it is a major purchaser of manufactured consumer goods, such as sugar, kerosine oil and leather.

It is obvious that given its sheer size and links with the manufacturing sector, the performance of the agricultural sector will have a significant impact on the process of growth and industrialization. Furthermore, increased agricultural productivity may also be vital for the solution of the massive problem of poverty and unemployment described in Chapter 2. None of this is novel: the pivotal role of the agricultural sector in the development process has long been recognized. Nor have India's policy-makers been unaware of the need to develop the agricultural sector. The following statement by the Planning Commission in the First Five-Year Plan document attests to the importance attached to agriculture by India's policy-makers.

For the next five-year period, agriculture including irrigation and power must, in our view, have the top-most priority. For one thing this emphasis is indicated by the need to complete the projects in hand, and further we are convinced that without a substantial increase in the production of food and of raw materials needed for industry, it would be impossible to sustain a high tempo of industrial development. It is necessary, however, on economic as well as on other grounds, first of all to strengthen the economy at the base and to create conditions of sufficiency and even plentitude in respect of food and raw materials.[1]

This intention to accord priority to agriculture was put into practice by allocating a lion's share of the total outlay of Rs 23 billion in the First Five-Year Plan to agriculture and community development, and irrigation. While these two categories accounted for 32 per cent of the total plan outlay of Rs 23 billion, industry accounted for only 7.6 per cent. The priorities, though, were reversed in the Second Five-Year Plan. The second plan, with its emphasis on import-substituting industrialization, increased the share of industry from 7.6 per cent in the first plan to 18 per cent out of a total outlay Rs 48 billion, and reduced that of agriculture and irrigation from 32 per cent to 22 per cent (Table 5.1). It is this reduction in the percentage share of plan outlay for agriculture that forms the basis for the widespread assertion that the Second Five-Year Plan neglected agriculture.

It should however, be noted that a smaller proportion out of a larger outlay is an increase in absolute terms. The absolute amount spent on agriculture and irrigation during the second plan was Rs 9.4 billion as against a sum of Rs 7 billion spent during the first plan. And it has steadily increased in the successive Five-Year Plans, with the sector's percentage share in total plan outlays remaining consistently above 20 per cent. Even so, it can be argued that given the size of the sector and the massive number of people dependent on farming for their livelihood, a much higher proportion of total expenditure should have been allocated to agriculture in the early years of planning. This, though, is an easy prescription to advance with hindsight. Moreover, there is no presumption that in the absence of technological and institutional change, increased investment would necessarily have resulted in increased agricultural productivity.[2] In sum, it may be an exaggeration to say that India's policy-makers have failed to appreciate the importance of agricultural development.

The policy-makers' laudable objective of creating conditions of plentitude of food and raw materials, though, has remained a pious hope. Growth in food production has barely matched the growth in population. Available estimates show that the per capita availability of food grains in the late seventies and early eighties was no

Table 5.1 Sectoral Allocation of Expenditure in the Five-Year Plans

	First Plan 1951–6	Second Plan 1956–61	Third Plan 1961–6	Annual Plans 1966–7 to 1968–9	Fourth Plan 1969–74	Fifth Plan 1974–8
Agriculture and allied sectors	14.8	11.7	12.7	16.7	14.7	11.9
Irrigation and flood control	22.2	9.2	7.8	7.1	8.6	9.5
Power	7.6	9.7	14.6	18.3	18.6	18.8
Village and small industries	2.0	4.0	2.8	1.9	1.5	1.3
Industry and minerals	2.8	20.0	20.1	22.8	18.2	24.1
Transportation and communications	26.5	22.0	24.6	18.5	19.5	17.8
Others	24.0	23.4	17.4	14.7	19.0	16.6
Total	100.0	100.0	100.0	100.0	100.0	100.0
Total plan expenditure (Rs billion)	19.6	46.7	85.8	66.3	158.8	286.5

Source: *Basic Statistics Relating to the Indian Economy: 1950–51 to 1978–79* (Central Statistical Organisation, Government of India, 1980).

higher than the 480 grammes per day achieved in the mid-sixties. The deceleration in the rate of growth of industrial output since the mid-sixties also appears to endorse the policy-makers' conviction that, without a substantial increase in the production of food and raw materials, it would be impossible to sustain a high tempo of industrial development.

This low growth performance of agriculture has given rise to a wide-ranging debate on India's agricultural policies. During the first fifteen years of planning, institutional reform of agriculture, styled as the integrated rural development approach, constituted the mainstay of India's agricultural policies. This included encouragment of cooperative farming, community development programmes, and land reform. For several reasons, including the failure of cooperative farming to take shape, growing scarcity of food, and the weight of opinion among influential foreign advisors, there was a major change in India's agricultural policy in the mid-sixties: from the integrated rural development approach to a technology-oriented agricultural production approach. The new strategy emphasized the application of modern science and technology to agriculture, supported by substantial investment in modern imputs, and price incentives for farmers to adopt them. The introduction of the new high-yielding varieties (HYVS) of wheat and rice, an integral part of the Green Revolution, also formed an important ingredient of the new strategy.

The failure of the new strategy to usher in the hoped-for era of agricultural prosperity has brought into sharp focus the debate between those who assign primacy to institutional change in agriculture, as a method of not only promoting productive efficiency but also securing social justice, and those who assign primacy to technological change. The institutionalists regard the new strategy to be not only of limited success in promoting agricultural growth, but also pernicious in its effects on equity and employment. They argue that the early attempts at institutional reform were feeble and much too narrow in scope, and that even those policies that were legislated were not fully implemented. What is needed is a radical programme of land reform, including not only policies of land redistribution but also policies designed to eliminate various institutional constraints facing agriculture.

The rest of this chapter reviews this debate, focussing on the theoretical foundations and factual basis of the two seemingly rival strategies. As much of this debate has taken place against the background of a low level of agricultural growth, we first briefly review the growth record of agriculture.

Growth record

Estimates of the growth rate of agricultural output are highly sensitive to the choice of the time period to which they relate. However, considerable importance is attached to a comparison of the growth performance since the year 1965 with that during the period 1950–65. For it was in the mid-sixties that the technology-oriented new agricultural strategy was adopted, and it is the argument of the critics that the strategy has made little difference to the growth performance during these two periods. Accordingly, we briefly review the growth performance during these two periods.

1950–65

The annual average compound rates of growth of total agricultural output, food grains output and non-food grains output during this period were 3.1 per cent, 2.9 per cent and 3.5 per cent respectively.

These growth rates are not low by historical standards. They not only compare favourably with the early record of the present-day developed countries, but also represent an appreciable increase over the rates of growth achieved during the pre-independence decades. During the period 1900–45, the rate of growth of total agricultural output was a mere 0.3 per cent.[3]

Food grains form a substantial proportion of total agricultural output in India. They have a weight of 68 per cent in the total agricultural output index, and account for 40 per cent of total consumption expenditure. Food grains output increased by 46 per cent from 61 million to 89 million tons during the period 1949–50 to 1964–65, with an annual average compound rate of growth of 2.9 per cent. Although this growth rate barely exceeded the rate of growth of population, it represented a considerable advance over the negligible rate of growth of 0.11 per cent achieved during the pre-independence decades.[4]

A substantial proportion of the growth in output of food grains over this period was on account of additions to the area under cultivation. John Mellor reports that over the period 1949–50 to 1960–1, increased area under cultivation was the single major factor contributing to the 35 per cent increase in output of food grains, with increased application of fertilizers accounting for less than 9 per cent of the increase in output. Over the period 1961–5, however, fertilizers contributed a substantial 34 per cent to the 9 per cent increase in total output of food grains.[5] This finding is of significance, for it suggests that by the early sixties, limits to increased area under cultivation as a source of growth were being reached, thereby necessitating a search for methods to increase productivity. This may have been one of the factors influencing the policy-makers to adopt the technology-oriented strategy in the mid-sixties, with emphasis on modern inputs for increasing agricultural productivity.

1965–81

The growth performance of the agricultural sector since the mid-sixties is marked by several features. First, there were the severe droughts of 1965–6 and 1966–7, which resulted in an absolute decline in the output of food grains from the peak level of 89 million tons in 1964–5 to 74 million tons in 1966–7. Second, even with the exclusion of these two drought years from the data, the recorded growth rate of agricultural output for the period 1967–81 turns out to be lower than that for the period 1949–50 to 1964–5 (Table 5.2). Third is the impressive surge in the growth performance of wheat.

Econometric studies incorporating sophisticated statistical techniques for the analysis of growth trends have, in fact, reached the conclusion that there is no appreciable difference in the growth performance of agriculture between the period 1949–50 to 1964–5 and the period since then. One such study by T. N. Srinivasan has analysed the growth trends for the period 1949–50 to 1977–8, and for the two sub-periods 1949–50 to 1964–5 and 1967–8 to 1977–8.[6] The study finds that over the period 1949–50 to 1977–8, the growth rate for food grains, all crops and non-food grains hovered around 3 per cent per annum, the first two being a shade under and the last a shade over 3 per cent. Of significance in this context is Srinivasan's finding that '. . . the output (and yield per unit of area) of food crops and all crops grew more or less uniformly over the entire period with no evidence of either acceleration or deceleration since 1967–8.'[7]

The one exception in this regard is the performance of wheat. There has been a truly revolutionary increase in the output and yield per acre of wheat since the mid-sixties. Total output of wheat

Table 5.2 Growth Rates in Area, Production and Yield, 1949–50 to 1980–1 (per cent per annum)

	Weight in the Production Index	Area			Production			Yield		
		1949–50 to 1964–5	1967–8 to 1980–1	1949–50 to 1980–1	1949–50 to 1964–5	1967–8 to 1980–1	1949–50 to 1980–1	1949–50 to 1964–5	1967–8 to 1980–1	1949–50 to 1980–1
Food grains	68.12	1.4	0.4	0.8	2.9	2.4	2.5	1.4	1.6	1.5
(a) Rice	33.98	1.3	0.7	1.0	3.4	2.2	2.4	2.1	1.4	1.5
(b) Wheat	12.16	2.6	2.9	2.8	3.9	5.5	5.8	1.3	2.6	3.0
(c) Jowar	4.86	1.0	−1.2	−0.1	2.5	2.0	1.3	1.5	3.2	1.4
Non-food grains	31.88	2.5	1.0	1.3	3.5	2.3	2.6	0.9	1.2	1.0
All crops	100.0	1.6	0.5	0.9	3.1	2.3	2.5	1.3	1.4	1.3

Source: Estimated on the basis of data in *Economic Survey* (Government of India, various issues).

increased from 16.5 million tons in 1966–7 to 36 million tons in 1980–1, with an annual average rate of growth of 5.7 per cent per annum compared to the 3.9 per cent achieved over the period 1949–50 to 1964–5. A substantial proportion of this increase in output was on account of growth in productivity. Measured in terms of yield per acre, average annual growth in productivity doubled from 1.3 per cent over the period 1949–50 to 1964–5 to 2.5 per cent over the period 1967–81 (Table 5.2).

In contrast is the performance of rice, India's dominant food crop. Available estimates show that the growth rates for area, yield and output were all appreciably lower for the period 1967–8 to 1980–1, compared to the period 1949–50 to 1964–5.

It is this low growth performance of the agricultural sector in general which forms the basis for the widespread suggestion that the technology-oriented strategy adopted in the mid-sixties has been a failure, and that the Green Revolution has been no more than a wheat revolution. As Ashok Rudra, whose sophisticated statistical trend analysis of the growth performance of agriculture also failed to detect a significant upward trend in the growth rate since the mid-sixties, puts it, 'the general conclusion that can be drawn is that there have indeed been breakthroughs in the production conditions for some crops in some regions, but no such thing has taken place for all crops and all regions. Thus for the country as a whole and agriculture as a whole, the strategy has not succeeded.'[8]

Is this a fair indictment of the new strategy? Is the strategy *per se* to be blamed for the uneven growth performance? Has the policy resulted in increased income disparities and the displacement of labour in agriculture? Were the policy-makers over-zealous and hasty in adopting the new strategy to the relative neglect of institutional reform, the avowed objective of agricultural policy prior to the mid-sixties? We first discuss the case for institutional reform of agriculture before reviewing the issues concerning the new agricultural strategy.

Institutional change

The case for institutional change in agriculture is based on the grounds of both equity and efficiency. The generally recognized institutional constraints facing agriculture are uneconomic size of farms, inequitable tenurial arrangments, wide disparities in land ownership, indebtedness and lack of access to credit and other inputs on the part of small farmers, inadequate marketing facilities, and low levels of health, literacy and education in rural areas. According to the institutionalists, it is these constraints, rather than the low level of technology, that have impeded the promotion of growth and equity in agriculture. For the most part, discussion on institutional change has centred on land-ownership patterns, tenurial arrangements and land reform policies.

The case for land reform

The prevailing distribution of land ownership, tenurial arrangements and the pattern of employment in agriculture are all relevant to the case for land reform on grounds of equity. Available evidence shows that the distribution of land ownership in India is highly skewed. Data reported by the National Sample Survey of India for the year 1960–1 shows that 63 per cent of a total number of 49 million rural households owned only 19 per cent of the total area of 324 million acres under cultivation, and operated farms ranging from less than 1 acre to 5 acres in size. At the other end of the scale were 18 per cent of the rural households who owned 62 per cent of the total area under cultivation and operated farms in excess of 10 acres in size.[9] Recent data for the year 1975–6 shows that a bare 3 per cent of the rural households owned 26 per cent of the area, while at the other extreme were 70 per cent of the rural households who accounted for 24 per cent of the cultivated area.[10]

It could, however, be argued that a skewed distribution of land ownership alone does not justify a policy of land redistribution. In so far as the productive efficiency and contribution of large landowners to national income is assured, equity can be promoted through fiscal devices. But this line of reasoning ignores a characteristic feature of land as an asset, which enables large landowners to reap rewards in excess of their contribution to the production process: this is that land, in essence, is an asset in fixed supply. Growth of population and money incomes exerts an upward demand pressure on a fixed supply of land, pushing up rents or the price of land. In this situation, large land-holders have an incentive to lease their land rather than cultivate it themselves. Hence the widely observed phenomenon of 'absentee landlords' in Indian agriculture. Even so, it can be argued that the price of land can be regulated through legislation; but such attempts at price controls can easily be thwarted because of the types of tenurial arrangement prevalent in Indian agriculture.

One such arrangement which has attracted wide attention is share-cropping tenancy. Under this arrangement, the landlord leases his land to the tenants in return for an agreed share of the produce. An arresting feature of this arrangement is that the tenant not only contributes his labour but also a part of the working capital – in some cases a part of the fixed capital also – to the production process. As Khusro puts it, 'share-cropping is distinguished from the services of a farm servant in that a servant serves but need not and does not give capital; a tenant does.'[11] An arrangement under which the tenant contributes both labour and capital and parts with a high proportion of the produce is obviously lucrative for the landlord. While the incidence of share-cropping varies from state to state in India, it is estimated that in the early sixties for the country as a whole, 25 per cent of the total area under cultivation was under one form of tenancy or another.[12]

The productive efficiency of share-cropping as opposed to wage-based owner-operated farms is a much debated issue. There is, though, a widespread suggestion in the literature that share-cropping as an institution is no less efficient than wage-based owner-operated farms.[13]

The cause for concern, however, is not so much the overall productive efficiency of the arrangement but the distribution of the gains between the landlord and the share-cropping tenants. While a 50–50 share for the landlord and the share-cropper is common, there are cases where the landlord's share is seen to exceed 50 per cent. The crux of the problem is that the tenants may have no legal redress against the disproportionately high rents they are charged, because most share-cropping and tenancy arrangements are in the nature of covert oral agreements between the landlords and the tenants. It is also reported that frequently the landlords style themselves as cultivators for purposes of land records and enter into a servant's deed with the cultivators, although the servants in effect contribute both labour and capital. In these circumstances the tenants are not only forced to pay high rents, but they may also be subject to eviction at the will of the landlord.

If the price of land, the asset in fixed supply, cannot be effectively controlled, the alternative is to ration the asset among the rival claimants to it. A policy of rationing would obviously involve fixing the maximum amount of land that can be owned by the large landowners and households, and redistributing the surplus land above the maximum amongst other claimants to it. Principal amongst such claimants would be the tenants who are at present cultivating the land, for it is they who have for long years contributed their labour and capital to the production process, and paid disproportionately high rents. It is this line of reasoning that underlines the old slogan 'land to the tiller', and the proposition that ownership of land should be conferred on the tenants. Such a policy of rationing and redistribution of land on grounds of equity, however, should also pay heed to considerations of productive efficiency. The issue here is the level at which the ceilings on ownership of land should be fixed, since too low a ceiling may render farms uneconomic in size and impair productive efficiency, and too high a ceiling may not provide enough surplus land for redistribution. The relationship between size of farms and productive efficiency in the context of land reform policies in India has been a much discussed issue. We first discuss this aspect before reviewing the record of India's land reform policies which have included both attempts at price control – fixation of land rents, and rationing of land in the form of imposition of ceilings and land redistribution.

A powerful argument in favour of land redistribution is the empirically observed phenomenon of the inverse relationship between farm size and productivity. Several studies have noted that productivity, measured in terms of the value of output per acre, decreases with increases in farm size.[14] In other words, the productive efficiency of small farms tends to be high relative to that of large farms, and a policy of land redistribution in favour of small farms would increase overall productive efficiency.

There are several explanations for the observed phenomenon of the relatively high productivity of small farms. One hypothesis is that the soil fertility of small farms tends to be high relative to that of large farms. In fact, Khusro has argued that when the data are adjusted for differences in soil fertility between various size-groups of farms, output per acre remains constant as farm size increases above a minimum efficient size.[15] However, more recent econometric studies show that the inverse relationship between farm productivity and farm size survives even after adjustments are made for differences in land quality due to soil fertility and irrigation. Another suggested explanation for the observed differences in productive efficiency between small and large farms is that the small farms tend to use labour more intensively than the large farms. Amartya Sen, for instance, argues that small farms operating with family labour tend to use labour up to the point where the marginal physical productivity of labour equals zero; whereas the large farms employing hired labour use it up to the point where the marginal physical product of labour equals the market wage. Because the small farms tend to use labour more intensively they are able to achieve a higher cropping intensity and a greater output per acre than large farms. Although this proposition has been disputed, there is statistical evidence to show that differences in the cost of labour in favour of the small farms is one of the principal reasons for their observed higher productivity.[16]

As stated earlier, these findings provide a powerful argument for land redistribution on grounds of productive efficiency. It should be noted too, that such a policy of land redistribution may also increase employment opportunities as small farms are relatively intensive in their use of labour compared with large farms. The issue, though, is what the optimum size of farm is from the point of view of both equity and efficiency. In other words, what is the minimum size of farm below which diseconomies of scale would set in, impairing productive efficiency?

Khusro has estimated that the economically viable size of farms, in terms of productive use of resources and incomes, tends to be between 7.5 and 15 acres.[17] Farms below 7.5 acres would not allow for the full utilization of a pair of bullocks (the plough unit), or the full utilization of family labour (the work unit); and farms below 15 acres would not fetch the adequate income of Rs 12,000 per annum per family (the income unit). While the three norms of plough, work and income units suggest differing optimum sizes of farm, Khusro argues that the feasible minimum farm size in the context of the prevailing conditions in Indian agriculture could not be less than 5 acres. In other words, land reform policies should regard 5 acres as the floor, below which farms would not be economically viable.

The facts of the Indian agrarian structure are that 63 per cent of rural households operate farms which are less than 5 acres in size, and together account for 19 per cent of the area under cultivation. A further 19 per cent of the households operate farms of 5 to 10 acres and account for 20 per cent of the area. An additional 18 per cent of the households operate farms in excess of 10 acres in size and account for 60 per cent of the area.[18] These data suggest that while a high proportion of the *rural households* operate farms below the optimum size, a large proportion of *the area under cultivation* is not subject to the disadvantages of small size.

Obviously, policies designed to bring up the large number of tiny farms to the minimum efficient size of 5 acres would increase productivity. Such policies would include consolidation of holdings at the lower end of the spectrum, the imposition of ceilings on large land holdings to bring the small farms up to the optimum level, and encouragement of cooperative farming. The issue, though, is whether a radical programme of land redistribution designed to reduce the size of farms which are at present above 10 acres and account for 60 per cent of the area would have an appreciable impact on productivity and growth. It is on this issue that debate is joined between those who advocate an urgent programme of land redistribution and those who emphasize policies designed to promote technological change. The advocates of a policy of land redistribution draw support from the observed phenomenon of the inverse relationship between farm size and farm productivity. As stated earlier, small farms are not only relatively efficient but also intensive in their use of labour. A policy of land redistribution through the imposition of ceilings on large land-holdings, therefore, would not only increase productivity, but also increase the demand for labour and wage rates for landless labourers. Hence it would promote both equity and efficiency.

The advocates of technological change in agriculture, however, argue that as a large proportion of the area under cultivation is above the minimum efficient size, there is no need for drastic land redistribution policies in the interests of efficiency. What is needed is provision of fertilizers, better seeds and irrigation facilities to the farms above 5 acres in size, to increase their production efficiency.[19]

There may be more than a germ of truth in this argument. Admittedly, a policy of land redistribution may increase productivity; but it is a costly exercise. A mere policy of land redistribution alone may not have much effect on productivity. It has to be accompanied by the provision of infra-structure, credit and marketing facilities for the small farmers who gain land from the redistribution policy. The issue, then, is whether or not the pay-off to investment in institutional change is likely to be higher than that to investment in technological change. Increased productive efficiency is a function both of improved allocation and utilization of existing resources, and of technological change involving the introduction of modern inputs and new methods of cultivation. The impact of land redistribution policies on productive efficiency arises principally through a better allocation of existing resources of land and labour. But there are limits to the gains in productivity arising from reallocation of existing resources. Ultimately, it is technological change that has to be relied upon for a major breakthrough in productive efficiency.

All this is not to say that there is no case for land reform. It is merely to note that the ambit of an efficient programme of land reform is wider than that of a mere policy of land redistribution. It includes not only policies of land redistribution but also policies designed to facilitate the effective utilization of land by the small farmers. The productive efficiency of small farmers would be relatively high in an environment characterized by technological change. In the absence of such change, the gains to be reaped from a radical policy of land redistribution may be limited, at best it could be a palliative to the massive problem of poverty and unemployment in the rural areas, but not a cure. Again, policies designed to promote security of tenure and an equitable distribution of gains between the share-croppers and the landlords are highly desirable from the point of view of equity. But it is arguable whether a policy of land redistribution in favour of the cultivators would necessarily increase productive efficiency, for, as stated earlier, the evidence in support of the proposition that owner-operated farms are more efficient than farms under share-cropping is inconclusive.

Land reform policies, centring on land rationing and the regulation of rents, are also unfortunately exceedingly difficult to implement. This, in fact, is the major problem confronting most policies of rationing and price control. More often than not, such policies result in the spread of black markets, corruption and widespread evasion of the legislation. These problems are compounded when such policies are attempted within the framework of a political democracy. India's experience with land reform policies since the fifties is illustrative.

The record of India's land reform policies

As stated earlier, India's agricultural policies prior to the mid-sixties set store on institutional change. The major policy measures included imposition of ceilings on land ownership and land redistribution, reform of tenurial arrangements, encouragement of cooperative farming among small- and medium-scale farmers, and community development projects. The community development projects were to be the instruments for ushering in cooperative farming and social change in rural areas.[20]

There are a number of studies reviewing the record of these policies.[21] We note here only the main points. There is a widespread suggestion in the literature that, save for the abolition of the Zamindari system, India's land reforms have been a failure. Although ceilings on land-holdings were set reasonably low, the legislation was not effectively enforced. Pranab Bardhan sums up the situation thus:

> Laws were frequently enacted with deliberate loopholes and telltale exemptions designed to induce fictitious transfers of land to close and distant relatives and to keep the size of permissible retentions high. These laws were executed by a local bureaucracy largely indifferent, occasionally corrupt, and biased in favour of the rural oligarchy.[22]

By the end of the year 1970, for the country as a whole, the declared surplus of land available for redistribution was only 2.4 million acres, and the area distributed just half of that, or 0.3 per cent of the total area. Legislation designed to control land rents and ensure security of tenure to the tenants frequently resulted in the eviction of tenants and the reclamation of land for cultivation by the landlords. In addition, mainly for administrative reasons, the community development and cooperative farming programmes were largely unsuccessful.

Yet, despite all its deficiencies, India's efforts at land reform cannot be dismissed as a total failure. The reforms to the extent that they were carried out, and perhaps the very threat of reforms, may have been factors of importance in the growth performance of agriculture prior to 1965. As stated earlier, much of the growth in output over this period was on account of increases in the area under cultivation. The abolition of the Zamindari system, which removed the land-owning tax intermediaries who were non-cultivators, and returned the land to the cultivators, may have been a factor in the growth in area under cultivation. Further, as Khusro states, although in the early years of reform there was large-scale eviction of tenants, the rate of eviction declined rapidly and the reforms made tenants conscious of their rights. The burden of exploitative rents on the tenants has also been reduced. It should be noted, too, that India's land reform experiment is distinguished by the fact that it has been attempted in the framework of political democracy. In sum, India's land reform policies, although not a total failure, have suffered from deficiencies of implementation, and have not achieved the hoped-for distributive justice and growth. The recognition that such policies are difficult to implement and have had only a limited impact on the growth performance of agriculture appears to have been a factor in the adoption of the technology-centred new agricultural strategy in the mid-sixties.

The new agricultural strategy

The agricultural policies which India has pursued since the mid-sixties have been christened a new strategy because of their emphasis on technological change, as opposed to the emphasis of earlier policies on institutional change. Generally regarded as the brain-child of American economists and the World Bank, the new strategy emphasized the application of modern science and technology to agriculture, supported by substantial investment in modern inputs, and the provision of price incentives to farmers to adopt them.

The intellectual lineage of the technology-oriented strategy is to be traced to the Chicago School thesis that 'farmers are everywhere capable of producing the right things in the right place in the right amounts and at low costs in terms of resources if they receive the proper economic signals.'[23] The crux of this thesis is that farmers are efficient and economically rational. They are profit maximizers, allocate resources efficiently and respond to market signals.

A lucid exposition of this thesis in the context of traditional agriculture was provided by the Chicago economist T. W. Schultz in a seminal book published in 1964;[24] citing various pieces of empirical evidence, Schultz argued that farmers in traditional agriculture allocate existing resources, such that factor rewards equal their marginal products. The fact that they do so shows that they respond to market signals; but they are poor. Their poverty is to be attributed to the nature of inputs and techniques of production they use. These are inputs and techniques of cultivation that have been in use for many years, and the rates of return to investment in them tend to be meagre. Given the low rates of return to existing factors of production, there is no inducement for additional work effort and savings. It is thus that traditional agriculture is efficient but poor. And it has reached a state of long-run low-level equilibrium.

The arresting feature of this thesis is its emphasis on economic factors rather than cultural and institutional attributes of traditional agriculture. The distinguishing characteristic of traditional agriculture that sets it apart from modern agriculture, according to this thesis, is the type of inputs and technology in use, and not its cultural and institutional attributes. As Schultz puts it, the basis for distinguishing between traditional and modern agriculture is not to be found in 'differences in particular insititutional arrangements, for example in whether farms are under resident or absentee ownership, whether they are small or large, whether they are private or public enterprises, and whether the production is for home consumption or for sale.'[25]

The policy implications of the thesis are that traditional agriculture needs to be jolted out of the low level of equilibrium by the introduction of modern inputs with relatively high rates of return and by the application of science and technology. As farmers are rational and respond to market forces, proper price incentives would induce them to adopt modern inputs.

Empirical foundations

As is well known, the Chicago school tradition of economics is grounded in empiricism. In fact, many of Schultz's propositions concerning traditional agriculture draw support from empirical studies, mostly relating to India. One illustration is Raj Krishna's econometric analysis of farmers' supply responses to price in the case of wheat, rice and cotton in India. The specific hypothesis he investigated was whether or not farmers responded to changes in the relative prices of output by varying the acreage sown to different crops. In other words, he was concerned with estimating the elasticity of substitution of acreage with respect to relative prices. The estimated short-run elasticities for wheat and rice in the Punjab for the period 1914–45 were 0.08 and 0.31, and the long-run elasticities were 0.14 and 0.59 respectively. In the case of cotton, relating to the period 1948–61, the short-run and long-run elasticities are put at 0.64 and 1.33.[26] All the reported elasticities are positive, and indeed quite high in the case of rice and cotton. Several other studies with widely differing methods of estimation data and time period also support the conclusion that Indian farmers do vary the acreage under different crops in response to changes in prices.

But a high elasticity of substitution of acreage with respect to price does not necessarily imply a high elasticity of output with respect to prices, because changes in output are not only a function of area planted but also of productivity or yields per acre. It could be argued that changes in acreage are a good approximation to changes in output, as increases in acreage are likely to be accompanied by increased use of inputs which would raise yields. This may be so in the case of individual crops or a group of crops. But if co-operant inputs are in short supply, it is doubtful if agricultural output as a whole would respond to prices. Moreover, most of these empirical estimates relate to the elasticity of substitution in output with respect to relative prices. For purposes of policy, the relevant issue is whether or not agricultural output as a whole responds to a change in the terms of trade – the prices of agricultural products sold by farmers relative to that of manufactured products purchased by the farmers – facing agriculture. Unfortunately there is little empirical evidence on this issue. What little there is relates to the elasticity of output of food grains with respect to prices. These are fairly low, in the region of 0.16 and 0.27.

The gist of the thesis, however, is that farmers do respond to prices. The available evidence supports this contention. In addition, the elasticity of output with respect to prices, although low, is positive.[27] In any case, a positive price policy for agriculture is but one facet of the new strategy. The emphasis of the strategy is on the introduction of modern inputs and technology into agriculture, with a positive price policy providing an incentive for the farmers to adopt the technology.

The strategy in practice

The design of India's new agricultural strategy reflects many of the precepts of the Chicago school concerning agricultural development. The technology-oriented new strategy adopted in the mid-sixties had three major strands. First was the explicit recognition of the need for price incentives to induce farmers to adopt the new technology and inputs. As Francine Frankel, summarizing the views of the Agriculture Minister, C. Subramaniam, on the issue, writes: 'The Agriculture Minister insisted this (the adoption of the new approach) required a reversal of past approaches to price policy, from a pre-occupation with low cost food grains for the urban poor, to a firm commitment to "renumerative and incentive prices to make this production process reasonably safe for farmers".'[28] The policy has been implemented since the mid-sixties, through minimum support prices for fifteen crops announced in advance of .he sowing season, and the annual announcement of government procurement prices for food grains for the public distribution system.

The second and vital strand of the new strategy was, of course, the introduction of the new high-yielding varieties (HYVs) of wheat and rice. The discovery of these new varieties was, in fact, a major argument in favour of the new strategy. Reports from Mexico had indicated that the new varieties of wheat were capable of absorbing high levels of fertilizers to give yields of 5,000 pounds per acre, more than twice those of traditional varieties. Similarly, in the case of rice, reports from the Philippines had indicated that the new varieties were capable of yielding 5,000 to 6,000 pounds per acre – nearly three times the maximum yield from local varieties. In addition to the introduction of the high-yielding varieties, the new strategy also emphasized the provision of subsidies to farmers to promote investment in tube wells and other improved implements and inputs.

The third facet of the strategy, as conceived in the mid-sixties, was the policy of gradualism, in the sense that it was to be confined at first to selected areas. The rationale for the policy was that, given the limited amount of resources at the disposal of the state, the strategy would yield better results if it was concentrated in selected areas. As C. Subramaniam, the Minister for Agriculture who spear-headed the strategy, put it, 'if we concentrate our efforts in a given area where we have assured water supply and we have the necessary extension services also concentrated in the area, then it should be possible for us to achieve much better results than by merely dispersing our efforts in a thin way thoughout the country.'[29] Implicit in this policy was the hope that once the dynamics were set in motion in the selected areas, they would eventually spread to other areas. It should be noted in this context that the new high-yielding varieties are resource intensive. They are not only intensive in the use of fertilizers, but also require more water than the traditional varieties. In addition, the new varieties require increased supplies of pesticides and germicides, as they are reported to be more prone to plant disease than the local varieties.

Initially the Ministry of Agriculture proposed to cover a total area of 32.5 million acres under food grains (12 per cent of the area) with the new varieties by the end of the decade of the sixties. It is estimated that by the end of 1978–9, nearly 70 per cent of the total area of 22 million hectares under wheat, and 40 per cent of the total area of 40 million hectares under rice were covered with the new high-yielding varieties.[30]

The strategy under attack

There is a vast body of literature, mostly critical, on the new strategy. For purposes of discussion, the criticism of the new strategy can be broadly grouped under three headings: (a) price policy (b) growth performance (c) employment and income distribution.

Price policy

As stated earlier, a positive and remunerative price policy towards agriculture constitutes one of the main elements of the new strategy. It has been argued that this policy may have been overdrawn in practice, with adverse consequences not only for equity and efficiency in agriculture, but also for the growth of industrial output.

This hypothesis is argued persuasively by Ashok Mitra.[31] The factual basis for the hypothesis is the steep increase in the price of agricultural products relative to that of manufactured goods since 1964–5. Mitra cites data to show that over the period 1963–4 to 1973–4, the weighted terms of trade between agriculture and industry had moved by almost 50 per cent in favour of agriculture. That the terms of trade had shifted perceptibly in favour of agriculture since the mid-fifties is also shown by R. Thamarajakshi's detailed estimates for the period 1950–1 to 1974–5 (Table 5.3).[32]

The primary and overriding reason for this steep increase in the relative price of agricultural products, according to Mitra, is the government's agricultural pricing policies. Principal amongst these,

Table 5.3 Indices of Terms of Trade between Agriculture and Manufacturing (1960–1 = 100)

Year	Net Barter Terms of Trade	Foodgrains Terms of Trade	Terms of Trade of all Agricultural Products	Income Terms of Trade
1951–2	100.82	104.47	116.89	67.07
1952–3	99.13	116.84	96.28	72.41
1953–4	103.74	112.54	102.83	88.40
1954–5	97.02	91.84	95.17	85.99
1955–6	94.78	92.02	89.10	88.20
1956–7	102.46	109.20	98.16	100.67
1957–8	98.46	107.11	96.07	92.15
1958–9	101.66	113.43	98.37	97.95
1959–60	101.68	105.88	98.85	94.43
1960–1	100.00	100.00	100.00	100.00
1961–2	100.69	98.38	97.64	106.20
1962–3	99.39	99.69	95.16	106.17
1963–4	97.39	101.59	96.77	108.90
1964–5	108.66	118.80	107.88	124.67
1965–6	114.47	120.60	110.17	123.95
1966–7	123.07	131.81	117.56	129.04
1967–8	125.02	148.10	123.74	149.99
1968–9	116.27	126.91	122.21	143.62
1969–70	125.72	131.05	126.72	167.08
1970–1	127.32	125.85	124.20	178.88
1971–2	120.08	122.65	119.29	181.31
1972–3	118.30	128.26	119.23	173.81
1973–4	136.98	134.40	134.14	206.11
1974–5	133.92	146.78	128.16	

Source: R. Thamarajakshi's estimates cited in A. Mody, 'Resource Flows between Agriculture and Non-Agriculture in India', *Economic and Political Weekly* (annual number, March 1981).

as stated earlier, are the minimum prices and procurement prices announced annually by the government. The level of the support prices and the procurement prices are set by the Agricultural Prices Commission, taking into consideration costs of cultivation and the need to maintain 'adequate' profit margins for the farmers. Admittedly, these prices are lower than those prevailing on the open market; but the case of the critics is that these prices mould the psychology of the market. Every increase in the procurement prices signals a rise in the open market prices by the same proportion. In other words, the system of procurement prices imparts a bullishness to the market. Furthermore, Mitra argues, each shift in the terms of trade in favour of farm products strengthens the ability of the large landowners – the surplus farmers – to hold back stocks and bid for still higher prices in the subsequent season.

If this were the case there would be a strong motivation on the part of farmers to lobby for higher procurement prices; not so much because higher procurement prices increase the returns from their sales of output to the government, but because of the impact of procurement prices on open market prices. In fact, the total amount of food grains procured by the government has amounted to no more than 11 to 12 per cent of total output in recent years, and it was less than 10 per cent in years prior to 1975.[33] The level of procurement prices, however, has increased steadily over the years. For instance, the procurement price for wheat went up from Rs 105 per quintal in 1976–7 to Rs 130 per quintal in 1981–2 and for rice from Rs 74 to Rs 115 per quintal over the same period. It is arguable whether these increases in price could be justified on the grounds of increases in costs of cultivation. In fact, the procurement prices paid by the government have often been higher than those recommended by the Agricultural Prices Commission. Even more revealing is the following comment in the government's Annual Economic Survey for 1981–2, in the context of rice: 'some State Governments have offered higher procurement prices than the support prices fixed by the Central Government and prices at which the Food Corporation of India is authorised to make purchases. Higher prices offered by the State Governments are bound to create confusion in the market. . . . It is important to maintain discipline in these corporations.'[34]

The confusion in the markets to which the official statement refers is apparently the impact which higher procurement prices are likely to have on open market prices. And the lack of discipline on the part of the corporations is apparently the result of political pressure for higher prices exerted by lobbies of the big farmers.

Political forces may thus have thwarted the objectives of the government's pricing policies. As stated earlier, the amount of food grains procured by the government for the public distribution system is relatively low. Raj Krishna, writing in 1967, has estimated that the government would have to purchase at least 21 per cent of the output by 1971 if it were to cater for 25 per cent of aggregate food demand through the public distribution system.[35] Yet by the end of the decade of the seventies, the government was purchasing no more than 12 per cent of the output: hardly an amount adequate to meet the food requirements of the poor dependent on the public distribution system. Furthermore, the public distribution system is concentrated mainly in the urban areas, but the majority of the poor in India are in the rural areas. As Ashok Mitra notes, a substantial proportion of the rural population, including landless labourers and households in possession of less than 2.5 acres of land, are forced to go to the open market for their requirements of food grains. It is thus that the big farmers may have gained at the expense of the poor who have to purchase their food grains on the open market at steeply increasing prices. This is hardly a prescription for equity.

It is also debatable whether 'high' prices have been a significant factor in the adoption of the new varieties of wheat and rice. The prospect of higher yields and the availability of subsidies for the adoption of modern inputs may have been factors of greater significance than the high prices.

All this is not to say that improved terms of trade and a positive price policy have no role to play in the modernization of agriculture. There are not many adherents to the traditional view, supported by the historical experience of the developed countries, that the terms of trade should be deliberately turned against agriculture as a method of siphoning the surplus from agriculture to promote industrialization. The irrelevance of such a policy to present-day developing countries, with respect to both equity and efficiency, has been amply demonstrated by the recent experience of many developing countries.[36] It is increasingly recognized that agriculture should be developed for its own sake, and that given the incentives, it is capable of generating increased supplies of food and raw materials. Improved terms of trade and a positive price policy for agriculture, however, do not necessarily imply an escalating price level for agricultural products. The relevant issue is not whether the terms of trade should favour agriculture, but what the optimum level of the terms of trade should be. While this is an unsettled issue, there are good grounds for arguing that the agricultural price level in India in recent years has been much too high to be justified on grounds of equity and efficiency.

Impact on growth of output

As stated earlier, one of the main criticisms of the new agricultural strategy is that it has had little positive impact on the growth rate of agricultural output. Admittedly, there has been no increase in the trend rate of growth of output since the mid-sixties. It has stayed constant at the rate achieved over the period 1950–65. It is, however, arguable whether the rate of growth of output could have been sustained at this level but for the adoption of the new strategy centred on the new high-yielding varieties. As stated in the section on the growth record of agriculture, much of the increase in output during the fifties and the early sixties was on account of increased area under cultivation. It is conceivable that the limits to the growth in area under cultivation as a source of growth in output may have been reached by the mid-sixties. Since then, it is continued increases in yield per acre which have sustained the growth rate of output. The contribution of the new strategy, centred on the introduction of new high-yielding varieties in conjunction with increased application of fertilizers and greater irrigation, to sustaining the growth in productivity may have been substantial.

Recent empirical studies lend support to this proposition. A recent study by Prahaladachar cites evidence to show that states which recorded comparatively large increases in food grain production between 1967–70 and 1976–9 were also the ones which, in general, had comparatively large proportions of their areas under food grains sown with the new varieties as well as irrigated. These states also fared better in respect of fertilizer use and credit.[37]

Another principal criticism of the Green Revolution is that it has mostly been a wheat revolution. It is a fact that the Green Revolution has not had the same dramatic impact on rice, India's principal crop, as it had on wheat; but that which has been achieved in the case of rice is not negligible. As stated earlier, for the country as a whole, more than 40 per cent of the area under rice was under new varieties by the end of the decade of the seventies. In the case of the principal rice-growing areas of the country, such as Tamil Nadu, 80 per cent of the area under rice is reported to be sown with the new varieties.

It is instructive in this context to examine the growth performance of rice in Tamil Nadu. Rice accounts for 35 per cent of the total cropped area, 67 per cent of the total irrigated area and over 70 per cent of the total output of food grains in the state of Tamil Nadu. According to the data reported by C. T. Kurien, total output of rice increased by 64 per cent over the period 1965–6 to 1975–6, from 3.6

million tons to 6 million tons.[38] Much of this increase in output is to be attributed to increases in yield per acre. While the total area under rice increased by a modest 8 per cent over the period, yields per acre increased by 54 per cent. The increase in yields per acre may largely be due to the introduction of the new varieties of rice, in conjunction with fertilizers and irrigation.

Kurien, however, argues that rice production over this period was subject to considerable year-to-year fluctuations, and the appreciable increases in production achieved during several of the years in the late sixties and the early seventies must be regarded as 'recovery growths'. The growth performance of rice, therefore, cannot be attributed to the new high-yielding varieties. Indeed, he argues that but for the 'recovery rates, the post-HYV performance was of the order of less than 6 per cent increase from year to year, compared with the 7 to 8 per cent which was frequent in the fifties. But it is conceivable that the recovery rates themselves may have been considerably lower than those recorded in the absence of the new varieties, especially as growth in output in the post-1965 period has been largely on account of increased yields per acre, whereas in the fifties the source of growth was increased area under cultivation.

The wide year-to-year fluctuations in the rate of growth of output induced by the vagaries of rainfall also points to the susceptibility of the new varieties of rice to environmental factors. By most accounts, the relative failure of the new varieties of rice is to be attributed mostly to environmental problems, including their proneness to disease in the rainy season and their requirement of controlled water-supply. In time, these obstacles are likely to be overcome through research, and it may not be over-optimistic to expect a rice revolution.

It is of significance in this context that in recent years, the traditional wheat-growing areas such as the Punjab and Haryana have adopted rice as an additional summer crop. Rice production in these areas is reported to be growing and gaining significance in terms both of absolute quantities produced and of growth rates. It is reported that this phenomenon is confined to the more progressive farms which possess the managerial skills and water control to make the new crop profitable. Presumably, these farmers have found it easy to transfer the managerial skills acquired in growing the high-yielding varieties of wheat to the high-yielding varieties of rice. This phenomenon illustrates again the importance of water control and irrigation facilities, and of managerial skills in adopting the new varieties. It is conceivable that the relatively low degree of success with the new varieties of rice in other areas of the country is largely due to the lack of such facilities.

Impact on equity and employment

The most significant and by far the most widely debated of the criticisms of the Green Revolution are that it has exacerbated income inequalities in rural India, and that it has had little positive impact on employment and real wages of agricultural labourers. There is a sizeable body of literature on these issues, too numerous to review in the confines of a brief chapter.[39] We discuss only the main points.

One of the major criticisms of the Green Revolution in the early seventies was that it had benefited mostly the large farmers – often at the expense of the small farmers. In support of this argument. data were cited to show that there was a strong positive relationship between size of farms and the proportion of farmers adopting the new varieties. There was also the suggestion that with the introduction of the new varieties, the inverse relationship between farm size and productivity no longer held. Indeed, there may now be a positive relationship between farm size and productivity. Because of the increased productivity of the new varieties, the large farmers may no longer be at a disadvantage relative to small farms with respect to labour costs. Implicit in all this is the suggestion that the new high-yielding varieties are not scale-neutral and their adoption requires relatively large farms.

Recent case-studies, however, paint a different picture.[40] The main conclusion of these studies is that the Green Revolution is scale-neutral. The technological characteristics of the new varieties do not impede the small farmers from adopting them. Further, the observed discrepancies in the rate of adoption and effective utilization of the new varieties between large and small farms is to be attributed to the nature of the institutional and infrastructural arrangements surrounding agriculture, and not to the Green Revolution *per se*.

Case-studies based on fairly large samples, relating to both rice- and wheat-growing areas, show that small farmers are progressively catching up with the large farmers in adopting the new varieties. A study by G. S. Bhalla, based on comprehensive household survey data, notes that in 1968–9, 46 per cent of irrigated large farms and 34 per cent of irrigated small farms had adopted the new varieties; but by 1970–1, both the small and large farms were on equal footing, with 62 and 66 per cent of the farms respectively adopting the new varieties.[41] However, the effective rate of utilization (i.e. proportion of total area under the new varieties) of the new varieties was relatively high for the large farms, the principal reason for the relatively low rates of utilization for the small farmers being their low resource base. The main constraints facing small farmers in adopting the new varieties were lack of access to credit, lack of irrigation facilities, inadequate supply of fertilizers and high prices of chemicals and fertilizers. Of these, lack of credit facilities appears to be the major constraint. It is reported that small farmers in certain areas in the Punjab and Harayana had frequently to resort to private money-lenders and big landlords with rates of interest varying from 18 to 40 per cent.

This is also the reason for the frequently observed relatively high yields and incomes experienced by the large farmers. Because of their access to credit and other resources for investment, they are able to reap higher rewards from the adoption of the new varieties than the small farmers. It is estimated that the variable costs per acre of new varieties are as much as five times as great as traditional varieties. Investment in durable capital is reported to be up to seven times greater on 'modern' farms than on traditional farms. But the returns from the adoption of the new varieties are also proportionately higher. The yields per acre sown to the new varieties are reported to be several times higher than that for the traditional

Table 5.4 Productivity of New Varieties and Traditional Varieties, 1968–9 to 1970–1 (yield per hectare in kgs)

1 Crop	2 New varieties	3 Traditional varieties	Ratio of 2 to 3
Wheat	2449	664	3.7
Rice	2136	948	2.3
Bajra	1620	331	4.9
Maize	1998	1007	2.0

Source: Estimates by J. B. Parker cited in J. S. Uppal (ed.), *India's Economic Problems: An Analytical Approach* (New Delhi, Tata-McGraw Hill, 1983) 3rd edition, p. 129.

varieties (Table 5.4). Given that the new varieties are expensive though profitable, small farmers, despite the advantages they possess with regard to labour use and cropping intensities, have been unable to adopt them to the same extent as the large farmers.

Employment effects of the Green Revolution

In discussing the employment effects of the Green Revolution, the effects of the new varieties on labour absorption need to be distinguished from those of mechanization. Most case-studies report that the use of labour in the cultivation of the new varieties of wheat and rice is considerably higher than that in the cultivation of the traditional varieties. They create additional demand for labour in peripheral activities such as weeding and the preparation of the soil for cultivation. Also, because the new varieties require the completion of agricultural operations in a shorter period of time, they create an additional demand for hired labour. According to one case-study, the new varieties of wheat and rice require 30 to 25 per cent higher labour-inputs per acre respectively than the traditional varieties.[42]

But the critics contend that these are short-term gains. The Green Revolution is not just a biological revolution centred on new varieties, water and fertilizers; it also provides incentives for mechanization. In the long run, large farmers tend to replace labour with capital. There is some evidence to show that mechanization through the introduction of power-driven tube wells, combine harvesters, threshers and tractors has been on the increase in the Punjab, Harayana and parts of Uttar Pradesh.[43]

The significant issues, though, are whether or not mechanization is necessarily associated with the adoption of the new varieties, and whether or not mechanization necessarily reduces employment. There does appear to be a complementarity between the new varieties and mechanization, but this is specific to large farmers. Because of their scale of operations they need to use tractors to cultivate the area under the new varieties. Small farmers, however, are able to adopt the new varieties and achieve a higher cropping intensity than the large farms without the use of tractors. Small farms also exhibit higher labour use per acre than large farms.[44] As stated earlier, an increasing proportion of small farmers are adopting the new varieties. All this suggests that there is no necessary complementarity between mechanization and the new varieties.

But has mechanization on the large farms reduced employment? Much of the discussion on this issue relates to the effects on employment of tractorization, because of the pronounced increase in tractorization on large farms. Tractorization has both an employment displacement effect and an employment creation effect. In the short run, it displaces labour employed in ploughing and transportation. But it also facilitates multiple cropping, and raises yields per acre because of better ploughing of land. These output effects may generate additional employment. The net employment effects of tractorization, therefore, depend on the extent to which the effects of employment displacement are compensated for by those of employment generation.

The empirical evidence on this issue is inconclusive,[45] but while tractorization alone may have little positive impact on employment, tractorization in combination with irrigation and the new varieties may increase employment. This, in fact, is the conclusion of Hanumantha Rao's case-study of tractorization in the Punjab.

But considerations of equity suggest that it would be preferable to increase employment through the development of small and medium farms, rather than through the stepping-up of output among large farms through tractorization. As stated earlier, small farms are intensive in their use of labour and are able to adopt the new varieties without tractorization. This, however, would require the provision of irrigation and credit facilities to the small and medium farms for the expansion of area under the new varieties.

Related to the issue of employment is the impact of the Green Revolution on income disparities and levels of living within agriculture. Most case-studies on this issue show that with the introduction of the new varieties, income disparities have widened. Not only have the large farmers gained more from the Green Revolution than the small farmers, but the owners of land and capital as a group have gained more than the agricultural labourers. These studies also indicate that while relative income disparities have widened, the absolute income levels of the lower income groups, including small and marginal land holders and agricultural labourers, have improved. There are also studies which show that while real wages of agricultural labourers were either constant or falling during the period 1956–7 to 1964–5, they rose sufficiently during the period 1964–5 to 1970–1 to offset the earlier decline.[46]

In sum, the Green Revolution, though it has not wrought any miracles, has been of considerable significance in sustaining the growth of agricultural output. Early doubts that the Green Revolution may be of limited significance and a waning phenomenon may have been misplaced. The full potential of the new varieties is yet to be realized. The various problems concerning equity associated with the Green Revolution may largely be institutional rather than technological. As Wolf Ladjensky, an astute observer of the Indian agricultural scene, observes:

> It is not the fault of the new technology that the credit service doesn't serve those for whom it was originally intended, that the extension service exists largely in name only, that tenurial legislation is deliberately miscarried, or that wage scales are hardly sufficient to keep body and soul together. All these are primarily man-made institutional inequities which, if corrected, could fuse a measure of economic or social justice with economic necessity, thereby adding another social dimension to the green revolution.[47]

It should be recognized that the new technology has literally sown the seeds for the modernization of agriculture. It may also have provided both the basis and the impetus for institutional reform: equity can hardly be achieved in the face of a stagnant agriculture. More to the point, as sociologists have been at pains to point out, the Green Revolution in India may have heightened class consciousness and the aspirations of the peasantry. Whether or not this discontent is likely to lead to a revolt of the peasantry and imperil the political stability of the country is a matter for speculation. But such a possibility alone should compel those in political power to initiate institutional reforms geared to the promotion of equity. The gulf between intent and practice in the past, with regard to the government's land reform policies, has been noted earlier. The Green Revolution may have provided the impetus to bridge the gulf.

But land reform should not be equated with a mere policy of land redistribution. A policy of land redistribution alone may be neither feasible nor sufficient as a solution to the problem of rural poverty and the plight of the landless. For, as often noted, there is simply not enough land to go around. A realistic programme of land reform should include not only the introduction of ceilings on land holdings and redistribution of land to the extent feasible, but also the implementation of tenurial legislation, compulsory consolidation of land holdings and complementary public works programmes. Beyond that is the need for institutional reform designed to provide credit, access to modern inputs at relatively low prices, marketing and irrigation facilities for medium and small farmers. As noted earlier, it is the absence of these facilities that has constrained the small farmers from adequate participation in the Green Revolution; such policies would also limit the gains from the Green Revolution accruing to the large farmers.

All these policies should go a long way in promoting growth and equity in agriculture. But could they also provide a solution to the massive unemployment problem facing the country? It is often argued that as the record of the manufacturing sector in providing employment opportunities has been none too encouraging, efforts should be made to absorb the growing labour force effectively in agriculture. Admittedly, agricultural growth, with emphasis on small and medium farms, should increase labour absorption in agriculture. Even so, there are limits to the ability of the agricultural sector to absorb a growing labour force. Such limits arise from both the supply and the demand side. On the supply side, increased labour productivity may reduce the demand for labour. On the demand side, growth in per capita incomes may result in a decline in the proportion of total incomes spent on food. In the current situation of massive poverty and relatively high income elasticity of demand for food, this prospect may seem far off; but it is an eventuality that cannot be ruled out. In any case, given the sheer size of the unemployment problem, the agricultural sector alone cannot be relied upon to provide a solution. Increasingly, employment opportunities may have to be found outside agriculture, in off-farm rural activites and in the manufacturing sector.

Admittedly, the employment record of the manufacturing sector over the years has been disappointing. The reasons for this are grounded in the specific industrialization policies which the country has adopted, analysed in Chapter 6. It is sufficient to note here that the Green Revolution has provided an opportunity for the augmentation and transfer of agricultural surpluses for purposes of industrialization. The utilization of this opportunity to promote the growth of industrial output and employment would depend on the policy stance adopted with respect to both agriculture and industry.

The conclusions of the chapter can be briefly summarized. India's agricultural performance, though impressive by historical standards, has been inadequate. The Green Revolution, though it has not transformed Indian agriculture, has served to sustain the rate of growth of output. The new technology may have widened income disparities in rural India, but this is to be attributed to institutional factors ingrained in the political economy of India, rather than to the new technology *per se*. The thesis that traditional farmers do respond to market forces, that they are economically rational and that the new technology is scale-neutral appears to be well founded. If practice has strayed far from theory, as in the case of the steep increases in farm prices that have occurred, the blame must lie with the inability or the lack of will on the part of the government to quell political forces, not the theoretical design of the strategy. In short, the problems of Indian agriculture belong primarily to the realm of political economy.

6
The Manufacturing Sector

It is often said that India is a land of paradoxes. Perhaps the most glaring of these is the presence of a sophisticated and diversified industrial sector in a desperately poor country. The spectrum of Indian industries ranges from traditional textiles to the modern petro-chemical, steel and engineering industries. India's diversified industrial structure is to be attributed to the policy of import-substituting industrialization initiated in the fifties and pursued with vigour through the decades of the sixties and the early seventies. The single-mindedness and technical expertise displayed by India's policy-makers in formulating the strategy, and the extent of industrialization that the country has achieved over a relatively short span of time have attracted much attention.

This admiration, though, has been punctuated with grave misgivings. Growth in manufacturing output has not been matched by a growth in manufacturing employment; nor has it been accompanied by a reduction in the concentration of economic power or in income disparities. The high degree of under-utilized capacity in several of the industries, low growth in productive efficiency, and the relatively poor performance of the state-owned enterprises have often been noted. Furthermore, there has occurred a marked deceleration in the rate of growth of manufacturing output since the mid-sixties.

These issues have been the focus of a wide-ranging debate. Few regard India's decision to industrialize as a folly. In fact, not even her decision to pursue a strategy of import-substituting industrialization with emphasis on investment in capital goods industries is seriously questioned. If one accepts India's ideological predilections in favour of establishing a 'socialist pattern of society', her decision to involve the State in direct production activity through the establishment of State-owned enterprises is also understandable. But it is the policy instruments which she has deployed in the pursuit of import-substituting industrialization that have come under heavy fire. These have consisted of an extensive system of controls over foreign trade, a panoply of bureaucratic controls over the size, pattern and location of industrial investments, and controls over the price and distribution of industrial raw materials. Debates during the sixties and seventies centred on the social costs and economic inefficiencies imposed on the economy by these policies.

The focus of the debate in recent years is the relatively low rate of growth of output experienced by the manufacturing sector since the mid-sixties. Several hypotheses, including that of a deficiency in domestic demand for industrial products, have been suggested to explain the deceleration in the growth rate of the sector. But the thought that it could largely be an aftermath of the trade and investment policies cannot be entirely dismissed. This chapter provides a review of India's industrial structure and performance, in the light of which recent policy debates are analysed.

Industrial structure

Is India an industrialized country? This may be regarded as a naïve question. India ranks twentieth among the nations of the world in terms of manufacturing output, and possesses a diversified modern industrial structure. Size of output, however, is but one among several criteria for judging the extent of industrialization – and a deficient one at that, for it says little about the contribution of the sector to employment and structural change. One set of criteria which attempts to include both qualitative and quantitative changes is that suggested by R. B. Sutcliffe. A country is counted as industrialized if 25 per cent of its national product arises in the industrial sector, of which at least 60 per cent is in manufacturing, and if at least one-tenth of the country's total population is employed in the industrial sector.[1]

In the year 1979–80, the industrial sector – defined to include mining, manufacturing, construction, electricity, gas and water supply – accounted for 24 per cent of India's total NDP. The share of manufacturing industries in the total value of industrial output was 69 per cent. Industrial employment as a percentage of total population was a bare 0.97 per cent. Thus, India just meets

Sutcliffe's first criterion, comfortably passes the second criterion but fails the third one miserably. In fact, the share of the industrial sector in total employment has stood unchanged at the relatively low level of 11 per cent since the decade of the sixties. Sutcliffe's study on the basis of data for the mid-sixties, in fact, classifies India among countries with a very small industrial sector in which manufacturing accounts for a predominant share of total industrial output. It may be apt to describe India as a semi-industrialized country.

Yet the industrialization which India has achieved is unique in some respects. First, she has been able to diversify the structure of her manufacturing sector relatively quickly. Second, she is one of the few developing countries which possesses a sophisticated modern industrial structure despite the low level of her per capita income. While, in 1957, the traditional food and textile industries accounted for 67 per cent of total manufacturing output, their share had declined to 35 per cent by 1978–9; that of the modern chemicals and engineering industries increased from 14 to 51 per cent over the same period (Table 6.1). These changes in the composition of manufacturing output are also reflected in the pattern of import-substitution the country has achieved. Padma Desai's detailed estimates, based on alternative measures of import-substitution, show that while the First Five-Year Plan years were marked by a high degree of import-substitution in consumer goods industries, the Second Five-Year Plan years were marked by a high degree of import-substitution in capital goods and intermediate goods industries.[2] This is a trend that appears to have continued into the Third Five-Year Plan years. It should be noted, however, that the industrial structure has changed very little since the mid-sixties.

The sequence of import-substitution in India conforms to the historically observed pattern. It generally runs from the establishment of consumer goods industries such as textiles, leather products and sugar, which are relatively less intensive in their use of modern technology and managerial skills, to those producing technologically sophisticated capital goods and consumer durables. India's industrialization, however, departs from the normal pattern in that the progression to the second stage of import-substitution has been swift; and she has both a higher proportion of industrial output to national product and a more sophisticated industrial structure than that warranted by the level of her per capita income. According to

Table 6.1 Composition of Manufacturing Output and Value Added (percentage shares)

Industry	Manufacturing output						Manufacturing value added					
	1951	1957	1965	1970–1	1975–6	1977–8	1951	1957	1965	1970–1	1975–6	1977–8
Food industries	28.8	27.4	20.9	19.9	17.2	16.8	1.62	18.9	10.6	9.3	8.2	9.9
Textiles	38.9	28.7	22.7	18.8	17.1	17.7	42.1	28.5	24.3	20.1	19.4	19.4
Rubber, chemicals and petroleum products	6.0	8.5	12.4	16.0	21.1	32.3	7.5	10.2	12.9	17.3	18.6	19.9
Non-metallic minerals	2.0	2.4	3.4	3.0	3.0	3.0	3.6	3.5	4.3	4.0	3.8	4.1
Basic metals	2.5	2.0	10.8	9.9	11.3	9.8	4.8	2.9	11.8	9.9	12.7	10.2
Engineering industries	7.6	16.6	19.8	19.9	19.1	18.9	10.8	21.2	25.3	24.9	26.0	25.9
All others	12.2	14.4	10.0	12.5	11.2	11.5	15.0	14.8	10.8	14.5	11.3	10.6
Total	100.0	100.0	100.0	100.0	100.0	100.0	100.0	100.0	100.0	100.0	100.0	100.0

Source: Estimated from data in J. Mellor, *The New Economics of Growth* (Ithaca, Cornell University Press, 1976) and *National Accounts Statistics* 1970–1 to 1977–8 (Central Statistical Organisation, Ministry of Planning, New Delhi, 1980).

the statistical studies of Chenery and Taylor, in large countries the proportion of industry in the national product rises rapidly from 16 per cent at an income level of $100 to 32 per cent at $400; it then levels off to reach a peak of 37 per cent at $1,200.[3] In India, the share of industry in the national product is around 24 per cent although the level of per capita income is less than $300. Moreover, as stated earlier, the technologically sophisticated chemical and engineering industries account for more than 50 per cent of the total value of manufacturing output.

This is to be attributed in large part to government policies, which have influenced the pattern of industrialization through controls over the composition of investment, the regulation of foreign trade, and their indirect influence on the pattern of income distribution and composition of demand. India's pattern of industrialization appears to conform to the so-called 'intentional pattern', rather than the normal pattern envisaged by the statistical studies. As will be outlined later in this chapter, this intentional pattern may be a factor of significance in the growth performance of the manufacturing sector.

The public sector

As stated earlier, State participation and intervention has been a key factor in India's industrialization process. The State has influenced the pattern of industrialization not only through the controls over foreign trade and investment but also through participation in direct production activity. The heavy presence of State-owned enterprises in capital goods-producing industries is a marked characteristic of India's industrialization. The decision to involve the State in direct production activity was based on both ideological and economic considerations. As Jawaharlal Nehru, the architect of India's planning, put it, 'planning should take place with a view to the establishment of a socialistic pattern of society where the principal means of production are under social ownership or control.'[4] The economic rationale for State participation was that the private sector would be unable or unwilling to meet the size of investment required and bear the risks involved in a large-scale programme of industrial development.

The Industrial Policy Resolution of 1956 gave a concrete shape to these objectives by demarcating the spheres of activity of the public and the private sectors. Seventeen industries, including several of the capital goods industries, were to be the exclusive preserve of the State. A second category was to consist of twelve industries in which the State would take the initiative in establishing new undertakings. The third category consisting of all the remaining industries was to be left to the initiative of private enterprise, although the State retained the option to participate in this category also.

It should, however, be noted that although the resolution stressed the primacy of the public sector in several lines of activity, it did recognize the complementary role of the public and private sectors. Indeed, over the years, with the growth in conflict between economic efficiency and political considerations, several compromises had to be forged. The import-substituting industrialization strategy had rendered domestic markets highly profitable to the private sector; and the latter could not be excluded from socially necessary investments such as steel on the grounds that it was unable or unwilling to undertake the investments. In the event, as Bhagwati and Desai note, a compromise was forged in the shape of a slackening of the public sector's share in investments combined with numerous restrictions on the growth of the private sector.[5]

The extent of State participation in manufacturing activity is shown by the various indicators in Table 6.2 and 6.3. The public sector has accounted for in excess of 50 per cent of the outlays ear-marked for the manufacturing sector in the various Five-Year Plans. In the year 1977–8, the public sector had a 31 per cent share in the total gross domestic capital formation in the manufacturing sector. Its contribution to the total GDP originating in the manufacturing sector, however, is relatively low at around 14.4 per cent. In terms of sectoral composition of investment in the State-owned enterprises, steel predominates (29%), followed by minerals and metals (23%), chemicals (24%) and engineering industries (10%). Public sector investments in these key capital and intermediate goods industries have been a factor of importance in the diversified industrial structure which India possesses. Indeed, most commentators regard the deceleration in public-sector investments as one of the principal reasons for the stagnation of the manufacturing sector since the mid-sixties.

The small-scale industries sector

The data in Table 6.1 relates to the registered sector which consists of large-scale industries. India's manufacturing sector also consists

Table 6.2 Share of the Public Sector in Gross Domestic Capital Formation, Gross Domestic Product and Employment in the Manufacturing Sector (percentage)

	(1) Gross Domestic Capital Formation	(2) Gross Domestic Product	(3) Employment
1960–1	–	4.2	10.8
1965–6	–	8.8	14.8
1970–1	22.0	12.5	17.0
1975–6	34.6	15.8	21.2
1977–8	31.4	15.9	24.4

Sources: Column 2 for years 1960–1 and 1965–6: Hazari and Oza, 'Public Sector in India', in M. Kidron and E. A. G. Robinson (eds), *Economic Development in South Asia* (London, Macmillan, 1970); and estimates on the basis of data in *National Accounts Statistics* 1970–1 to 1977–8 (Central Statistical Organisation, Government of India, 1980).

Public and Private-Sector Investments in Industry by Plans

(1) Plan	(2) Total Investment (Rs billion)	(3) Public Sector Investment (Rs billion)	Percentage of column 3 to column 2
Second Five-Year Plan	18.1	9.6	53.0
Third Five-Year Plan	31.4	18.2	58.0
Fourth Five-Year Plan	60.4	34.8	57.6

Source: J. C. Sandesara, 'Industrial Growth in India, – Performance and Prospects', *Indian Economic Journal* vol. 30, no. 2, p. 127.

of a substantial number of traditional village industries and 'modern' small-scale industries. They are modern in the sense that they produce a diversified range of industrial products and are frequently found to use modern technology. Estimates of the contribution of the small-scale sector to total manufacturing output are highly sensitive to the matter in which the small sector is defined. Official definitions of the sector have changed frequently. In the mid-seventies, all those firms with an investment in plant and equipment not exceeding Rs 0.75 million were designated as small firms. More recently, this definition has been revised to include all firms with an investment in plant and equipment not exceeding Rs 2

Table 6.3 Composition of Value Added: Unregistered Sector (percentages)

Industry	1970–1	1977–8
Food products	10.5	10.3
Beverages, tobacco and tobacco products	6.0	5.5
Textiles	25.6	24.4
Leather and leather products	3.9	3.9
Rubber, petroleum and chemical products	4.4	4.7
Wood and wood products	12.6	13.8
Paper and paper products	2.9	2.6
Non-metallic mineral products	5.4	6.9
Metal products and parts	6.7	6.6
Machinery, machine tools and transport equipment and parts	8.8	8.3
others	13.2	19.0
Total	100.0	100.0

Source: *National Accounts Statistics* 1970–1 to 1977–8 (Central Statistical Organisation, New Delhi, 1980).

million. On the basis of this definition, the Planning Commission reports that in the year 1979–80, the village and small industries sector contributed 49 per cent of the total gross value of output of the manufacturing sector and 51 per cent of the total value added.[6]

The criteria underlying the latest official definition of the small-scale sector, however, are not clear. Admittedly, there is no unique definition of a small firm, but it is usually identified by the relatively small size of its labour force, its organizational structure and the degree to which it is subject to State legislation. Unlike the large firms, owners of the small firms also perform entrepreneurial and managerial functions. Small firms are usually exempt from State regulations and legislation concerning minimum wage laws, labour safety and welfare; and a paternalistic form of relationship exists between the owners and their labour force. It is thus that the small-scale sector is often referred to as the unorganized sector; and because of its exemption from factory legislation it is referred to as the unregistered sector.

The official definition, however, puts several of the firms in the organized, registered sector into the small-scale sector. These firms may hardly qualify for inclusion in the small-scale sector by virtue either of their ownership or of their organizational pattern. Indeed, many of them may be no more than off-shoots of large firms, hived off and accorded a separate identity in order to qualify for government subsidies. Thus, the Planning Commission's estimate of the contribution of the small-scale sector to total manufacturing output, based on the official definition of the small-scale sector, may be an overestimate. If the small-scale sector is identified as the unregistered sector, the contribution of the modern small-scale sector to total manufacturing output turns out to be around 16 per cent. This figure moves up to 21 per cent if the contribution of the village industries is included in the total production of the small-scale sector.

The industrial performance of the small-scale sector has been the subject of extensive discussion, as will be detailed later in the chapter. Suffice it to note here that small firms in India operate in a wide range of industries, both traditional and modern. While textiles account for 25 per cent of the total value added of the unorganized sector, the modern group of metal products and engineering industries account for 15 per cent of the total value added (Table 6.3).

Growth performance

The index number of industrial output shows that the annual average compound rate of growth of output increased from 5 per cent during the First Five-Year Plan to 7 per cent during the Second Five-Year Plan and 9 per cent during the Third Five-Year Plan period. Over the fifteen-year period 1951–65, total industrial output increased at an annual average rate of 7.4 per cent. The index of manufacturing output exhibits a similar trend. The growth performance of the sector since 1965 presents a marked contrast: over the fifteen-year period 1965–80, the growth rate was only 3.8 per cent per annum (Table 6.4). In fact, if the exceptionally high rate of increase of 9.7 per cent achieved in 1976 is excluded from the data,

Table 6.4 Estimated Growth Rates of Industrial Output

Types of Industries	(1) Weight (1960)	(2) 1951–5	(3) 1955–60	(4) 1961–5	(5) 1965–70	(6) 1970–5	(7) 1975–6	(8) 1976–80	(9) 1951–65	(10) 1965–80
1. Basic industries	25.11	4.7	12.0	10.4	6.2	5.4	14.7	2.8	9.3	5.5
2. Capital goods industries	11.76	9.8	13.1	19.7	−1.4	5.6	10.6	4.0	14.5	3.2
3. Intermediate goods industries	25.88	7.8	6.4	6.9	2.4	2.8	7.5	3.6	7.0	3.2
4. Consumer goods industries	37.25	4.8	4.4	4.9	4.1	1.5	8.3	4.0	4.7	3.5
(i) Durable consumer goods	5.68	–	–	11.0	8.4	1.6	13.2	8.0	–	6.1
(ii) Non-durable consumer goods	31.57	–	–	3.8	2.7	1.5	9.8	3.1	–	3.1
5. Total industrial output	100.00	5.3	7.4	9.0	3.3	3.7	9.8	3.6	7.4	3.8

Sources: Columns 2 to 4 from S. L. Shetty, 'Structural Retrogression in the Indian Economy since the mid-Sixties', *Economic and Political Weekly* (annual number, February 1978), and estimates based on data on index number of industrial production, *Reserve Bank of India Bulletin* (various issues). Index numbers with base 1970=100 have been converted to base 1960=100.

the rate of growth over the second period turns out to be a modest 2.5 per cent per annum.[7]

It is this marked difference in the growth rates of manufacturing output over the two periods that has been the focus of recent debates. The first period is often regarded as one of satisfactory performance and the second period as one of stagnation; a variety of hypotheses have been offered to explain this stagnation. But was the performance of the sector over the earlier period, in fact, satisfactory? Is the stagnation over the second period entirely unrelated to the performance of the sector over the first period?

Whether or not the performance of the sector was satisfactory over the first period turns on the chosen criterion of performance. If growth rates are the criterion, the performance of the sector over the first period is commendable. But growth rates are one among several criteria for adjudging the performance of the sector. Equally relevant are the productive efficiency of the sector, its contribution to employment generation and its effect on income growth. It is the consensus that the performance of the sector was far from satisfactory on all these counts. It is also generally acknowledged that many of the observed economic inefficiencies and social costs incurred by the sector over the first period can be traced to the specific foreign trade and industrial licensing policies deployed by the government in the pursuit of import-substituting industrialization. Furthermore, there are grounds for arguing that the stagnation of the manufacturing sector in the second period is a consequence of the policies pursued during the first period. An elaboration of this thesis requires a review of the industrialization experience during the first period.

The strategy and its consequences

The main features of the import-substituting industrialization strategy and its consequences have been analysed in detail in the seminal studies by Bhagwati and Desai, and Bhagwati and Srinvasan;[8] we note only the main points here. The main policy instruments of the strategy were tariffs and quantitative restrictions on imports, coupled with a detailed system of foreign-exchange allocation and a complicated system of industrial licensing. In addition there were price and distribution controls over key industrial inputs. The stated objectives of the system of industrial licensing and controls were to regulate industrial investments according to plan priorities, limit the concentration of ownership of industries, protect and promote small-scale industries and promote balanced regional development.

Bhagwati and Desai conclude from their detailed analysis that these policy instruments lacked any sort of economic rationale and were subject to *ad hoc* bureaucratic decision-making; that the industrial licensing and import control policies had served to eliminate competition to existing firms from both prospective domestic rivals and imports; and that the policy of allocating import licences on the basis of existing capacity had created an artificial and wasteful incentive to overbuild capacity. Further, the policies had imparted a bias in favour of producing for the relatively profitable domestic markets, and against exporting. In sum, the policy instruments, far from promoting the stated objectives, had contributed to widespread economic inefficiencies in resource allocation, increased concentration of incomes and wealth, and slow growth in employment.

Inefficiencies in resource allocation

These indictments of India's foreign trade and industrial licensing policies are supported by an array of empirical evidence, principal among which are the estimates of effective rates of protection (ERP) and domestic resource costs (DRC) for various Indian industries. Both these measures provide an indication of the extent to which the domestic prices for various industrial goods diverged from their international prices as a consequence of the policy measures. And if the opportunity cost of producing a good domestically is reckoned to be its import price, these measures provide an indication of the costs to society of producing the good at home rather than importing it.

ERP is a conceptual method of assessing the degree of protection afforded to the value-added process of an industry by the entire tariff structure, including tariffs on imports of final products and inputs. An industry is said to be protected if the domestic prices of its products exceed the international prices. Value-added, by definition, is the final value of the product minus the value of all purchased material inputs used in the production process. In other words, it is the rewards accruing to labour and capital, the primary factors of production. A tariff on the import of a good, referred to as the nominal tariff, would increase the domestic price of the good and its domestically-produced substitutes over and above the international price of the good, by the height of the tariff. To this extent the value added of the domestic industry, measured in domestic prices, could be expected to increase over and above its value added measured at international prices. But if the imported inputs of the industry are also subject to a tariff, the increase in the value added product of the industry would be lower than that in a situation where the imported inputs bear no duty. In other words, a tariff on the final product of the industry which increases its domestic price is analogous to a subsidy and a tariff on its imported inputs would be analogous to a tax. Thus, the extent of protection or degree of effective protection enjoyed by the industry would depend on the mix of subsidy and tax elements in the tariff structure.

It is therefore, conceivable that the degree of protection afforded to the various industries by the tariff structure could be quite different from that indicated by the nominal tariff rates on the final goods. Estimates of ERP take account of the tariffs on both final outputs and inputs in measuring the degree of protection. In essence, ERP measures the increase in the rewards accruing to the primary factors of production in the various industries, resulting from the tariff structure. Operationally, it is the excess of value added of an industry in domestic prices over that measured in international prices, as a percentage of the latter.

It should be noted that not only tariffs on imports but also quotas – and indeed any policy measure such as the Indian domestic industrial licensing system which limits competition – could raise domestic prices over and above international prices and hence the ERP. The reported estimates of ERP for various Indian industries discussed below implicitly take account of all these factors. Usually, a ranking of industries by their ERP is supposed to indicate the direction of resource pull; resources could be expected to move from industries with relatively low ERP to industries with relatively high ERP. But, as Bhagwati and Desai note, for various reasons this may not always be so. For instance, the industrial licensing system, as stated earlier, may increase ERPs for specific industries. But it does so only by limiting entry into an industry for new firms. In these cases, high ERPs would be associated with movements of resources, not into the industry, but away from it. The main analytical significance of ERP, however, is that it indicates the extent of price distortions caused by the trade and industrial licensing policies, and the differential impact of these policies on the various industries. A wide dispersion in estimated ERPs would be indicative of widespread price distortions and economic inefficiencies in resource allocation, regardless of the specific direction of resource movements.

Estimated ERPs for sixty-nine Indian industrial sectors for the year 1968–9 show an enormous dispersion.[9] They range from 27 per cent in the case of woollen yarn to an incredible 3,354 per cent for Khandsari and Gur. Further, in the case of four industries – animal husbandry, rubber, starch and man-made fibres – value added at international prices turns out to be negative. These are obviously high-cost industries which would not have survived international competition but for the high degree of protection afforded to them. In addition, there are also industries for which ERPs are found to be negative. The tariff structure penalised these otherwise efficient industries. The haphazard nature of the incentives provided by the policy instruments are all too clear. Other facts of significance that emerge from these estimates are that the capital goods industries received less protection than either the intermediate goods or the consumer goods industries; and that in general, import-substituting industries received a much higher degree of protection than industries oriented towards exports.

Closely related to the concept of ERP is the concept of DRC. ERP, as stated earlier, is defined as the ratio of value added of an industrial activity in domestic prices to its value added in international prices. DRC is defined as the total value of domestic resources including labour, capital and non-traded material inputs expended by an industry in earning or saving a unit of foreign exchange. DRC is thus a ratio of cost to benefits, the costs being the value of domestic resources expended by the industry and the benefits being its net foreign exchange contribution. In estimating the total costs, labour and capital – the primary factors of production – are evaluated at their social opportunity costs or shadow prices. The foreign-exchange contribution of the industry is arrived at by evaluating its output at international prices (c.i.f. import prices if it is an import-substitution industry and f.o.b. export prices if it is an export industry), and deducting from this the value of all imported inputs, also evaluated at international prices. DRC thus indicates the social opportunity costs of the domestic resources expended by an industry in earning or saving a unit of foreign exchange. For this reason DRC is referred to as the domestic resource cost of foreign exchange, and is expressed as a proportion of the official exchange rate.

A ranking of industries by their DRCs would indicate their comparative advantage in the earning or saving of a unit of foreign exchange. A wide dispersion in DRCs between industries would be indicative of inefficiencies in resource allocation, because by shifting resources from industries with high DRCs to those with relatively low DRCs, the country could increase its foreign exchange earnings or savings at a much lower total DRC. But in the presence of widely differing degrees of protection, relatively inefficient industries with high DRCs could continue to function and reap high rates of private returns. In other words, because of the protection from competition which they enjoy, they could be privately profitable though socially unprofitable.

Estimates of DRCs for the years 1964–5 and 1968–9 for a total of sixty-nine Indian industrial sectors reported by Bhagwati and Srinivasan show a wide dispersion.[10] For the year 1968–9, DRCs range from Rs 5.9 per dollar in the case of printing and publishing to Rs 65.8 per dollar in the case of silk textiles. In the case of thirty-four sectors the DRCs were found to exceed Rs 15 per dollar. The official exchange rate during this period was Rs 7.50 per dollar. Thus, in the case of several industries, the domestic costs of earning or saving a unit of foreign exchange far exceeded the official valuation of foreign exchange.

But even if the true social opportunity cost of foreign exchange is put at double the official rate, DRCs in thirty-four out of the sixty-nine sectors are found to exceed it two to threefold. These relatively high-cost industries were no doubt able to survive because of the tight protection afforded to them by the controls over the import and domestic industrial licensing policies.

As noted in Chapter 4, another feature of India's industrialization experience is the high degree of under-utilized capacity in many of the Indian industries. Frequently cited reasons for this are the shortage of inputs – including imported inputs – and in some cases, lack of demand. However, as Bhagwati and Desai argue, the import licensing policies of the government could also have contributed to the excess capacity in several industries. One of the guiding principles in allocating licences for imported inputs was installed capacity, so that the only way an entrepreneur could avail himself of imported inputs and increased production was by installing more capacity. It is thus that the import control régime could have created an incentive for overbuilding capacity.

Productive efficiency

Three recognized features of the performance of India's manufacturing sector over the period 1951–65 are growth in capital intensity, growth in labour productivity and a decline in overall productive efficiency. Data reported by Asit Banerjee show that capital intensity, measured by the ratio of the value of fixed assets at constant prices to the amount of labour employed, increased by 300 per cent over the period 1951–64, from Rs 3,402 to Rs 13,784.[11] This estimate is based on data from the Census of Manufactures for the periods 1951 and 1964. The two sets of data are not strictly comparable because of differences in the coverage of industries. However, Raj Krishna and Mehta's estimates for a comparable group of twenty-nine industries also shows that capital intensity increased by nearly 100 per cent between the six-year period 1946–51 and the period 1958–63.[12] Both these studies also report divergent movements in the labour productivity and capital productivity indices. Raj Krishna and Mehta's study shows that while labour productivity increased by 42 per cent over the period 1946–63, capital productivity declined by 18 per cent. Asit Banerjee's estimates also show that while the productivity of labour increased by 3.3 per cent per annum over the period 1946–64, productivity of capital declined by 6.2 per cent per annum.

These movements in the three indices are not entirely unrelated. The growth in labour productivity may be a consequence of capital deepening. Increased mechanization of existing industries and the establishment of new capital-intensive industries could have contributed to the productivity of labour. Indeed, if the manufacturing industries are characterized by production functions showing constant returns to scale, an increase in the capital-labour ratio would result in an increased labour productivity and a decline in the productivity of capital.

But the divergent movements in the labour and capital productivity indices preclude an unambiguous judgment on overall growth in the productive efficiency of the sector. One method of overcoming this problem is to estimate an index of 'total factor productivity'. This index relates the total value of output to the total amount of labour and capital used in the production process, with labour and capital weighted by their respective prices. In other words, it is the ratio of the value of output to the total costs of inputs. Alternatively, total factor productivity can be estimated by the production function approach. The two approaches would yield the same result under certain conditions.[13]

While Raj Krishna and Mehta estimate total factor productivity by the former approach, Asit Banerjee relies on the production function approach. Both sets of estimates show that total factor productivity declined by 1.6 per cent per annum over the period 1946–64.[14] Bhagwati and Srinivasan also cite evidence to show that cost reductions and improvements in the quality of products manufactured were not the hallmarks of the manufacturing sector over this period.

Factors promoting capital intensity

It is a matter of debate whether the growth in capital intensity of the manufacturing sector is to be attributed primarily to change in the industrial composition in favour of capital-intensive industries, or is due to a progressive substitution of capital for labour in the production process. Available evidence, however, appears to favour the former view;[15] as stated earlier, the composition of the manufacturing sector shifted progressively in favour of relatively capital-intensive investment and the intermediate goods sectors. Further, within the consumer goods sector there appears to have occurred a shift in favour of inherently capital-intensive industries.

The factors promoting this change in industrial composition appear to have been ingrained in the foreign trade and industrialization policies pursued during the first two decades of planning. The most important of these policies is the priority accorded to the establishment of capital goods industries in the Five-Year Plans, especially in the Second Five-Year Plan. But the trade and licensing policies appear to have reinforced this bias in favour of capital-intensive industries through their effects on factor prices and demand patterns.

One of the frequently cited reasons for the capital intensity of the manufacturing sector in relatively labour-abundant developing countries is factor price distortions. Factor prices are distorted in the sense that the market prices of labour and capital do not reflect their true factor endowments. Trade union power and minimum wage legislation serve to raise the price of labour above its opportunity cost; and the price of capital tends to be lower than its opportunity cost not only because of various forms of subsidy on capital, but also because of overvalued exchange rates which result in artificially low prices for imported capital equipment. A result of all this is that profit-maximizing entrepreneurs prefer to invest not only in relatively capital-intensive methods of production but also in the production of goods which are inherently capital-intensive.

In the Indian context, factor price distortions appear to have been pronounced because of both the overvalued exchange rate and the system of import licences.[16] While the overvalued exchange rate understates the opportunity cost of imported capital goods, the import licensing system may have encouraged the use of imported goods by those who were fortunate enough to acquire the licences. For while those who had licences could obtain imported materials and equipment at the imported price inclusive of the tariff, those without such licences had to buy indigenous inputs sold at a premium far above the imported price. The premium was a consequence of the protection afforded to indigenous industries through the system of quotas and tariffs on imports.

Another direct consequence of the system of import controls was the incentives it provided for the establishment of relatively capital-intensive consumer goods industries, producing luxury goods. As noted earlier, consumer goods industries enjoyed a relatively high degree of effective protection. This was largely the outcome of a policy which banned the import of such goods on the grounds that scarce foreign exchange had to be conserved, but at the same time permitted their domestic production. To the extent that such industries could acquire licences for the importation of inputs – and there is evidence to show that many of them did – the policy framework was conducive to the establishment of relatively capital-intensive consumer goods industries.

It should also be noted that the import licensing system in general may have generated a demand for such luxury goods, through the rents it conferred on certain sections of the population. It has often been noted that the exorbitant premiums which the import licences fetched on the market and the bribes paid to the bureaucrats in charge of allocating such licences were a major source of black money in the economy. Anne Krueger, for instance, has estimated that in the year 1964 government restrictions of various sorts generated rents to the tune of Rs 14.3 billion in the economy, with import licences accounting for Rs 10.3 billion – or 73 per cent of this total.[17] These rents accruing to the high-income groups in society were apparently a major source of demand for various durable consumer goods.

In addition to all this, the pricing policies of State-owned enterprises also appear to have been a factor in promoting the capital intensity of the industries in the private sector. Besides, the performance the state-owned enterprises may have been a factor of significance in the low productive efficiency of the manufacturing sector.

Productive efficiency of the state-owned enterprises

The low levels of productive efficiency of the State-owned enterprises have often been noted.[18] While not all of these enterprises were unprofitable, several recorded substantial losses, and in many the rates of return on capital were markedly below those of the industries in the private sector. It could, however, be argued that the basic purpose of State-owned enterprises is the promotion of social objectives and not private profitability. This appears to be the philosophy that underlies the no-profits, no-loss principle advocated for State-owned enterprises; a principle which may have influenced the Indian government in exercising price controls in the case of State-owned enterprises such as steel. In the face of such price controls, the monetary returns of such enterprises would obviously be low.

One consequence of this policy, though, may have been the promotion of capital-intensive operations in the private sector, for the private sector enterprises were able to obtain many of the key industrial inputs produced by State-owned enterprises at relatively low prices. In other words, the capital inputs they obtained were heavily subsidized by the State. This, too, amounts to a distortion of the price of capital and may have been a factor in the growth of the capital intensity of the manufacturing sector.

There is, however, little evidence to suggest that State-owned enterprises were socially efficient. Managerial inefficiencies, excessive over-manning, deficiencies in the design and implementation of projects, and the scant attention paid to accepted economic criteria of costs and benefits in the formulation of investment plans in many of these enterprises have often been noted.[19] It would, however, be an exaggeration to say that these problems are endemic to State-owned enterprises, or that their managers tend to be profligate because they are not answerable to share-holders. For professional managers, be they in the public or the private sector, could be expected to shoulder the same sort of responsibilities and be guided by the objectives of growth and efficiency in their enterprises. It is size and technology which differentiate enterprises, and not the nature of their ownership.

State-owned enterprises, however, are not always manned by professional managers. Quite often, top management positions in these enterprises are filled by political appointees and traditional civil servants. Even when they are filled by professional managers, political interference and bureaucratic regulations could stifle their zeal for innovation and enterprise. As Yair Aharoni succinctly puts it:

> When State-owned enterprises become a device for political patronage, when they are used to pay political debts or to accumulate power, when their managers are recruited on the basis of loyalty rather than ability, these enterprises become feudal bastions of certain ministry, a concentration of economic and political power is created, and the economic goals for which the enterprises were formed and financed may not be achieved.[20]

This description appears to fit the Indian State-owned enterprises. Several studies have shown that top managerial positions in many of these enterprises are held by political appointees and civil servants with little expertise in industrial management, that they are subject to excessive government scrutiny and political interference, and that professional managers are poorly paid, relative to the Civil Service and the private sector.[21]

Employment

The factors contributing to the growth in manufacturing employment are capital accumulation, technical change and the composition of industry. Obviously, growth in capital accumulation and technical change contribute to growth in output and hence to employment. But the growth in employment associated with the growth in output is a function of the type of technical change which the manufacturing sector experiences, and the composition of industry in the sector. If the growth in capital accumulation is accompanied by changes in the composition of industry in favour of capital-intensive industries, it could contribute to growth in labour productivity and output, but relatively little to employment growth.

As noted in the previous sections, this, in fact, has been the experience of India's manufacturing sector. While manufacturing output increased at an annual average rate of 7.6 per cent over the period 1951–65, factory employment increased at only 3 per cent per annum.[22] Again, as noted previously, this period was characterized by a change in the composition of the manufacturing sector in favour of capital-intensive industries, with predictable consequences for the growth in employment. As John Mellor notes, if all the incremental investment between 1951 and 1965 had been distributed in the same proportions in each industry as in 1951, employment in the organized manufacturing sector would have been 2.3 times greater than the actual level in 1965.[23] Ranadev Banerji and James Reidal's statistical study on the factors contributing to the growth in manufacturing-sector employment in Taiwan and India also reaches similar conclusions. In both countries, capital accumulation was the primary factor contributing to growth in employment. But Taiwan experienced a higher rate of growth of employment than India because the structural change which her manufacturing sector experienced was in favour of labour-intensive industries.[24]

This, however, reflects the differing policy orientations of the two countries. Taiwan initiated a switch in policy in 1960 from an inward-oriented import-substitution strategy to an outward-looking export-promotion strategy, whereas India persisted with an inward-looking import-substitution strategy. Arguably, because of differences in size, population and resource endowments, India may not be able to emulate Taiwan's experience. But, as Banerji and Reidal note, even during the import-substitution stage Taiwan's industrial structure was much more heavily weighted towards labour-intensive industries than was that of India. In any case, the contrasting experiences of India and Taiwan show that the composition of the manufacturing sector could have a significant effect on employment growth. And as argued in the previous sections, apart from India's basic policy objective of emphasizing capital goods industries, her import control and industrial licencing policies may have contributed significantly to the structural change which the manufacturing sector has experienced in favour of inherently capital-intensive industries.

Employment and the small-industry sector

India's policy-makers, though, were not unaware of the fact that large-scale capital goods industries had a limited employment potential. It was in recognition of this fact that the Mahalanobis industrialization strategy advocated the development of a small-industries sector as a sort of adjunct to the heavy-industry-oriented large-scale manufacturing sector. It was the hope that small-scale industries would provide immediate large-scale employment, promote a more equitable distribution of national income and facilitate an effective mobilization of capital and skills which might otherwise remain unutilized. This policy has been reiterated in successive Five-Year Plans, including the Sixth Five-Year Plan, and also forms an integral part of the rural employment strategy advocated for India by John Mellor.[25] And since the mid-fifties there has been in operation an elaborate programme of financial and technical assistance to the small-industries sector. It is also a fact that in response to the financial and technical assistance provided by the government, the small-industry sector has grown at a faster rate than the organized sector in terms of the number of units and value of output and exports. But has the small-scale sector fulfilled the objectives of the policy-makers in terms of employment generation and the promotion of equity?

As noted earlier in this chapter, the small-industry sector contributes around 16 per cent to the total value of manufacturing output. According to the Planning Commission's estimates, in 1980, the sector provided employment to 24 million people as against the 4.5 million people employed in the medium- and large-scale industries.[26] This is a remarkable improvement over the figures for the year 1955, when the small-industries sector is reported to have accounted for 13 million jobs out of the 16.2 million jobs provided by the manufacturing sector as a whole.[27]

These figures, however, are to be viewed with caution. The small-industries sector is a heterogenous group consisting of the traditional village industries, urban household industries, and the modern units in the urban areas employing hired labour. A substantial proportion of the reported employment in the small-scale sector in 1980 is on account of the traditional village industries. These are household enterprises employing little hired labour; they are labour-intensive in their production process and sell their products in local markets.[28]

While these industries are likely to continue to be important, it would be unrealisitc to rely heavily on them as a major source of employment. It is often argued that the Green Revolution in agriculture has opened up new vistas for these industries, for the increased farm incomes would be a source of demand for their products. This, however, is a debatable proposition. As P. N. Dhar notes, the chances for these industries to expand may be limited, because as incomes rise, demand shifts from 'inferior' traditional products to 'superior' modern products.[29] In recent years, the products that have made their appearance in the rural areas are bicycles, sewing machines, torches, transistor radios, etc. These are goods with a high income elasticity of demand, and are produced in the urban areas in the modern small industries and firms in the organized sector. It is also worth noting that, for all its much-vaunted objective of promoting rural small-scale industries, the government's subsidized credit facilities have mostly accrued to the modern small industries and not to the traditional village industries. According to the Planning Commission, up to June 1976, 69 per cent of the total credit provided by the nationalized commercial banks to the small-scale sector accrued to 11 per cent of the bigger units in the sector which accounted for 55 per cent of the total production.[30] Presumably, many of these units were bogus small units set up as separate entities by large firms in order to qualify for financial assistance.

It is modern small industries which have developed faster than the other groups in the small-scale sector. In the year 1980, they accounted for nearly 72 per cent of the total value of output of the sector at current prices, but their share in the total employment generated by the sector as a whole amounted to only 32 per cent. These statistics belie the popular belief that small industries in general tend to be labour-using and capital-saving in their production processes. Indeed, several studies have found modern small enterprises to be frequently more capital-intensive in their production process than large firms. In industries such as hand tools, rubber products, bakery products, footwear and bicycles, the ratio of fixed capital to output of the modern small industries is reported to exceed that of the large firms by a wide margin.[31] The popular belief is based on the assumptions that capital intensity varies directly with the scale of production, and that the wage rates paid by small firms are relatively low. Both these assumptions may be suspect. In most modern industries such as machine tools, bicycles and transistors, the basic technology tends to be identical for both large and small firms. While small firms may economize on capital in ancilliary activities such as material handling and packing, the core of the production process may permit little substitution of labour for capital.

It is a fact that the total wage bill for small industries in general tends to be lower than that for the large-scale sector. It is estimated that the annual wage rate per employee in the small-scale sector was Rs 1,560 in 1972, whereas in the factory sector it was Rs 4,290.[32] It should, however, be noted that these two figures may not be strictly comparable. There may be considerable differences in the nature of the products produced and the skill levels of the labour employed between the various industries in the two sectors. The observed differences in the wage rates between the two sectors may, in part, reflect these differences in product composition and levels of labour skill. Further, within the small-scale sector there may be considerable differences in the wage rates paid by modern small enterprises and by traditional enterprises. Modern small enterprises located in the urban areas may have to compete with large firms for skilled labour, and pay comparable wage rates, especially when they produce products similar to those produced by the large firms. When they are confronted with distorted factor prices, and they have access to cheap credit, modern small enterprises are as likely as large enterprises to adopt capital-intensive technologies. After all, they too are profit maximizers.

Again, not all small firms may be immune from trade union pressure and labour problems of the sort experienced by large firms. Several modern small firms located on industrial estates – many though not all of which are located in the vicinity of large enterprises – argue that labour disputes tend to be frequent on the estates. A dispute in one of the units on the estate is likely to spread to all other units, and solidarity among the labourers on the estates tends to be high.[33] For all these reasons the generalization cannot be made that all small enterprises are at an advantage with regard to labour costs relative to the large firms.

There are also several other explanations of an institutional nature for the observed capital intensity of the modern small enterprises. Most such enterprises are managed by family groups rather than professional managers. Because of this managerial constraint, they operate on a one-shift basis, whereas large firms employing professional managers operate on a multiple-shift basis. Hence the observed relatively high capital-output ratios and low level of employment per unit of investment in modern small enterprises. It is also reported that factory space on industrial estates tends to be under-utilized, and that capital costs of construction on the estates have been excessively high. This again contributes to the capital intensity of the small firms. Yet another factor contributing to the capital intensity of the modern small enterprises may be the sub-contracting arrangements between small and large firms. Such sub-contracting arrangements, whereby the large firms farm out the production of components and parts they need to the small enterprises, are not all that widespread in India. But in the case of such arrangements that do exist, the technical specifications, drawings and designs required for the production of the components are supplied by the large firms. More often than not, these are capital-intensive technologies imported by the large firms under technology licensing agreements with foreign firms. These are farmed out to small firms without any alterations or adaptations of the designs and specifications to suit local factor endowments. The small firms often claim that they themselves carry out such adaptations.[34] But it is unlikely to be widespread because of the research expenditure and skills involved, which may be beyond the means of the small firms. The large firms stand to gain from such arrangements because overhead costs, including costs of labour welfare, tend to be relatively low in the small firms; but there may be little difference in the capital costs of manufacturing these components between the large and small firms.

All this should not be construed as an indictment of the government's stated objective of developing the small-scale sector. Admittedly, the small industries do possess several advantages relative to the large firms. Their overhead costs in terms of buildings and land tend to be relatively low; they can be located in rural areas; they can interact with large firms through sub-contracting arrangements; traditional village industries tend to be intensive in the use of labour; and industries such as the handloom industry have a proven export potential. But the policies pursued towards small enterprises appear to represent yet another case of good intentions gone astray.

A main policy deficiency is the inability or unwillingness of the government to distinguish between genuine small industries in need of financial and technical assistance, and the bogus units set up with the express purpose of qualifying for such assistance. Also, the credit policies pursued by the government, the main beneficiaries of which were the bigger units in the small-scale sector, may have promoted factor price distortions and hence the capital intensity of modern small enterprises. Nor have the import control policies been of much assistance to the genuine small firms. Bhagwati and Desai cite evidence to show that despite the government's avowed objective of supporting the small-scale sector in the interests of equity, the import licensing system actually discriminated against the small-scale sector.[35] One of the frequent complaints voiced by managers of small-scale enterprises in interviews with researchers is their lack of access to raw materials and inputs. Often, they are forced to purchase these inputs on the black market at exorbitant prices. It is conceivable that, but for these quirks in official policy, the contribution of the small-scale sector to employment, equity and income growth could have been much more impressive.

The post–1965 stagnation

To say that the manufacturing sector has stagnated since the mid-sixties may be an exaggeration. But it is a fact that the industrial sector has experienced a marked decline in the rate of growth of output since 1965. This decline in the growth rate cuts across all the industry groups, though it is marked in the case of capital goods. The rate of growth of consumer goods industries has generally been lower than that for the industrial sector as a whole, but the decline in their growth rate over the period 1965–75 is noticeable (Table 6.3). It should also be noted that the weight of the consumer goods industries in the overall index of industrial production declined from 48.37 in 1956 to 27.83 in 1976 (Table 6.5). Admittedly the growth rate of output picked up during the period 1975–80. But, as noted earlier, much of this increase is to be attributed to the

Table 6.5 Weights of Major Industrial Groups in the Index of Industrial Production

Category	1956	1960	1965	1970	1976
Basic industries	22.13	25.11	26.84	32.28	36.14
Capital goods industries	4.71	11.76	18.67	15.74	16.76
Intermediate goods	25.59	25.88	23.60	20.95	19.27
Consumer goods	48.37	37.25	30.89	31.03	27.83

Source: S. L. Shetty, *op. cit.*

exceptional performance of the sector during the year 1976. Further, the growth rates for the four-year period 1976–80 are generally lower than that for the period 1951–65.

While the facts of deceleration in the rate of growth of industrial output are not in dispute, the reasons for the deceleration in the growth rate have been the subject of a lively debate among Indian economists. Such is the variety of the explanations and hypotheses offered, that they lend credence to the popular view that if you have six economists they are likely to come up with seven opinions. These explanations are worth reviewing not only for their ingenuity but also for the light they shed on India's industrialization experience.

Decline in investment

One of the early explanations for the deceleration in the growth of industrial output, provided by Srinivasan and Narayana, was that it was due to the decline in investment, especially public-sector investment.[36] This explanation has some merit for the period 1965–74. As noted in Chapter 4, there was a sharp decline in the share of public-sector savings after 1965, until the year 1974–5. Also noteworthy is the fact that gross domestic capital formation in industry, as a percentage of GDP, during the late sixties and the early seventies was generally lower than the 5 per cent rate registered in 1965–6. Admittedly, these relatively low levels of investment during this period have been a factor in the deceleration in the growth of industrial output. But since the year 1973–4, gross domestic capital formation as a percentage of GDP has recovered to the level achieved in 1965–6. Indeed, over the entire period 1960–1 to 1978–9, the observed rates of capital formation show wide year-to-year fluctuations without any discernible trend (Table 6.6). In

Table 6.6 Gross Domestic Capital Formation in the Industrial Sector (Rs billion)

(1) *Year*	(2) *Total Capital Formation*	(3) *Gross Domestic Product*	(4) (2) as percentage of (3)
1960–1	7.07	150.20	4.7
1961–2	6.26	159.80	3.9
1962–3	8.24	171.00	4.8
1963–4	6.74	196.60	3.4
1964–5	9.73	230.44	4.2
1965–6	12.22	241.12	5.1
1966–7	19.41	276.91	7.0
1967–8	14.49	323.34	4.5
1968–9	13.12	334.03	3.9
1969–70	15.67	370.00	4.2
1970–1	19.76	402.63	4.9
1971–2	22.67	435.31	5.2
1972–3	18.98	478.70	4.0
1973–4	32.27	589.40	5.5
1974–5	46.88	696.00	6.7
1975–6	41.16	741.62	5.5
1976–7	35.00	806.00	4.3
1977–8	44.52	902.00	4.9
1978–9	61.25	977.00	6.3

Source: J. C. Sandesara, 'Industrial Growth in India – Performance and Prospects', *Indian Economic Journal* vol. 30, no. 2.

sum, while the thesis that a relatively low rate of investment is the cause of the deceleration in the rate of growth of industrial output has some merits, it cannot provide a full explanation.

Demand deficiency

If the diagnosis that a decline in investment is the cause of industrial stagnation is correct, the obvious prescription is that public-sector investment should be increased. This prescription, however, is seen by many to be of limited use. Deepak Nayyar, for instance, has no quarrel with the diagnosis that the cause of the stagnation is the decline in public-sector investment, but he sees little merit in the prescription of increased public investment in capital goods and basic goods industries.[37] He argues that the limits to increased public investment in basic and capital goods may have been reached, and that additional investments would only add to the existing under-utilized capacity in these industries. Further, according to Nayyar, the private sector need not wait upon the public sector to increase its investment. It has accumulated surpluses, and if only the domestic market for industrial goods were profitable, it would come up with the investment.

Indeed, Nayyar's explanation of the stagnation is that the manufacturing sector is constrained by a rapidly shrinking home market for its products. He provides some evidence for this thesis in terms of the relatively low proportion of consumer expenditure accounted for by the poorest 50 per cent of the population. He seeks reasons for the decline in domestic demand for industrial products in the increasing inequalities in income distribution; and he is sympathetic to Ashok Mitra's thesis, elaborated in Chapter 5, that income inequalities have been aggravated by the movement in the internal terms of trade in favour of agriculture. Nayyar also believes that demand for luxury products by the upper-income groups sustained the manufacturing sector over the 1951–65 period, but that it has petered out since then. In other words, the economy has reached the limits of import-substituting industrialization. He also sees no salvation for the manufacturing sector in the export markets; according to Nayyar, exports are a consequence of growth in national income and not the other way round. And, in any case, for a large country such as India, it is not exports but the home market which is vital. Nayyar's solution to the problem is increased public investment, oriented towards employment creation and increased income for the poor.

This thesis, too, has some merit. As stated in Chapter 4, although the evidence in support of the conclusion that consumer expenditure has declined is not strong, there is reason to believe that there has occurred little growth in such expenditure. Again, while the evidence on increased inequality in incomes is inconclusive, it cannot be disputed that there has been no reduction in the proportion of the population living in abject poverty. But Nayyar's assertion that exports are a consequence of growth in national income and that export growth is not the solution to the problem of low growth in demand is open to debate. We return to this issue in Chapter 9.

Speculative activities of the private sector

Prabhat Patnaik's explanation of the stagnation casts doubts on the feasibility of Nayyar's solution.[38] The villain of the piece in Patnaik's explanation of the stagnation is the private sector – consisting of the agricultural landlords and the industrial capitalists – which is ever eager to make short-term profits through speculation. And the public sector, caught in the political stranglehold of the private sector, aids, abets and promotes the speculative activities of the private sector. The scenario which Patnaik sketches begins with a rise in the surplus or stocks of commodities held by the private sector. At the first signs of an excess supply of commodities on the market, the public sector readily buys up the stocks at existing prices. This liquefaction of the private sector provides it with the wherewithal to engage in speculative activities. Any attempt on the part of the public sector to increase public investment on the strength of the stocks of wage goods it now holds would be frustrated by the activities of the private sector. For with the first signs of an increase in prices on the markets, the latter would swiftly move from cash into commodities and stock up the wage goods and inputs released by the public sector.

Attempts at increasing public investment, therefore, would only result in inflationary pressures and the diversion of public expenditure into non-developmental expenditure such as the subsidization of essential commodities. This scenario, according to Patnaik, mirrors the situation in the Indian economy in the seventies. This is an arresting thesis. But one may wonder how the landlords and the capitalists – the villains of the piece – possess the information, expertise and ingenuity with which Patnaik credits them. It is also a puzzle why speculation with a given stock of commodities should be more profitable than expansion of production at assured prices with the aid of relatively inexpensive wage goods and inputs provided by the public sector.

High capital-output ratios

Ashok Desai will have none of this. He dismisses all of the aforesaid explanations, and a few others, citing data to show their weak empirical foundations.[39] Desai's strictures are directed at most of the long-held beliefs; he provides data to show that the terms of trade did not turn in favour of agriculture, income inequalities did not increase, there has been no reduction in real wage rates and no reduction in the ratio of fixed investment to GNP during the seventies. All this is provocative. Admittedly, Desai does pick many holes in the data used by the authors he criticizes; but the data he cites are equally suspect. The agriculture–industry terms of trade data he cites are simple ratios of agricultural prices to prices of manufactured goods, and lack the sophistication displayed in the estimates provided by Thamarajakshi, cited in Chapter 5. Desai's data on investment in machinery and equipment, although at constant prices, are gross figures unadjusted for depreciation; and the rising trend in fixed investment during the seventies which he cites is hardly perceptible. But Desai's strictures on the data on the demand and supply of consumer goods cited by the authors he criticizes appear to be well-founded. It is conceivable that data on the production of several items of consumer goods consumed by the poor go unreported, and the data on capacity utilization in many of the luxury goods industries do tend to be misleading. Indeed, the welter of data from different sources on various aspects of the Indian economy such as savings, investment, industrial and agricultural output with their differing concepts, base periods, weights and the frequent changes in methodology and coverage they undergo all pose insurmountable problems to the researchers. Desai's article abundantly illustrates these problems.

While certainly casting doubt on the empirical validity of the explanations which he evaluates, Desai's own explanation of the stagnation at the same time is appealing. According to him, the problem is supply-oriented. A persistently high rate of industrial investment, combined with a low rate of industrial growth, indicates high capital-output ratios. He cites data to show that while capital-output ratios in India have generally been high by international standards, they have not only increased over the years, but are also much higher in the public-sector industries than in the private-sector industries. Capital-output ratios are high in public-sector industries not so much because their capital costs tend to be high, but because their capacity-utilization rates are low; and the high levels of under-utilized capacity in public-sector industries are to be ascribed primarily to over-manning in these industries. Desai's thesis is that the political power exercised by the 'petty-bourgeois haute proletariat' has led to this trend towards over-manning. And because no-one in these industries can be dismissed and no one wants to be found overtly doing nothing, such over-manning has resulted in a low work ethic, low work-loads and a tendency towards idleness. In short, an inefficient and largely unproductive industrial base is being maintained with the support of government revenues. In the face of the low levels of public-sector savings, such revenues have come from the credit system: that is, through money creation.

These are not the only explanations for the stagnation. There are also others based on long-term structural changes occurring in the economy. One such explanation, offered by Sudipto Mundle, is that the stagnation is but a transient phase in the long-term reorganization of capital which is occurring in the economy. The reorganization is characterized by a change in the industrial structure in favour of capital-intensive industries and capital-intensive technologies, with old traditional industries yielding place to new modern industries. Once this reorganization is complete, capital accumulation and output growth are likely to re-emerge.[40] It is conceded, however, that this emerging pattern of industrialization is unlikely to generate employment and a demand for mass consumer goods. It is, therefore, a puzzle as to how this pattern of industrialization could be sustained over time. One other factor which has figured prominently in several of the explanations is the adverse effects of foreign private capital and technology on India's industrialization. This aspect is discussed at length in Chapter 7.

Towards a synthesis

It is obvious from the foregoing review that no one factor can be singled out as the primary reason for the post-1965 stagnation of the manufacturing sector. Shrinking domestic markets, increasing capital-output ratios, deceleration in the growth of public investment and social and economic inefficiencies in public-sector enterprises have all contributed to the stagnation. But these various supply and demand factors cannot be regarded as mutually exclusive. They influence each other. For instance, Deepak Nayyar's contention that the stagnation is the result of a deficiency in domestic demand for manufactured goods may be valid, but the factors responsible for this deficiency in demand are to be traced to the slow growth in manufacturing-sector employment and the persistent disparities in income distribution. Admittedly, the movement in the internal terms of trade in favour of agriculture and the relatively low growth performance of the agricultural sector may have contributed both to the low growth in real incomes and to the growth in the disparities in income distribution. It may also have increased the input costs for agro-based industries. But an equally significant factor contributing to the low growth in employment and incomes for the poor is the industrial licensing and trade policies pursued by the government during the fifties and the sixties. The consequences of these policies for resource allocation, productive efficiency, employment and income distribution have been narrated at length in the previous section. The rise in the capital-output ratio and productive inefficiencies in the public-sector enterprises which figures in Ashok Desai's explanation of the stagnation can also be traced to these policies.

But curiously enough, most commentators are reluctant to acknowledge the contribution of the import-substituting industrialization policy framework to the stagnation of the manufacturing sector in recent years. Deepak Nayyar, for instance, dismisses the Bhagwati-Srinivasan analysis of the economic inefficiencies and social costs perpetrated by the industrial licensing and trade policies of the government in the past as irrelevant to an explanation of the post–1965 stagnation. This analysis – labelled neo-classical – is regarded as static in conception, which ignores inter-temporal considerations. As Nayyar asks, 'Why did the industrial sector perform satisfactorily until 1965 in spite of these policies, and why did it not respond to liberalisation, thereafter, or now?'[41]

The short answer to these questions is that the pre–1965 performance of the sector was hardly satisfactory. While protection from both international and domestic competition enabled the sector to register high growth rates measured in domestic prices, its performance was far from satisfactory in terms of resource allocation, productive efficiency and international competitiveness. The stagnation in the growth rate of output since 1965 may well be a culmination of these inefficiencies, brought to a head by the severe droughts of 1965 and 1966 and the military conflicts with Pakistan and the Bangladesh War. The sector has failed to respond to liberalization, because spasmodic attempts at liberalization of the industrial licensing policy and a haphazard system of export subsidies simply do not constitute liberalization in any real sense.[42] As Bhagwati and Srinivasan note, the so-called liberalization following the 1966 devaluation was short-lived, and by 1968 the economic policy had lapsed back into the earlier restrictive régime.

Indeed, when Nayyar pleads for a reorientation of public investment towards employment creation and incomes for the poor, he is in fact asking for a major restructuring of economic policy. Such a restructuring would not be effective unless it also involved a correction of factor price distortions, positive incentives for the development of genuine small industries and village industries, promotion of competition in the economy with a view to increasing productive efficiency and cost consciousness, and an agricultural policy directed at providing technical assistance and credit facilities for the small farmers. And despite Nayyar's agnosticism concerning the benefits of an export-led strategy for a country such as India, the restructuring would also entail the promotion of exports, for they would be one method of promoting competition and generating employment. This aspect is discussed in detail in Chapter 9.

Such a policy framework for India has often been suggested, and recent Five-Year Plans have recognized the need for an employment-oriented industrialization strategy. The pertinent issue, though, is why India has persisted with a policy framework which has been proved to be demonstrably inefficient. A succinct answer is provided by Angus Maddison, when he states that the industrial strategy 'won support from the bureaucratic establishment because it added to their power, it was supported by politicians because it encouraged their patronage, it met no opposition from established industry because it did not interfere with vested interests and it was supported by intellectuals who generally identified capitalism with colonialism . . . it aroused no opposition because it conflicted with no vested interests.'[43] This is a theme that is echoed in Ashok Desai's explanation of the stagnation.

The main conclusions of this chapter can be briefly summed up. India possesses a diversified and sophisticated industrial sector, but the industrialization she has achieved has not been matched by growth in employment opportunities and reduction in income disparities. Further, the rate of growth of manufacturing output has decelerated since the mid-sixties. There are a number of explanations for both the low growth in employment opportunities and the deceleration in growth rate of output, but the proximate and overriding reason appears to be the policy instruments deployed in the pursuit of the import-substituting industrialization strategy.

7

Private Foreign Investment and Technology

The familiar academic debates on the role of private foreign investment (PFI) and technology in the development process have often been rehearsed in the Indian context. India, too, has her 'dependencia' theorists who argue that PFI has distorted the pattern of industrialization, reduced indigenous control over the future pattern of the economy, contributed to the concentration of incomes and economic power, and that the economy has suffered from an excessive dependence on foreign technology.[1] It is argued that this excessive dependence on foreign technology has inhibited the development of indigenous technologies and products appropriate to Indian conditions, and has been a factor of significance in the slow growth of the industrial sector. There are also those, decidedly a minority, who believe that imported technology has been widely diffused in the economy and that imports of technology and associated equipment have contributed to industrial expansion and the prevention of monopolistic conditions.[2] The data and information required to assess the various claims made in favour of and against PFI and technology are unfortunately not available. In fact, there is very little published data on the composition, size and pattern of PFI beyond the year 1973. Moreover, the very nature of the subject, with its heavy political overtones, permits few settled conclusions. Given these constraints, this chapter briefly reviews the role of PFI and technology in the Indian economy, mainly with a view to highlighting the major analytical issues.

Official policy

Most developing countries still in the shadow of yesteryear's colonialism and jealous of their political independence are wary of foreign economic domination. Recent exposés of attempts by some multinational companies to destabilize foreign régimes, and of the bribing of foreign officials, have heightened the innate hostility of developing countries towards PFI. But they also recognize that it is a powerful conduit for the transference of the technology, managerial skills and capital they need for their development programmes. It is thus that most developing countries display an ambivalent attitude towards PFI and technology. On one hand, they have wooed PFI by offering various tax incentives, generous depreciation allowances and various forms of subsidies; on the other hand, they have instituted various forms of control on the operations of foreign firms.

These attitudes are reflected in India's official policy towards PFI and technology. Successive policy statements, beginning with the Prime Minister's 1949 policy statement on foreign capital, have recognized the technological and financial contribution of PFI to the economy. Foreign firms have been assured that there would be no restrictions on the repatriation of capital and remittances of profits, and that there would be no nationalization without compensation. Foreign firms have also been offered various forms of tax exemptions and tax concessions.[3]

While the broad framework of policy has not been hostile to foreign enterprise participation, PFI has been subject to a detailed set of regulations concerning its sectoral allocation and the nature of its participation. PFI is excluded from certain 'key' industries and 'inessential' consumer goods industries; in certain others, both foreign capital and technical participation are allowed; while in a third category of industries, foreign enterprise participation is restricted to technical collaboration. There are also stipulations concerning the extent of foreign equity participation, maximum rates of royalty to be paid on the import of technology, and the duration of technology licensing agreements between Indian and foreign firms. While there have been exceptions, the government's preference has, in general, been for joint ventures and technology licensing agreements, as opposed to the operations of wholly foreign-owned subsidiaries. In fact, the 1973 Foreign Exchange Regulations Act (FERA) required existing big foreign companies to shed their equity in favour of local shareholders, generally to less than 40 per cent unless they were in a priority sector or were major exporters. Forging a link between foreign enterprise participation and exports has for long been an integral part of the policy framework, with foreign firms in export-oriented industries enjoying special privileges.

The Indian regulatory framework is regarded as more complex than that of most other developing countries. Foreign investors and Indian firms importing technology from abroad not only have to meet with the regulations concerning foreign enterprise participation in the economy but also have to comply with all the import and industrial licensing policies outlined in Chapter 6. In practice, all this has meant a detailed bureaucratic scrutiny of the applications for foreign investment and technical collaboration. The delays, expense and confusion caused by this policy of considering each case on its merits have been a major cause for complaint on the part of both Indian and foreign firms.

The complex nature of the regulatory framework is to be ascribed in the main to the challenge that PFI poses to policy-makers. The problem is how best to reconcile the conflict between the objective of economic nationalism – the desire to preserve and promote national control and ownership of the economy – and the objective of maximizing the economic contribution of PFI and technology to industrialization and development. The import-substituting industrialization strategy initiated in the mid-fifties, with its associated controls on imports and industrial licensing policies, not only spurred on the process of industrialization but also created widespread monopoly rents in the system. Foreign firms sought to capture these monopoly rents through investment and technology-licensing agreements with Indian firms. The Indian firms operating in the highly profitable domestic markets also found joint ventures and technology licensing agreements to be a method of obtaining the scarce resources of technology, managerial skills and foreign exchange. The government in its turn, while recognizing the contribution of foreign enterprise participation to industrial development, has sought to limit the share of monopoly rents accruing to foreign firms through a complex web of rules and regulations. Whether or not the regulatory framework has been successful in attaining these twin objectives is difficult to judge. While this issue is examined later in the chapter, it is sufficient to note here that the regulatory framework has had an impact on the composition and organizational pattern of foreign enterprise participation in India.

Magnitude and composition

In relation to her size, the total amount of private foreign capital in India is not very high. In 1978, the most recent year for which data are available, the total stock of private foreign capital in India was $2,500 millon. This compares with figures of $2,880 million for Malaysia, $13,520 million for Brazil, $6,000 million for Mexico and $3,320 million for Argentina.[4] The gradual tightening of restrictions on inflow of PFI since 1973 is reflected in the meagre inflow of private foreign capital in recent years. Data cited by Sanjaya Lal and Sharif Mohammad in a recent study shows that during the period 1966–79, the total amount of new foreign equity capital approved by the government amounted to only about $70 million, and the net inflow (after deducting dividends and repatriation) was negative. In 1979 alone, net foreign investment in Brazil was of the order of £2,220 million, in Mexico $668 million, and in Singapore $815 million.[5]

A more meaningful estimate of the extent of PFI in India would be its share in the total private capital formation in the country. Unfortunately, comparable figures on this statistic are not readily available. However, available data show that the total stock of PFI as a percentage of the total value of gross assets of 1,650 Indian joint-stock companies in the private sector amounted to around 22 per cent in 1973.[6] Data on the proportion of private foreign investment in individual industry groups in the Indian manufacturing sector are also not readily available. However, rough estimates provided by Lal and Mohammad in the study cited earlier give some indication of the relative share of foreign firms in various branches of Indian manufacturing industry. The study employs dividends paid abroad as a percentage of total dividends paid, as a proxy for the share of foreign firms in India's manufacturing industries for the year 1977–8. This measure is estimated for a group of twenty-eight industries, and is based on the balance-sheet data for large manufacturing enterprises published by the Reserve Bank of India. It is shown that in one industry (other chemicals), the foreign share was over 50 per cent; in eight of the twenty-eight industries, the foreign share was in the range of 25 to 50 per cent, and in seven industries it was less than 10 per cent.

Meagre as they are, these various sets of data show that although the amount of PFI in India is not insignificant, it is not large enough

Table 7.1 Sectoral Distribution of Private Foreign Investment in India

	1948 Rs million	Per cent	1961 Rs million	Per cent	1967 Rs million	Per cent	1969 Rs million	Per cent	1971 Rs million	Per cent	1972 Rs million	Per cent
Plantations	523.0	20.4	1005.0	19.0	1072.0	16.4	1225.0	16.7	1199.0	15.6	1205.0	14.8
Mining	115.0	4.5	109.0	2.1	44.0	0.7	37.0	0.5	63.0	0.8	67.0	0.8
Petroleum	223.0	8.7	1481.0	28.0	1276.0	19.5	1315.0	17.8	1158.0	15.1	1226.0	15.0
Manufacturing	710.0	27.8	1868.0	35.3	3226.0	49.0	3920.0	53.1	4857.0	63.3	5235.0	64.2
(a) Food, beverages and tobacco	101.0	14.2	337.0	18.0	350.0	10.1	405.0	10.3	435.0	9.0	466.0	8.9
(b) Textile products	280.0	39.4	140.0	7.5	161.0	5.0	177.0	4.5	252.0	5.0	244.0	4.7
(c) Transport equipment	10.0	1.4	86.0	4.6	229.0	7.1	257.0	6.6	277.0	5.7	282.0	5.4
(d) Machinery and tools	12.0	1.7	79.0	4.3	213.0	6.3	250.0	6.4	314.0	6.5	344.0	6.6
(e) Metals and metal products	80.0	11.3	267.0	14.3	495.0	15.3	612.0	15.6	733.0	15.0	812.0	15.5
(f) Electrical machinery	48.0	6.8	120.0	6.4	284.0	8.8	413.0	10.5	528.0	11.0	587.0	11.2
(g) Chemicals	80.0	11.3	476.0	25.5	946.0	29.3	1158.0	29.5	1496.0	30.8	1608.0	30.7
(h) Others	99.0	6.8	363.0	19.4	584.0	18.0	648.0	16.5	822.0	17.0	892.0	17.0
Services	988.0	38.6	821.0	15.6	929.0	14.2	880.0	12.0	396.0	5.2	416.0	5.1
Total	2559.0	100.0	5284.0	100.0	6542.0	100.0	7377.0	100.0	7673.0	100.0	8149.0	100.0

Source: *Reserve Bank of India Bulletin* (various issues).

to dominate and influence the course of the economy.

Since independence, significant changes have occurred in both the composition and the organizational pattern of foreign enterprise participation in the Indian economy. Foreign capital and enterprise have been fanning out toward technologically-intensive fields of manufacturing industry, and away from the traditional strongholds of plantations and extractive industries. More than 60 per cent of the total stock of PFI in the seventies was accounted for by the manufacturing sector. Within the manufacturing sector, chemicals, metal and metal products and the machinery industries have been major hosts to private foreign capital (Table 7.1).

Another major development is that the Indian economy has played host to almost all the diverse forms of foreign enterprise participation. At one extreme is the operations of subsidiaries wholly owned and controlled by foreigners, and at the other extreme are the technical collaboration agreements between Indian and foreign firms. The latter involve no foreign financial participation; the payments received by foreign firms are in the form of royalties and technical fees for the technology and know-how they supply to Indian firms. In between are a variety of hybrids, including joint business-ventures between Indian and foreign firms and technical collaboration agreements which also involve minority foreign equity participation.

The most significant of these organizational changes is the growth in the number of technical collaboration agreements between Indian and foreign firms. Over the period 1957–76, the government approved more than 4,800 technical collaboration agreements, including agreements between foreign subsidiaries in India and their parent firms, pure technical collaboration agreements between India and foreign firms, and agreements involving minority foreign financial participation. It should be noted that not all of the agreements in the last group involve inflows of capital from abroad. In several cases, the equity held by foreign firms may merely represent payment made by Indian firms in lieu of royalties and technical fees paid for the import of technology.

Technical collaboration agreements are also heavily concentrated in technologically intensive fields of manufacturing activity. More than 50 per cent of the 3191 agreements approved by the government between the years 1957–70 related to electrical machinery, non-electrical machinery, machine tools and transport

Table 7.2 Technical Collaboration Agreements Classified by Industry, 1957–70

	1957	1958	1959	1960	1961	1962	1963	1964	1965	1966	1967	1968	1969	Jan- Dec. 1970	Total 1957- Dec. 1970
1. Electrical equipment, apparatus, components, etc.	4	6	9	46	69	63	52	35	22	21	24	16	16	21	404
2. Industrial machinery (other than textile machinery)	6	3	8	34	47	29	40	68	40	44	19	25	32	43	433
3. Machine tools & accessories	–	4	6	26	35	17	26	33	14	19	21	15	3	12	231
4. Transport equipment	5	7	13	38	23	26	24	26	7	12	11	4	6	14	261
5. Basic chemicals	7	8	18	25	37	4	4	26	14	10	11	7	4	4	179
6. Chemical products	3	2	9	8	13	38	24	25	20	5	12	5	7	10	181
7. Heavy electrical equipment (generation and distribution)	7	6	4	35	27	–	2	20	10	8	13	10	4	5	151
8. Iron & steel products	2	5	11	25	17	12	13	21	9	12	2	7	2	6	124
9. Instruments	–	–	1	19	9	12	21	20	17	7	8	–	7	1	124
10. Textile machinery	1	1	4	15	15	4	5	15	18	10	1	7	3	6	105
11 Materials handling & construction equipment	1	1	4	18	19	4	4	13	8	8	9	3	7	5	104
12. Castings & forgings	1	–	1	9	10	5	12	27	5	6	1	1	1	–	79
13. Drugs & pharmaceuticals	4	8	4	11	7	9	6	6	5	3	5	5	1	3	77
14. Ceramic & glassware	2	3	2	10	11	10	5	8	3	4	–	2	3	2	65
15. Paper & paper products	2	2	–	9	10	5	5	4	5	2	1	2	1	1	49
16. Metal & metal products	2	1	1	3	6	6	8	5	1	1	5	2	2	4	47
17. Technical consultancy	–	2	1	–	–	5	9	6	1	1	4	2	2	5	38
18. Agricultural machinery & implements	1	–	3	4	2	3	3	2	2	3	2	4	9	4	42
19. Fertilizers	–	–	–	–	2	1	1	–	3	3	–	1	–	1	12
20. Pesticides	1	2	2	1	1	–	–	–	–	–	1	2	–	–	12
21. Others	32	42	49	44	43	43	37	47	38	23	32	11	25	36	500
Total	81	103	150	380	403	298	298	403	242	202	182	135	135	183	3191

Source: *Journal of Industry and Trade* (various issues).

equipment (Table 7.2). These organizational changes which have occurred in recent years reflect the preference of policy-makers for forms of foreign enterprise participation which involve very little foreign ownership of equity or control over operations. The changes in industrial composition of PFI and technology imports reflect the impact of the industrialization policies of the country. The foregoing has sketched the salient features of private foreign enterprise participation in the Indian economy. The widely debated analytical issues are the impact of PFI and technology on the balance of payments, employment and growth of the economy.

Balance-of-payments issue

One of the principal criticisms of PFI in India is that it has had an adverse effect on the balance of payments. This criticism is based on the evidence that annual outflows of foreign exchange on account of PFI, in the form of profits, dividends and royalties, have exceeded inflows of private foreign capital. Over the period 1964–72, the total gross inflow of private foreign capital including retained profits of foreign companies was Rs 2,400 million, whereas the total amount of dividends and profits remitted abroad during this period amounted to Rs 3,000 million, resulting in an excess of outflows over inflows of foreign exchange of the order of Rs 600 million.[7]

The fallacies in this line of reasoning have been widely noted. First, the two sets of figures being compared may not be logically related. The outflow of dividends and profits relates to a stock of capital accumulated over a number of years and it would necessarily exceed annual inflows. Second, the inflow–outflow comparison is too partial in its approach to the balance of payments. It neglects all the direct and indirect export-generating and import-saving effects of PFI, besides failing to take into account its contribution to technology, managerial and labour skills. Third, the inflow–outflow comparison approach can be dismissed as unsatisfactory on theoretical grounds. The balance of payments is a general equilibrium phenomenon. In other words, it is an integral part of the economy. Any positive contribution to the total productivity of the economy *pari passu* improves the balance of payments. As Kindleberger argues, the two sums – the debt source payments and the capital inflows – have nothing to do with each other, except in a narrow balance-of-payments context. In so far as each act of investment has been productive and contributes to total productivity, the problem of debt servicing is taken care of. The problem arises only when past investments have been unproductive or resources have been misallocated, resulting in a loss of production.[8]

The critics of PFI in India do not deny these arguments. Their case is that the direct contribution of PFI to exports and import-substitution has been negligible and that domestic investment would have been a preferable alternative to it. Data are cited to show that the ratio of exports to total production of foreign subsidiaries in India during the sixties was a meagre 4.3 per cent.[9] This, however, is hardly surprising. The sixties were the heydays of import-substituting industrialization. Much of the stock of PFI in India was oriented towards the highly profitable domestic markets. Indeed, received theory on the determinants of PFI accords considerable importance to the role of tariffs and quotas on imports in attracting foreign firms to developing countries.

The much more relevant issue is the contribution of foreign firms to import substitution. The basic issue here is the relative productive efficiency of foreign firms. Are they superior in their productive performance, relative to Indian firms? If it can be shown that their productive efficiency is no higher than that of Indian firms, it can be argued that, in the absence of PFI, domestic investment would not only have resulted in an equivalent amount of import substitution but it would also have been much less expensive. In this case, while PFI would be a mere substitute for domestic investment, it would result in an outflow of foreign exchange in the form of dividends and profits. If this were the case, the inflow–outflow approach to the balance-of-payments effects of PFI would suffice and the critics would be justified in arguing that it had adversely affected the balance of payments.

This, in fact, is the case of the critics of PFI in India; but the data cited in support of this contention are both selective and inadequate. The one piece of evidence cited relates to the relatively high import-intensity of foreign firms. It is shown that during the period 1964–70, the ratio of imports to total production of foreign subsidiaries and Indo-foreign joint ventures was around 35 per cent. This compares with a figure of around 20 per cent for both Indian firms operating with know-how imported through technical collaboration agreements and Indian public enterprises.[10]

These data, though, are hardly adequate to support the critics' case. The various groups of firms may differ considerably from one another in the nature and composition of products they produce and the markets they serve. As such, a comparison of the import intensity ratio between these groups of firms may be meaningless. Further, the data cited show that the import intensity of both foreign subsidiaries and Indian firms operating with imported know-how declined during the period 1964–70. The Reserve Bank of India reports that nearly 90 per cent of imports in the case of the subsidiaries was on account of raw materials. The decline in the ratio of imports to value added, from 54.9 per cent in 1964–5 to 32.5 per cent in 1969–70, presumably reflects the success of the subsidiaries both in economizing on raw materials and in substituting domestic materials for imported materials.

In the case of joint ventures between Indian and foreign firms, however, not only is the import intensity high but it also depicts a rising trend from 35.1 per cent in 1964–5 to 53.9 per cent in 1969–70. It should be noted that joint ventures in which foreign firms have a minority share in the equity are the officially favoured method of foreign enterprise participation. A possible reason for the relatively high import intensity of joint ventures may be the 'over-pricing' of the materials and equipment supplied by foreign firms to the ventures. In the absence of a majority stake in the equity, foreign firms may have resorted to 'over-pricing' of equipment as a method of maximizing their share of the revenues from the ventures. However, the principal objective of Indian firms in entering into joint ventures with foreign firms may be to acquire the materials and equipment they need. It does not, therefore, necessarily follow that their import intensity would have been any less if they had not contracted joint ventures.

There is also some evidence to show that the productive efficiency of foreign firms in India is, in fact, higher than that of locally-owned firms. A case-study of the productivity differences between foreign firms and locally-owned firms in a sample of thirty-four industries reports that on average, labour productivity of the former exceeds that of the latter by 66 per cent, capital productivity by 60 per cent and total factor productivity by 55 per cent.[11] Again, available data on profitability show that the ratio of gross profits to capital employed for foreign firms in India was 40 per cent higher than that for Indian firms. Admittedly, all these indicators, estimated on the basis of data expressed in market prices, are a crude approximation for productive efficiency. In an economy rife with controls on foreign trade and domestic investment, market prices may be highly distorted, and may not reflect the true social opportunity costs of outputs and inputs. The relatively high ratio of return earned by foreign firms may also in part reflect the monopoly position they enjoy in various lines of industrial activity. It is, however, arguable whether the verdict that PFI has adversely affected the balance of payments and made a negative contribution to the Indian economy is justified.

All this points to the complex nature of the problem of assessing the balance-of-payments affects of PFI. It may, in fact, be impossible to assess the balance-of-payments effects of PFI at the macro level, and each project may have to be assessed individually. Such a method of analysis – which also suggests a way of resolving the problem posed by distorted market prices – is the now-famous Little-Mirlees (LM) approach to the balance of payments. It is worth pausing to review the approach, not only because of its theoretical elegance but also because it has been shown to be operationally practical in the context of a group of PFI projects in India.[12]

The LM approach

The balance-of-payments effects of a project are, by definition, the net savings in terms of foreign exchange resulting from the project. Net savings accruing to the economy are equal to the total value of output minus all the material and non-material input costs. In other words, it is the value added of the project minus the total wages costs of the project. In the LM method, all the inputs and outputs of the project are evaluated in terms of foreign exchange. If they are importables they are valued at c.i.f. import prices, and if they are exportables they are valued at f.o.b. export prices. The justification for such a procedure is that international prices, through trade and balance of payments, represent the true social opportunity costs of inputs and outputs. This method not only resolves the problems posed by distorted domestic market prices, but also provides a direct method of estimating the foreign-exchange contribution of the project.

How to evaluate labour? In the LM method, it is valued at its shadow wage rate, meaning its opportunity cost or marginal product in an alternative occupation. This marginal product is again valued in terms of foreign exchange. It is possible that increased employment resulting from the project may give rise to increased consumption. In this case, the increased value of consumption in foreign-exchange terms has to be deducted from the value added of the project, to arrive at the balance-of-payments effects of the latter. Further, in the case of PFI projects, foreign capital inflows are added to the benefits of the project and outflows of foreign exchange in the form of dividends and royalties are deducted. In addition, any externalities resulting from the project in terms of labour and managerial skills are added to the benefits. These externalities are difficult to quantify; the precise number arrived at is largely a matter of subjective judgment.

The balance-of-payments effects of the project are thus the net savings from the project, expressed in terms of foreign exchange. But how is the choice to be made between competing projects when investment funds are limited? The deciding criteria suggested are the ones normally used in investment appraisal – the net present value criteria, or alternatively the internal rate-of-return criteria. In the former case, the time streams of the net foreign-exchange benefits accruing from the project over its life are discounted back to the present. The discount rate used for this purpose is based on the social opportunity cost of capital to the economy. If the resulting present value of the benefits of the project is positive, it is accepted. The alternative is to use the internal rate-of-return criteria. The internal rate of return – or the 'yield' of the project – is by definition the discount rate that equates the present value of the benefits of the project to its capital cost. In this case, if the internal rate of return is greater than the predetermined social opportunity cost of capital, the project is to be accepted.

That the LM method is operational is shown by case-studies such as that of Deepak Lal on four chemical projects in India.[13] These projects were in the nature of joint ventures involving foreign collaboration, both financial and technical. The social opportunity cost of capital in India was assumed to be around 6 per cent.

In general, Lal's results show that although these projects were privately profitable, they were socially unprofitable. The internal rate of return for these projects was higher than the social opportunity cost of capital only in the presence of the high tariffs on competing imports which the government had imposed. Clearly, in these cases the country would have been better off importing the products rather than producing them at home. It could, though, be argued on 'infant industry' grounds that these were relatively new projects which could become efficient in the future. Also, as Lal argues, there may be no alternative to PFI in high-technology industries such as chemicals, if the establishment of such industries is deemed essential.

The critics of PFI in India, however, appear to argue that domestic investment in general would have been a preferred alternative. It could be so in cases where the required technology and managerial skills are available from domestic sources. But if these have to be imported from abroad through licensing agreements and management contracts, and paid for in foreign exchange, domestic investment may be no less expensive than PFI. In any case, generalizations based on casual empiricism are no substitute for detailed case-studies. As Paul Streeten argues, 'the important point for analysis and policy is to envisage the various alternatives, against which any operational assessment has to be made, and to assess the benefits and costs of each, measuring what is measurable and judging what is not.'[14] The LM approach outlined above provides such a method for analysing the various alternatives. Obviously, more case-studies such as the ones conducted by Deepak Lal are needed before passing judgment on the balance-of-payments effects of PFI.

Employment effects of PFI

This is also a controversial issue. The advocates of PFI argue that one of its principal benefits is the jobs it creates, especially when employment opportunities are constrained by a shortage of capital. The critics, though, argue that at best the employment which PFI creates is a mere substitute for existing employment, and at worst it destroys rather than creates employment. The principal basis for this argument is that the technologies perfected by foreign firms tend to be relatively capital intensive. Furthermore, foreign firms tend to fashion local firms in their own image: either because of a preference for foreign technologies or because of the need to survive in a competitive milieu, local firms tend to imitate the capital-intensive technologies of foreign firms. Local firms may also be forced to substitute capital for labour because of the wage policies pursued by foreign firms. Their high-wage-rate policies based on international standards tend to push up wage rates in local labour markets, forcing locally-owned firms also to adopt capital-intensive technologies.[15]

It is a fact that the technologies of foreign firms often tend to be capital-intensive. Part of the reason for their capital intensity is their structural characteristics. They mostly tend to be relatively large in size; and scale of operations and capital intensity appear to go together. Techniques perfected in the capital-rich and labour-scarce developed countries tend to be capital intensive. It is also presumed that the highly differentiated products they produce embody capital-intensive technologies. The evidence on this issue, though, is mixed. Differentiated products may be intensive in their use of skilled labour rather than capital. There is also evidence to show that foreign firms do pay relatively high wage rates.

The significant issue, however, is whether or not foreign firms are invariably capital-intensive in their operations. When the influences of size and product composition are controlled for, do foreign firms tend to be relatively capital-intensive in their operations? Do they respond to incentives to adapt and restructure their technologies to local market conditions? There are a number of case-studies attempting to compare the choice of techniques of foreign firms with that of locally-owned firms in developing countries. While these case studies do detect a difference in the factor proportions between the two groups of firms, the direction of difference is not always the same. There are studies, pertaining to Kenya for instance, which show foreign-owned firms to be less capital-intensive in their operations than locally-owned firms.[16]

One such case-study for India, by Agarwal, reports that in the case of twenty-two out of a sample of thirty-four industries, foreign firms were more capital-intensive in their operations than locally-owned firms.[17] For the thirty-four industries as a whole, the weighted average productive capital per employee for the foreign firms was seen to exceed that of locally-owned firms by 16.1 per cent, with wide variations around the average for individual industries. Also value added per employee – a proxy for capital intensity – for the foreign firms was seen to exceed that of the locally-owned firms by 66.6 per cent. The experience of Indian firms operating with know-how imported through technical collaboration agreements, discussed later in the chapter, appears to be similar.

Agarwal ascribes the capital intensity of foreign firms mainly to their ease of access to capital markets. They not only have access to the capital markets in their home countries but are also favoured customers on the local capital markets. Data are also cited to show that foreign firms pay relatively high wage rates. From this it is inferred that the relatively high capital-intensity of foreign firms is in large part due to the high wage–interest ratios they face.

The findings of this study, however, are subject to a number of qualifications. The definition of productive capital includes not only expenditure on plant and equipment but also expenditure on buildings for factories, offices and housing for personnel. As Agarwal notes, foreign firms typically spend more on buildings than local firms. It is arguable, however, whether expenditure on buildings should be included in the measurement of capital intensity. The more relevant concept would be the degree of mechanization of the direct production process. Expenditure on buildings could, in fact, generate employment in the typically labour-intensive construction industries in the developing countries.

There are also various other well-known problems associated with the measurement of capital. The study acknowledges these problems, and emphasizes the differences in value added per employee between the two groups of firms as a proxy for capital intensity. But there need not necessarily be a correlation between capital intensity and value added per employee. The relatively high value added per employee for the foreign firms may in large part reflect their efficiency in labour use and managerial skills. That this may be the case is, in fact, argued by Agarwal in a companion article to the one under discussion.[18]

Even so, Agarwal's detailed data for individual industry groups and the statistical tests of significance which he reports suggest that the presumption that foreign firms in India tend to be relatively capital-intensive cannot be rejected altogether. Nor can it be denied that they have ease of access to capital. But could ease of access to capital alone influence their choice of techniques in the direction of capital-intensive technologies? And could lack of access to capital be the reason for the relative labour intensity of locally-owned firms? There is no presumption that easy access to capital would necessarily result in the choice of capital-intensive technologies. A case-study for Brazil, for instance, shows that large Brazilian firms were not at any great disadvantage relative to foreign firms in raising capital; yet the Brazilian firms had adopted labour-intensive technologies and foreign firms had instituted capital-intensive technologies.[19]

The study for Brazil argues that it was not so much differences in access to capital and the costs of capital, but the permissive market environment in Brazil that had influenced the foreign firms to choose relatively capital-intensive technologies. (By permissive market environment is meant the absence of effective competition on product markets, a consequence of the import-substituting industrialization policies pursued by Brazil.) Given the permissive market environment and the resulting high monopoly profits, foreign firms had adopted tried-and-tested capital-intensive technologies rather than incur the costs involved in searching for labour-intensive technologies. Locally-owned Brazilian firms, for their part, had adopted the labour-intensive technologies with which they were familiar. Their value added per employee, however, was relatively low because they lacked the managerial and labour skills required to operate the labour-intensive technologies efficiently.

India's experience could be similar. As described in Chapter 6, India's import-substituting industrialization policies provided highly profitable domestic markets, sheltered from international competition. Admittedly, this permissive environment may have encouraged both foreign and domestic firms to invest in inherently capital-intensive industries and in relatively capital-intensive methods of production. But the former could have responded to such incentives much more so than the latter, because of their familiarity with and access to capital-intensive technologies. In addition, fiscal incentives such as generous depreciation allowances, tax rebates and tax holidays provided to attract PFI may have contributed to the capital intensity of foreign firms.

In sum, the observed capital intensity of foreign firms could be due more to the nature of the product markets facing them than to their ease of access to capital. Policies designed to promote competition on product markets and subsidization of labour rather than capital could influence foreign firms to adopt cost-minimizing labour-intensive technologies. Such policies would include a more liberalized import régime, and encouragement of production for exports. These would expose foreign firms to international competition and force them to seek cost-minimizing labour-intensive technologies. With their endowment of managerial skills they would be likely to utilize such techniques effectively. This solution, though, is not without its problems. A liberalized import régime may reduce the inflow of PFI, and extensive export efforts may be impeded by restrictions on exports placed by the importing countries. The trade-off against these losses, however, is the increased employment which such policies would create.

In any case, it may be unrealistic to expect foreign firms to make a major direct contribution to the solution of the massive unemployment problem facing countries such as India. Because of their structural characteristics they do tend to be capital-intensive in their operations. The need is to ensure that domestic policies do not further encourage their natural proclivities for capital-intensive technologies; to provide them with incentives to seek labour-intensive technologies; and to institute fiscal measures to transfer the maximum benefit possible from their operations to the local economy.

Technical collaboration agreements

The large number of technical collaboration agreements entered into by Indian firms with foreign firms for the import of technology and know-how has raised several controversial issues. Has India imported too much and the wrong kind of technologies under these agreements? Have Indian firms paid too high a price for these technologies? Are such agreements a viable alternative to PFI?

On the basis of the available information, it is difficult to assess whether or not excessive imports of technology have occurred. The number of agreements contracted by different industries is a poor guide to the extent and nature of technology imported. It is a fact, however, that in the early years a number of collaboration agreements were approved in 'inessential' consumer goods industries, such as toys, footwear and toothpaste. Private firms may justify importing such know-how on the grounds that it is unavailable from indigenous sources. It has been frequently argued, nevertheless, that several items of consumer goods produced by foreign firms and locally-owned firms utilizing imported know-how are inappropriate to the requirements of low-income countries such as India. They tend to be over-specified, over-packaged and over-differentiated, and cater mainly for the needs of upper-income groups. Such products, as stated earlier, are also supposed to embody capital-intensive methods of production. The usual response to this sort of criticism is that the skewed income-distribution patterns in the developing countries generate a demand for such products. The best policy, in this case, would be to correct the income-distribution pattern. But once these industries have been established, there may be little logic in denying them access to technology that is not available at home.

Are imported technologies over-priced, and has India paid too much for the technologies she has imported? It is frequently argued that the prices charged by foreign firms for the technologies they transfer are exorbitant. This criticism is based on the thesis that knowledge, once produced, becomes a 'free good'. The marginal cost of replicating an existing invention is trivial compared to the average costs of research and development. If it were sold on the open market, it would become freely available as it could be produced at little or no cost. Foreign firms have monopolized what ought to be free goods, and charge prices far in excess of marginal costs.

This thesis, however, ignores the fact that unless firms engaged in research and development can appropriate a fair share of the returns from such activity, they will have little incentive to invest in the production of knowledge. It also ignores the organizational costs associated with technology transfers. Such transfers include not only technology embodied in blue-prints and designs, but also human skills and information required to make the embodied knowledge operational. For these reasons, it would be illogical to argue that the price of technologies should approximate their marginal costs.

In practice, the prices charged lie between the marginal costs of replicating the technologies and the average costs of their production. Where exactly they settle between these two limits depends on the relative bargaining strength of the sellers and buyers of technology. It is possible that because of lack of information about alternative streams and sources of technology, technology-importing firms in developing countries strike a poor bargain; hence the attempts of developing countries such as India to regulate prices through the imposition of ceilings on rates of royalty paid and limitations on the duration of agreements.

Such government intervention may have increased the bargaining strength of Indian firms; they could plead inability to pay higher rates of royalty because of the ceilings. But a policy of imposing ceilings on royalties across the board has its limitations. If ceilings are too high, firms may end up paying too high a royalty; if they are too low, they may not be successful in importing the kind of technology they need.[20] Moreover, there are any number of channels available by which firms can circumvent the regulations. These include paying a premium on equipment imported from the suppliers of technology; fees such as inspection charges for approving the product; and increased commission on sales when the product is exported through the foreign firm's marketing channels. There is evidence to show that Indian firms have resorted to such channels in the face of the ceilings on royalties imposed by the government.[21] This suggests that the value they place on the technology is higher than that indicated by the government's price ceilings.

Even so, in many cases, Indian firms may have paid too high a price. The basic problem here is one of lack of information. Government assistance in collecting and disseminating information about alternative sources and streams of technology could be much more valuable than a policy of imposing across-the-board ceilings. It should also be noted that Indian firms are in a better bargaining position now than they were in the early years of industrialization, for with the advent of Japan and West Germany as significant sources of supply of technology, the monopolistic position enjoyed by the UK and USA has waned. Indian firms have also gained in experience. As one Indian executive puts it, 'In the initial years of operation it was impossible to know the cheaper sources of supply. In the 1950s when technical collaboration agreements were a new phenomenon, it is possible that the foreign firms took the Indian firms for a ride, but we have learned our lesson now.'[22]

The total payments for imported know-how in the form of technical fee and royalties have increased substantially over time: from Rs 40 million in 1964–5 to Rs 186 million in 1972–3; their rate of increase has also been higher than that of dividend payments. While these figures reflect the growth in the number of technical collaboration agreements, they do not substantiate the thesis that the payments made by India for imported know-how have been excessive. These payments have to be related to the benefits derived from imported know-how in the form of its contribution to the productivity and growth of Indian industry. But such an analysis is beset with several conceptual and data problems.

The available evidence on this issue is confined to inter-firm efficiency comparisons between three groups of firms: those that had imported know-how under technical collaboration agreements (TCA firms), Indian firms with neither foreign technical nor financial connections (IF firms) und foreign subsidiaries (FF firms). The results of one such study, confined to a sample of eighty-six firms in four industry groups, are reported below.[23] The study attempted to take account of differences in size and product composition between the three groups of firms by a careful selection and scrutiny of available information. Even so, the conclusions of the study are subject to the well-known limitations of exercises in inter-firm efficiency comparison, and are to be regarded as tentative. First, the study showed that TCA firms were much more capital-intensive in their operations than IF and FF firms in all four industry groups. Second, capital productivity was relatively low for TCA firms. Third, the experience of TCA firms in terms of total factor productivity varied between industries. The TCA firms in the electrical machinery and chemical industries were more efficient than comparable FF and IF firms; but they were less efficient than comparable IF firms in both the metal products and non-electrical machinery industries. Fourth, during the period 1964–70 the IF firms registered a considerable improvement in total factor productivity, and the rate of growth in their productivity was much higher than that of the other two groups.

This mixed bag of conclusions permits no generalizations. It does, however, sound a note of caution against the widespread advocacy of technology licensing agreements as a preferred alternative to PFI. Such agreements may not always be an efficient conduit for the transfer of technology. Their success depends both on the extent and quality of knowledge transferred by foreign firms, and on the ability of recipient firms to assimilate and absorb the borrowed technology. Technical collaboration agreements by definition involve no foreign financial participation or managerial control, and the returns to the foreign firms are in the form of royalties and technical fees. Foreign firms may not regard these returns as an adequate compensation for their investment in research and development. In addition, they may regard the technology recipients as a possible source of competition for their products in third markets. Transfers of technology under licensing agreements may also result in an erosion of their monopoly over technology, unless the production and transmission of knowledge on a continuous basis is central to their activity. In other words, 'appropriability' – or the ability of foreign firms to capture fully the returns from their investment in research and development – may be relatively low in the case of technology licensing agreements. Hence the extent and quality of knowledge transferred under technology licensing agreements may be low relative to that under PFI.

'Appropriability', or the lack of it, may also be the reason for the various sorts of restriction clauses – such as restrictions on exports, sources of supply of raw material and equipment, production standards, non-disclosure clauses – frequently stipulated by foreign firms in technical collaboration agreements. Nearly 53 per cent of the 1951 agreements surveyed by the Reserve Bank of India were found to contain export restriction clauses of one sort or another, and 30 per cent were found to contain restrictions on sources of supply of materials and equipment.[24] Export restriction clauses are a device by which foreign firms attempt to guard the markets for their own products in third countries against competition from their licensees. Restrictions on sources of supply of materials and equipment may tie Indian firms to a particular source of supply, and enable foreign firms to charge a mark-up on the plant and equipment they supply. Such mark-ups would be a source of revenue in addition to the royalties they receive. The essential point is that all such restriction clauses are in the nature of a device to increase the 'appropriability' of foreign firms. Such restriction clauses are increasingly frowned-upon by governments of developing countries, including that of India, and their elimination constitutes one of the principal demands made in the declaration on the New International Economic Order. Inimical though they are to the development effort, their elimination may reduce the flow of technology to the developing countries. This, again, is a dilemma posed by foreign enterprise participation to the developing countries.

There is also no presumption that technical collaboration agreements are necessarily a relatively less expensive channel for the import of technology and know-how. As Raymond Vernon notes, on economic cost differences alone it is difficult to establish a universal preference between PFI and alternatives to it (such as licensing agreements). Assuming that royalty rates in the case of licensing agreements would be of the order of 3 to 4 per cent of sales, and that the annual costs of borrowing capital would be in the range of 15 to 20 per cent, Vernon estimates that the annual payments for technology and capital for a 'typical' local firm would be around 20 per cent of the capital. This compares with the figure of 20 per cent for the aggregate technical fee and profits made by foreign-owned subsidiaries in developing countries.[25]

Finally, an important determinant of the success of a technology transplant is the capacity of the recipient firms to absorb the technology. This includes their ability both to implement technologies which need no alteration and to restructure and adapt imported technologies to suit local conditions. The former requires managerial and labour skills at the plant level, and the latter is a long-run problem involving investment in research and development. While foreign firms can be of assistance in solving these problems, the extent of the assistance they render may depend on the mode of transfer adopted. Available evidence indicates that foreign firms in India have done little to adapt and restructure technologies transferred under technical collaboration agreements; it is only when they have had a financial stake in the ventures that they have provided such assistance.[26]

The relatively high capital intensity and low productive efficiency of TCA firms, reported above, may be a consequence of their low absorptive capacity. In the absence of managerial and labour skills required to assimilate the imported technologies, they may not only have been inefficient in the use of capital but also have substituted capital for labour in the production process.

All this is not to say that technical collaboration agreements in general have been ineffective and should be discarded altogether. It is just that the euphoria for them in the recent literature on technology transfers may not be justified. They can be effective if domestic research and development is directed towards improving the absorptive capacity of the economy, and if efforts are made to assemble and disseminate information about alternative streams and sources of technology. In any case, they could be complements to PFI; but not a total substitute.

The foregoing review points to the complex ramifications of the role of private foreign capital and technology in India. While individual cases of PFI may have ranged from the enormously beneficial to the disastrous, it is impossible to arrive at any generalizations. The arguments presented to support the thesis that its contribution to the Indian economy has been entirely negative are not convincing. The available data and information do not permit such a conclusion. It should also be noted that many of the problems associated with PFI, such as its high capital intensity and the monopoly rents earned by foreign firms, may be grounded in the type of industrialization and trade policies which the country has adopted. India's experience with technical collaboration agreements appears not to have been entirely happy, but there is no reason for discarding them. The need is for efforts directed at increasing the absorptive capacity of the economy. It is conceivable that over the years India has gained in experience, not only in negotiating with foreign firms, but also in adapting and restructuring the imported technology. Her reported success in recent years as an exporter of technology to other developing countries may be due to her growing ability to adapt imported technology.

8

Foreign Aid in India's Development Process

For long, the aid debate has been enveloped in a cloud of cynicism. In the popular view, aid is no more than charity bestowed on the poorer nations of the world by the relatively affluent, guided by considerations of morality that the limited income and wealth of the world ought to be shared more equitably. In the view of the radical 'new left', aid is yet another instrument of world monopoly capitalism designed to exploit the countries of the Third World. Indeed the World Bank and USAID are regarded as the creation of world monopoly capitalism, designed to propagate the capitalist creed in the Third World. These institutions are accused of using aid as a bargaining ploy for obtaining favourable treatment to foreign private investment in the Third World countries; for obtaining ease of entry for export of goods and services from the West; and for the promotion of economic policies beneficial to the aid donors.[1]

Less cynical but no less damaging to the 'aid cause' is the left-wing critique of the efficiency of aid in the development process. Representative of this school is the view of the Oxford economist Keith Griffin: 'If anything, aid may have retarded development by leading to lower domestic savings, by distorting the composition of investment and thereby raising the capital-output ratio, by frustrating the emergence of an indigenous entrepreneurial class and by inhibiting institutional reform.'[2]

Aid has also been assailed by right-wing economists, suspicious of government interference in economic affairs. Representative of this group is Professor Peter Bauer's view that aid is neither a necessary nor a sufficient condition for development.[3] It is shown to be unnecessary because several developing countries, such as Hong Kong, Singapore, Malaysia, Thailand, Nigeria and Mexico, made rapid progress between the last quarter of the nineteenth century and the middle of the twentieth century without much aid. Aid is not a sufficient condition for development because many countries which have received substantial aid have made little progress. In the absence of other essential ingredients for development, such as human skills, institutions and attitudes conducive to progress, aid is likely to be wasted. Apart from casual empiricism, Bauer's case against aid also rests on the premise that aid encourages profligacy on the part of aid recipients. It encourages misallocation of resources, weakens domestic savings efforts, and allows recipient governments to indulge their fetish for ostentatious projects.

India's attitude towards aid

Foreign aid has been assailed by differing spectrums of political opinion in India as well. Echoing Peter Bauer's view that aid encourages profligacy on the part of the recipient governments is the right-wing economist Professor B. R. Shenoy's thesis that it has encouraged the growth of the public sector and inefficient bureaucratic policies in India. It is also the implication that, but for aid, Indian policy-makers would have followed more efficient policies involving a greater degree of reliance on private enterprise and the market mechanism.[4]

At the other end of the spectrum is the radical left-wing view that 'concentration of economic power and strengthening of Indian big business control over the Indian economy has been contributed to a great extent by foreign aid whether it was given to the public sector or the private sector and whether its source was capitalist or socialist countries'.[5] Indeed, according to this view, the significant achievement of the World Bank – one of the principal aid donors to India – has been to integrate India in the world capitalist system so that the international investors get a huge market for capital and technology in which to maximize their profits.[6] It is also implied that the Bank and western capitalists have had the cooperation of India's policy-makers in this endeavour.

India's recourse to a massive loan of $5.8 billion – or Rs 51 billion – from the International Monetary Fund (IMF), under the Extended Fund Facility in 1981, has heightened these criticisms. This loan represents the largest ever extended to any member country by the IMF. The critics argue that a loan of this size from the IMF *ipso facto* amounts to a crippling of India's economic sovereignity. For, according to the critics, the IMF is an instrument of neo-classicalism.

As one critic puts it, 'it has the most sweeping theory in the interests of imperialism', because 'as per the terms and conditions of the IMF loan, a borrowing country has to open its door for free entry of transnational corporations and banks, liberalise imports, give up national planning, orient itself for exporting its best products, restrain wages, and curtail public welfare programmes.'[7]

Admittedly, the conditions governing the IMF loan require the liberalization of the foreign trade régime and the promotion of domestic economic stability. But to say that these stipulations amount to economic imperialism is surely an exaggeration. Many economists outside the IMF have, in fact, advocated a liberalized foreign trade régime for India, and an increased role for market forces in the allocation of resources. They can hardly be accused of being advocates of imperialism, unless an advocacy of a greater play for market forces is equated with imperialism.

In any case, India's policy-makers have long maintained that aid is only a temporary expedient. Indeed, 'self-reliant growth' has been one of the principal objectives repeatedly espoused in successive Five-Year Plan documents. Admittedly, the interpretation of 'self-reliance' has been subject to change and revision over time. While the Third and Fourth Five-Year Plans interpreted it to mean termination of aid, later Five-Year Plans have interpreted it to mean reduction in the dependence on aid. Thus, the Sixth Five-Year Plan interprets 'self-reliance' as a means of gaining a more equal relationship with the world economy and reducing the country's vulnerability to international pressures and disturbances. This is to be achieved not only through a reduction in the dependence on aid but also by according equal weight to export promotion and efficient import-substitution.[8] The official policy constitutes a much more pragmatic approach to aid and international economic relations, especially in its recent formulation.

Given these attitudes to aid, what has been the role of aid in India's development process? Has it in fact been counterproductive, as the critics of aid allege? What are the prospects for 'self-reliant growth'?

Magnitude of aid to India

In absolute terms, India has received more economic aid than most other developing countries. Indeed, no other developing country

Table 8.1 Utilization of Foreign Aid (Rs million)

		I Five-Year Plan 1951–6	II Five-Year Plan 1956–61	III Five-Year Plan 1961–6	Annual Plans 1966–9	IV Five Year Plan 1969–74	1976–7	1977–8	1978–9	1979–80
I	Loans	1,264	7,250	19,083	22,005	35,239	10,017	8,096	7,275	8,500
	(a) Multilateral agencies	338	2,228	3,240	4,249	7,354	4,574	3,662	3,803	
	(b) Bilateral sources	926	5,022	15,843	17,547	27,885	5,443	4,434	3,472	
	USA	903	396	6,395	7,737	9,472	565	185	198	
	UK		1,219	1,704	2,237	4,953	178	155	137	
	West Germany		1,199	2,197	1,873	3,110	737	400	612	
	Canada		157	116		2,209	129	247	192	
	Japan		160	882	1,223	1,425	620	417	489	
	USSR		748	2,073	1,365	2,242	258	242	215	
II	Grants	702	1,606	1,062	2,258	1,596	2,458	2,660	3,668	2,890
	USA	443	855	311	106	126				
	UK	43	5	8	55	54	1,537	1,701	2,219	
	West Germany		6	20		250			14	
	Canada		603	544	1,675	915	469	156	36	
	USSR		12	38		6				
III	Commodity Aid	51	5,448	8,532		1,540				
IV	Total Aid	2,017	14,304	28,677		38,277	12,475	10,756	10,943	11,390
	% of grants to total	34.8	11.2	3.7		4.2	19.7	25.2	33.5	
	% of commodity aid to total	2.5	38.1	30.0		4.0				

Source: *Basic Statistics Relating to the Indian Economy: 1950–51 to 1978–79* (Central Statistical Organisation, Government of India). Figures for 1979–80 from *Report on Currency and Finance, 1980–81*, Reserve Bank of India, Bombay.

may have received aid from such diverse sources or in such diverse forms as India. In several years – for example, in the sixties – aid-flows to India have run into billions of rupees (Table 8.1); yet in per capita terms, very few developing countries have received less aid than India. Even during the mid-sixties, when net aid-flows to India were at their peak, per capita aid-flows to India averaged around $2 per annum. These figures are meagre compared to the per capita aid-flows of $58.5 for Egypt, $115 for Jordan and $8.6 for Pakistan in 1978.[9] The picture is much the same for earlier years.[10]

The per capita aid figures reflect a significant fact about aid: that the distribution of aid among the developing countries conforms to no consistent set of humanitarian or economic criteria. Indeed, detailed statistical studies on aid distribution have failed to detect any correlation, either between the shares of different countries in total aid-flows and their per capita GDP, or between their per capita aid receipts and per capita GDP. Nor is there any correlation between aid flows and *earlier* growth rates, returns on investment or domestic savings.[11]

The only inference which the observed pattern of aid distribution permits is that it is guided by donors' preferences and not by recipients' needs. The preferences of donors are largely politically determined.

India's low per capita aid receipts are in part a reflection of these facts of aid. She is a relatively large country, and she is not politically affiliated to any one large donor country. India, though, may not have fared any better even if she were politically affiliated to a major donor. As long as nation-states are regarded as the relevant entities for aid allocation, large nations will inevitably be at a disadvantage. For aid donors are likely to limit the expansion of aid to large countries in the knowledge that they cannot afford to neglect the other countries. As Robert Cassen puts it, 'If all aid were equally divided on a per capita basis, there would be little left over for other countries – India's population is, after all, about equal to the combined populations of Africa and South America.'[12]

It is conceivable that, but for multilateral aid arrangements, India's aid receipts would have been even lower. In this context, the role of the Aid India Club in co-ordinating aid to India has been significant. The Club, established by the World Bank in 1958, is a consortium of aid donors including the World Bank, the USA, the UK, Germany, Japan, Italy, Austria, France, the Netherlands and

Belgium. The consortium technique is of advantage to large countries such as India. As Bhagwati states, it enables the relatively generous countries at consortium meetings to persuade the conservative members to be more liberal. And from the point of view of the donor countries, consortia are equally useful in avoiding duplication of effort and in making the overall evaluation of the recipient country's economy before aid more meaningful. The multilateral aspect also tends to make the assistance programme of each member country of the consortium *appear* apolitical.[13] An overwhelming proportion of aid to India has come from the members of the consortium.

Nominal and real aid-flows

The foregoing statistical picture of aid to India is flawed in one respect. It does not distinguish between the nominal and real amounts of aid India has received. Foreign aid, strictly defined, relates to a transfer of real resources from the donor countries to the recipients. Furthermore, the giving of aid should not involve any expectations of commercial gain on the part of the donors. To the extent that aid-flows confer commercial gains on the donors, the real amount of resources transferred will be less than the nominal amount of aid-flows. Thus, grants which are in the form of outright gifts constitute 'full transfers', whereas loans which have to be repaid and bear an interest rate do not.[14] Loans qualify as 'aid' only to the extent that they bear a concessionary rate of interest, and have longer maturity periods than commercial loans. In other words, there may be a 'grant element' in aid loans. Thus, loans which bear the same rate of interest as commercial market rates would have a zero grant element, whereas outright grants which bear no interest would have 100 per cent grant element. For loans which bear concessionary rates of interest, the grant element would be between zero and 100 per cent. The Development Assistance Committee (DAC) of the OECD stipulates that to qualify as aid, a loan must have at least a 25 per cent grant element.

The grant element in aid loans has to be estimated and added to the amount of outright grants, to arrive at the 'real' magnitude of aid. The grant element of a loan is estimated by discounting each future stream of repayments on the loan – including amortization and interest payments – at an appropriate discount rate, back to their present value, and then deducting the sum of the present values from the principal or the face value of the loan. The difference between the two figures indicates the grant element of the loan. The present value estimates are sensitive to both the rate at which the future repayment streams are discounted and the time period over which the repayments are made. With higher rates of discount and longer periods of repayment, the present value of the future repayment streams will be lower and the grant element of the loan higher. The use of a relatively high discount rate implied that the opportunity cost of the loan to the donor (yields from investments alternative to the aid donation) is relatively high and hence involves the donor making a greater sacrifice.

The choice of a discount rate in estimating the grant element of aid loans is a contentious issue. The 1980 Report of the DAC, however, uses a rate of 10 per cent, reckoning that it is the conventionally-used market rate of interest. On this basis, the Report estimates the grant element in the DAC members' commitments of $355.37 million in loans to India for the year 1979 to be around 75 per cent.[15] Another estimate of the grant element in loans from all bilateral donors to India during the Third Five-Year Plan is around 65.8 per cent.[16] It should be noted that it is only since the late sixties that the terms and conditions of US loans to India have grown softer, and also that during the years 1956–69, when aid-flows to India were at their peak, grants – as distinct from loans – accounted for less than 10 per cent of total aid-flows (Table 8.1).

Tying of aid

Another factor which reduces the amount of real resources transferred from a given amount of nominal aid is the practice of 'aid-tying'.[17] Aid may be tied by source, by projects, or both. Source-tying compels the aid recipients to purchase goods and services from a specified source, usually the donor country, even though it may be a relatively expensive source. Project-tying not only prevents the aid recipients from spending the aid funds on alternative projects but also enables the donors to engage in monopolistic pricing practices. In addition, aid donors may be able to charge excessive prices for spare parts, inputs and raw materials which follow the machinery and equipment supplied under tied aid. Besides, aid-tying may lead to resource misallocation and the importation of machinery and equipment unsuitable to the resource endowments of aid recipients.[18]

However, as Bhagwati has noted, aid recipients may have opportunities for untying of aid *de facto* even though it is tied *de jure*. They can do this by switching existing imports financed from funds other than tied aid from donor countries to other sources. The extent to which recipient countries can exploit such substitution possibilities depends on the extent to which they have access to more than one source of foreign exchange, the extent to which donor countries permit such substitution, and the ability and willingness of recipients to behave in this way.

The motives behind the practice of aid-tying are not far to seek. Source-tying is justified by donor countries – especially by deficit countries – on grounds of balance of payments. But surplus countries have also argued that, but for aid-tying, their balance of payments would experience deficits. Project-tying is a method of ensuring demand for industries with spare capacity, and for disposal of surpluses in the donor country. Food aid under the P.L. 480 programmes of the USA is perhaps one of the most conspicuous examples of aid-tying for surplus disposal. Also, there are obvious political gains for donor countries if particular projects – especially the conspicuous and dramatic ones – can be identified with their aid donations. The essential point, though, is that aid-tying practices reduce the real worth of nominal aid-flows to the recipients.

Available evidence shows that 66 per cent of bilateral loans to India during the Second Five-Year Plan were source-tied, and that this proportion had increased to 83 per cent during the Third Five-Year Plan.[19] Similar estimates for later years are not available. Nor are there any estimates of the excess costs of source-tied aid to India. There is, however, little reason to believe that the excess cost of tied aid to India could be any less than those experienced by other developing countries. UNCTAD has estimated such costs to be in the region of 10 to 20 per cent of nominal aid-flows to Pakistan, Iran and Tunisia during the sixties.[20]

These estimates, however, do not include costs due to the tying of aid to projects. Apart from allowing monopolistic pricing practices on the part of donors, project-tying of aid may give rise to excess capacity in import-intensive industries. When aid is tied to projects, and recipient countries have limited access to other sources of foreign exchange, they may be unable to finance imports of raw materials and spares. It has been argued that the frequently-observed excess amounts of spare capacity in Indian industries are due to a shortage of imported raw materials. It is also a fact that until the mid-sixties, an overwhelming proportion of aid-flows to India was project-tied. During the Second Five-Year Plan, nearly 80 per cent of the aid loans authorized to India were for projects; this figure was round 60 per cent for the Third Five-Year Plan. Since then, there has been an increase in the amount of non-project aid, with its share in the total disbursement of aid being in excess of 45 per cent.[21]

Admittedly, there are no definitive estimates of either the grant element of aid or the excess costs of tied aid to India. The available evidence summarized in the foregoing, however, shows that the 'real' amount of aid which India has received could be substantially lower than the nominal aid-flows. This, though, is a feature which India shares with other aid recipients.

Efficiency of aid

It is easy to dismiss aid as of little importance to India as it has amounted to no more than a couple of dollars per head. Aid, however, was never intended to be the sole solution to the poverty problem. No developing country, especially a large country such as India, could expect aid to be the major source of finance for its development programme. The role of aid should be construed as a supplement to the country's domestic savings effort and foreign-exchange earnings. It could also be of significance in sustaining consumption and investment in the short run when recipient countries are faced with bad harvests and unexpected shortfalls in foreign-exchange earnings.

Viewed thus, aid has been of importance to India. It was a significant factor in sustaining her consumption and investment levels both during the balance-of-payments crisis in the mid to late-fifties and the bad harvests during the sixties. Aid accounted for a substantial proportion of plan outlays and imports during the years 1956–69 (Table 8.2). Since then the importance of aid to India has declined. In part this reflects India's efforts at reducing dependence on aid, assisted by a remarkable increase in domestic savings rates, and in part it indicates the deteriorating international aid situation in general. These considerations have also governed the decision to reduce India's dependence on aid further, to 6 per cent of the total Sixth Five-Year Plan outlays of Rs 97.5 billion in the public sector and 10 per cent of the projected import value of Rs 58.8 billion.[22]

Table 8.2 Aid and the Five-Year Plans

	Gross aid (Rs crores)	Amortization and interest payments (Rs crores)	Net aid (Rs crores)	Net aid as % of total plan outlays	Net aid as % of investment	Net aid as % of NNP	Net aid as % of imports
First Five-Year Plan (1951–6)	201.7	23.8	177.9	9.1	5.4	0.38	4.9
Second Five-Year Plan (1956–61)	1,430.4	119.4	1,311.0	28.1	19.2	1.0	26.9
Third Five-Year Plan (1961–6)	2,867.7	542.6	2,325.1	27.2	20.6	2.7	37.5
Annual Plans (1966–9)	3,229.6	982.5	2,247.1	33.9	20.0	2.8	37.5
Fourth Five-Year Plan (1969–74)	4,183.7	2,445.0	1,738.7	11.2	6.0	0.9	17.6
Fifth Five-Year Plan (1974–9)	7,309.5	3,770.4	3,539.1	8.9	5.3	1.0	12.8

Source: *Sixth Five Year Plan* (Planning Commission, Government of India, New Delhi).

Has aid been counter-productive?

The costs and inefficiencies associated with India's import-substituting industrialization strategy have been recounted in Chapter 6. Some critics have argued that foreign aid was a factor in promoting the strategy. Implicit in the criticism is the suggestion that in the absence of aid, India would have followed an alternative strategy emphasizing investment in agriculture and the production of wage goods. It has also been suggested that the policy-makers may have deliberately opted for ambitious investment outlays in the knowledge that the ensuing foreign-exchange crises would precipitate large inflows of aid.

Table 8.3 Utilization of Aid by End Use (percentage)

	1966–74	1974–8	1978–9	1979–80
Food aid	7.4	6.8	28.4	–
Agricultural development	4.3	16.3	28.3	40.5
Industrial development	63.2	41.5	16.0	18.3
Power	4.4	5.0	9.5	17.8
Transport and communications	9.4	7.4	7.8	5.4
Others	11.3	23.0	10.0	18.0
Total	100.0	100.0	100.0	100.0
Total aid utilization (Rs million)	57,048	38,793	7,275	8,500

Source: Estimated from data in 'Report on Currency and Finance – 1980–81' (Reserve Bank of India).

It is a fact that until the mid-seventies, an overwhelming proportion of foreign aid and credits was earmarked for industrial development. From 1951–2 to 1973–4, industrial development accounted for more than 60 per cent of total foreign aid, whereas the share of agriculture was less than 10 per cent. It is only since the mid-seventies that the share of agriculture has increased relative to industry, reaching 40 per cent in 1979–80 (Table 8.3).

It is, however, arguable whether the availability of aid for purposes of industrial development has been a factor of importance in the chosen strategy of import-substituting industrialization pursued by India. It is conceivable that even in the absence of aid, India would have pursued her heavy-industry-oriented investments, albeit at the expense of price stability and with a further reduction of investment in agriculture, her economic philosophy, especially in the early years of planning, was shaped by deep-seated political and ideological considerations. In addition, the Mahalanobis growth model provided the intellectual underpinnings for the heavy-industry-oriented investment strategy. The strategy may, however have suited the preferences of aid donors for projects with a large foreign-exchange component, which would provide a demand for the goods and services they export. Thus, while the availability of aid may have facilitated the pursuit of the import-substituting industrialization strategy, it may be an exaggeration to say that it was one of the principal reasons for the strategy. The increased share of agriculture in total aid utilization in recent years indicates the shift in emphasis, from industrial development to the promotion of agriculture by multilateral aid donor agencies, and the growth in importance attached to agriculture by India's planners.

It may also be far-fetched to argue that the decision to 'plan big' was predicated on the assumption that it would result in increased aid-flows. Self-reliant growth, interpreted as growth without dependence on aid, has been one of the basic objectives of Indian planning. Indeed, the decision to 'plan big' was based on the assumption that the investments would be largely financed by domestic savings. As stated in Chapter 4, India's savings record, though it may not have always matched the policy-makers' expectations, appears to have justified their optimism. What the planners may not have foreseen is the import intensity of the investments, which precipitated foreign-exchange crises such as the one during the Second Five-Year Plan years. In other words, the balance-of-payments crises may have been more due to the economy's inability to transform domestic savings into investment, either domestically or through foreign trade, rather than to a shortage of domestic savings as such; and the lack of transformation capabilities through foreign trade may have been compounded by the pessimism displayed by India's policy-makers with regard to exports in the early years of economic planning. In sum, while the policy-makers could be criticized for their failure to foresee the balance-of-payments consequences of their policies, they cannot be accused of deliberately engineering a balance-of-payments crisis in the hope that it would attract increased aid-flows.

Viewed thus, the principal contribution of aid to India has been in supplementing the foreign-exchange earnings of the country. In the context of the so-called 'two-gap analysis' of the role of aid in the development process, foreign aid to India is to be regarded as bridging the foreign-exchange gap rather than the savings gap. If the economy were characterized by a savings gap, it is conceivable that inflows of aid would have substituted for domestic savings. Aid inflows would have been utilized for maintaining domestic consumption levels, with a consequent negative relationship between inflows of aid and domestic savings. Statistical studies, however, have failed to detect a statistically significant negative relationship between aid inflows and domestic savings in India.[23] Foreign aid, though, appears to have a statistically significant positive impact on investment. In fact, Pramit Chaudhuri's multiple regression analysis of the effects of national income and aid-flows on investment shows that not only was the impact of aid on investment positive and statistically significant, but it was also much stronger than that of income.[24] It is to be inferred from these results that within the confines of India's chosen strategy of development, foreign aid has not been counterproductive. Nor can aid be regarded as a major factor in the promotion of the chosen strategy of import-substituting industrialization.

Commodity aid

Much more controversial has been the debate on the impact of commodity aid on the Indian economy. Commodity aid – principally wheat under the United States P.L. 480 programmes – bulked large in aid-flows to India during the years 1958–71. These imports were to be paid for in non-convertible Indian rupees, most of which were later given as grants and long-term loans to India. These aid-flows averaged in excess of 30 per cent of the total value of aid to India during the years 1958–71.

Commodity aid to India has attracted two sorts of criticism. First, the expenditure by the government of the loans and grants generated by the commodity aid was inflationary. Second, and more important, is that food imports have had a depressing effect on India's agricultural production. While the first criticism appears to be plausible, the second seems to rest on weak premises.

Isher Ahluwalia's incisive econometric study of price and output behaviour in India during the sixties lends some support to the first criticism.[25] Ahluwalia's results are derived from simulation exercises performed on a fairly comprehensive macro-economic model for India. When both food imports and the accompanying government current expenditure from the counterpart funds are assumed to be zero, the model predicts that the price level would have declined by 3.2 per cent on average per annum over the period 1961–8. However, if imports of food grains are assumed to be zero but government expenditure is held constant, the model predicts that the price level would have increased by an average of 4.6 per cent per annum over the period. These results suggest that increased government expenditure did bring about an increase in the price level. But the model also shows that the government expenditure had a positive effect on real output.

The second criticism, relating to the impact of food aid on agricultural production, is based on the premise that agricultural supplies respond positively to prices and that food imports depress domestic food prices. In fact, there is some suggestion in the literature that by depressing food prices, food imports turned the domestic terms of trade against agriculture. There is also evidence in support of the view that agriculturalists do respond to price incentives; but much of this evidence relates to shifts of acreage and output between crops in response to changes in relative prices. The elasticity of agricultural output as a whole with respect to prices is found to be fairly low, at around 0.16.[26] The conclusions of several statistical studies on the impact of food imports on agricultural production accord with these facts. For instance, Ahluwalia's study, referred to earlier, concludes that the main effect of food-grain imports was to shift output from food grains to commercial crops, with a slight positive effect on agricultural output as a whole. It is thus that the second criticism relating to food imports appears to rest on weak premises.

It could, however, be argued that, but for food imports, the government would have been compelled to invest more in agriculture and related activities. The government could also have stockpiled food and released it during the years of bad harvests. It should be noted, however, that the decision to invest in industrialization programmes was a conscious political decision, and that imports of food grains was a method by which food prices were maintained at relatively low levels for the urban consumers. In any case, it is one thing to argue that the chosen development strategy was ill-conceived and quite another matter to argue that food-grain imports depressed agricultural production.

The main conclusion to be drawn from this brief review of the role of foreign aid in India's development process is that aid has been a factor of some importance in India's development process, although not a major factor. Many of the criticism concerning the impact of aid on India's development strategy and growth process may have been overstated. Since the late sixties, the importance of aid in India's Five-Year Plans has declined. Increased domestic savings rates, the sharp increase in remittances from Indian immigrants in the Gulf countries and improved agricultural performance all appear to have been factors responsible for the declining importance of aid in India's development plans. But prospects of India achieving a further reduction in her dependence on aid may depend crucially on the strength of her exports. Recent events suggest as much. During the late seventies, India enjoyed a comfortable foreign-exchange position, due mainly to the inflow of private remittances from abroad, increased aid-flows and improved agricultural performance. But the oil price hike in 1979 reversed this position, and in 1980–1 India's balance of payments experienced a massive deficit. It is this sizeable deficit in the balance of payments that has been a factor in the recent decision, cited earlier, to borrow from the International Monetary Fund under the Extended Fund Facility. Added to this is the growing debt burden due to amortization and interest payments on past loans – a burden which is likely to grow heavier with the recent loan from the International Monetary Fund. The growing debt burden, the dim prospects for a decline in the real price of oil, and the none-too-encouraging international aid situation all suggest that it is imperative for India to increase her export earnings. India's export performance, policies and prospects form the subject of Chapter 9.

An earlier version of this chapter appears in J. S. Uppal (ed.), *India's Economic Problems: An Analytical Approach* (New Delhi, Tata-McGraw Hill, 1983).

9

Foreign Trade

Compared to most other developing countries, India is an exceptionally closed economy. The share of imports and exports in her national income is well below 10 per cent (Table 9.1). Admittedly, part of the explanation for India's relatively low dependence on foreign trade is her vast size and the diversity of her regions and resource endowments. It would be an exaggeration, though, to say that India's is a continental economy such as that of the United States, a characteristic feature of which is a low dependence on foreign trade; for size and diversity of regions are not the only characteristics of a continental economy. The regions must be interdependent, they must be at a similar stage of development in terms of income levels and the magnitude of resources they possess, and they must be knit together by an efficient system of transportation and communications. All this would facilitate regional specialization and inter-regional trade based on comparative costs. The United States may be one such classic case of a continental

Table 9.1 Ratio of Exports and Imports to GDP for Selected Countries (percentage)

	1960		1970		1979	
	Exports	Imports	Exports	Imports	Exports	Imports
USA	5	4	6	5	9	10
Brazil	6	7	7	7	7	10
Indonesia	13	13	13	16	31	24
Malaysia	53	39	41	36	50	42
South Korea	3	13	14	24	30	37
Pakistan	6	10	8	11	13	24
India	5	8	4	5	7	8

Source: *UN Yearbook of International Trade Statistics* 1980–81, vol. II.

economy. India, though she is a continent in the geographical sense, is as yet far from being a continental economy. While some of her regions are highly developed, others are economically backward by most criteria of development.

Yet the notion that India is a continental economy appears to have shaped the objective of 'self-reliance', an enduring theme in India's economic philosophy. Successive Five-Year Plans, including the most recent Sixth Five-Year Plan have endorsed self-reliance as an objective of development planning. This in itself could be unexceptionable. Broadly interpreted, self-reliance means no more than relying on one's endowments and resources with a view to maximizing one's economic gains. And such maximization of gains may require exchanging those goods and services which one is relatively efficient at producing for goods and services which others are efficient at producing. Indeed, the hallowed doctrine of comparative cost advantage of international trade theory is no more than an enunciation of the principle of self-reliance. Simply put, the doctrine states that countries should specialize in those goods whose opportunity cost of production at home are low relative to those of other countries and should exchange them through trade for goods whose opportunity cost of production at home are relatively high. Such a pattern of production and trade would raise the potential economic gains for the trading partners.

In India, however, self-reliance appears to have been equated with self-sufficiency. As Michael Lipton and John Firn put it, self-reliance in the Indian context does not mean, 'let us do what we are good at doing', but rather, 'leave us all that we are in principle able to do – the in-principle principle.'[1] A country of India's size has the ability to do quite a lot in principle, and this ability to do a number of things is exploitable through the provision of protection against competition from imports from abroad. One illustration of the in-principle principle at work is provided by the twin criteria of 'essentiality' and 'indigenous non-availability' that govern the allocation of import licences. Imports are not permitted under the regulations, if it could be shown that there is domestic production of the imports demanded, regardless of cost and quality considerations.[2]

The in-principle principle, in fact, represents an extreme version of the thesis that the doctrine of comparative cost advantage is much too static in conception. The doctrine ignores the changes in the quantity and quality of factors of production that may occur – partly as a result of the production process itself – over time. Further, it pays little heed to scale economies, externalities and 'learning by doing', most of which are characteristics of large-scale manufacturing activity. These can be nurtured and exploited, especially in a country of India's size, if only manufacturing activity can be afforded protection from international competition. Further, it is argued that because of various sorts of imperfections in the factor markets, such as factor price rigidities and lack of mobility of factors of production between sectors, market prices may not reflect the true opportunity costs of production in developing countries. Typically, they tend to overstate the opportunity costs of production in the manufacturing sector relative to those in the agricultural sector.[3]

The proponents of the traditional doctrine, while accepting these criticisms, would argue along the lines of the pioneering studies by Bhagwati and Ramaswami – that the best method of correcting such market imperfections and distortions is through a system of domestic taxes and subsidies and not through intervention in international trade.[4] These criticisms of the traditional doctrine, however, have served to sanctify the penchant for self-sufficiency and import-substituting industrialization on the part of developing countries such as India. In sum, although the size of the country may be a factor in the low proportion of foreign trade to national income in India, it has been accentuated by the strong bias towards import-substituting industrialization in her policy framwork.

Recent development experience, though, has served to rekindle the faith of policy-makers in the contribution of foreign trade to the development process. In part this is due to the demonstrated success of countries such as Taiwan and South Korea with an export-led strategy of growth, and in part it is due to the awareness of the social costs and economic inefficiencies imposed by interventionist trade policies. It is thus that most developing countries, including India, have tended to emphasize export promotion as an integral part of their economic policies since the late sixties. This, however, is not the end of the fascinating debate on the role of foreign trade in the development process. There is a widespread view in India that the pendulum might have swung too far to the other extreme in favour of outward-looking economic policies; that it has hardly conferred the hoped-for benefits; and that in any case,

Table 9.2 Structure of India's Imports (percentages; selected years)

	Total value of imports (Rs million)	Food and beverages	Raw materials and intermediate products	Mineral fuels	Machinery and transport equipment	Consumer goods	Others	Total
1950–1	6,509	18.5	34.0	8.5	24.8	3.0	11.2	100.0
1955–6	6,788	8.0	40.7	8.2	30.0	4.0	9.1	100.0
1960–1	11,397	11.1	36.6	6.1	29.2	2.3	14.4	100.0
1970–1	16,342	20.1	43.5	7.7	24.0	1.9	2.9	100.0
1975–6	52,652	25.7	34.7	22.6	15.9	1.0	0.2	100.0
1979–80	90,218	3.2	21.3	37.4	15.3	3.0	20.2	100.0

Raw materials and intermediate products include crude materials, chemicals (excluding medicinal and pharmaceutical products), basic metals and metal products. Consumer goods include the category of other manufactures and medicinal and pharmaceutical products.

Sources: Years 1950–1, 1955–6 and 1960–1 estimated from data in *Basic Statistics Relating to the Indian Economy* (Planning Commission, 1969); 1970–1 and 1975–6, *UN Yearbook of International Trade Statistics* 1980–81, vol. I; 1979–80, *Report on Currency and Finance* 1980–81, vol. II (Reserve Bank of India).

export-led growth could hardly be a panacea for India's economic problems. In fact, the role of foreign trade has been the great divide in Indian economic policy debates. This chapter analyses the structure of India's foreign trade and provides a brief review of these debates.

Imports

The course and pattern of India's imports reflects the capital-intensive industrialization strategy she has pursued. Imports are mostly geared to the production of capital goods and equipment destined for the production of goods and services for the home market. The structure of imports is heavily oriented towards capital goods, industrial raw materials, and petroleum and petroleum products (Table 9.2). Food, in years of drought conditions, has been the only consumer good which has been imported in any significant quantity. Imports of manufactured goods as a proportion of the total value of manufactured output steadily declined until the late seventies. The increase thereafter is accounted for by the import liberalization policies and the rise in the price of imports (Table 9.3).

Table 9.3 Manufactured Imports of India as Percentage of Gross Value of Manufactured Output (selected years)

1 Year	2 Total value of manufactured imports (Rs million)	3 Total value of output of manufactures (Rs million)	Column 2 as percentage of column 3
1950	3,514	21,985	16.0
1957	6,913	30,260	20.4
1961	7,056	45,229	15.6
1965	8,094	75,355	10.7
1970	9,650	134,550	7.2
1978	37,210	191,409	19.4

Data are at current prices. Output figures relate to gross output of the registered manufacturing sector. Data on output from J. Mellor, *The New Economics of Growth* (Appendix Table 10) (Ithaca, Cornell University Press, 1976, for 1951 to 1965; *National Accounts Statistics 1970–71 to 1977–78*, and *Annual Survey of Industries, Summary Tables, 1978–79* (Central Statistical Organisation, Government of India) for 1970 and 1978–9. Data on imports from *Basic Statistics Relating to the Indian Economy 1950–51 to 1968–69* (Planning Commission, Government of India, 1969) and *Report on Currency and Finance* 1980–81 vol. II (Reserve Bank of India, 1982).

Table 9.4 Imports: Annual Average Growth Rates

	Total imports (Rs million)	Growth rate	Volume index of imports (1968–9 = 100)	Growth rate
1951–2	9,709		63	
1952–3	6,713	−5.8	47	−1.3
1953–4	5,758		44	
1954–5	6,564		55	
1955–6	7,064		55	
1956–7	8,406		65	
1957–8	10,849		74	
1958–9	9,063	6.1	66	+1.9
1959–60	9,608		73	
1960–1	11,214		85	
1961–2	11,071		80	
1962–3	11,356	4.8	87	+5.0
1963–4	12,229		89	
1964–5	13,490		97	
1965–6	13,941		102	
1966–7	20,784		99	
1967–8	20,076		110	
1968–9	18,616	−4.5	100	−2.1
1969–70	15,817		84	
1970–1	16,340		87	
1971–2	18,120		105	
1972–3	17,333	27.2	99	
1973–4	29,553		114	−0.8
1974–5	45,180		100	
1975–6	56,250		99	
1976–7	56,740		99	
1977–8	60,250		130	+8.9
1978–9	68,140	20.5	140	
1979–80	89.080		145	
1980–1	124,650			

Source: Estimated from data in *Basic Statistics Relating to the Indian Economy 1950–51 to 1968–69* (Planning Commission) and *Report on Currency and Finance* (Reserve Bank of India, various issues).
Growth rates are estimated on the basis of year-to-year variations.

The ten-year period 1956–66 and the latter half of the decade of the seventies have been the only two periods of accelerated growth in imports (Table 9.4). The strategy of import-substituting industrialization was initiated in 1956, and the period 1956–66 represents the period of rapid industrialization centring on the production of capital goods. Much of the growth in the value of imports during this period was on account of imports of technologically-intensive equipment required for the production of capital goods, and of industrial raw materials. The decline in the rate of growth of imports during the latter half of the decade of the sixties was on account of the industrial recession during this period. There was, though, an appreciable increase in the rate of growth of value of imports during the first half of the seventies, but much of this was on account of the steep increase in the prices of imported goods, especially that of oil. There was, in fact, little change in the rate of growth of the volume of imports during this period. During the second half of the decade of the seventies, however, the total volume of imports increased at an annual average rate of 8.9 per cent, reflecting the relaxation in the import control régime. The bulk of the growth in imports during this period was on account of chemicals, paper and paper board, metal products, texile yarn and fabrics.

Exports

The heavily domestic-market-oriented import and industrialization strategy has had predictable effects on India's export performance and export structure. It is a widely noted fact that export promotion was a relatively neglected aspect of India's economic policy during the first fifteen years of planning. One of the suggested explanations for this neglect of exports is that India's policy-makers at that time had assumed that India's exports – consisting mainly of traditional products such as tea, jute manufactures and cotton textiles – were faced with a stagnant world demand, and that there were few opportunities for transforming domestic savings into investment through foreign trade.

Indeed, export pessimism was a major theme in development economics during the fifties. Well known in this context is Ragnar Nurkses' thesis that while exports served as an engine of growth for the countries of new settlement such as Argentina, Australia, New

Zealand and Canada in the nineteenth century, the engine had lost steam for the developing countries in the twentieth century. This was because of the low levels of demand for primary products in the developed countries; a consequence of both the relatively low income-elasticities of demand for such commodities, and the growth in substitution of synthetic materials for raw materials in the production process of manufactured products in the developed countries.[5] Analogous is the Prebisch-Singer thesis that developing countries specializing in the production and export of primary products experienced a long-run deterioration in their terms of trade.[6] Exports of primary products were faced with low income- and price-elasticities of demand, and increased supplies of such commodities only served to depress their prices relative to those of manufactured goods imported by the developing countries. Thus, while the traditional doctrine of comparative cost advantage points to potential gains from free trade, there was no guarantee that the developing countries specializing in the production and exports of primary products could reap a fair share of such gains. The suggested remedy for the problem was industrialization behind tariff walls.

This pessimism concerning exports appears to have been a self-fulfilling prophecy in the case of India during the decade of the fifties. In the early fifties, India had a sizeable share of the world markets in several agriculture-based exports: 86 per cent in the case of jute manufactures, 50 per cent in the case of tea and 18 per cent in that of cotton textiles. But by 1960, her share of world markets in jute manufactures had declined to 73 per cent; in tea it had fallen to 30 per cent; and in cotton textiles her share remained below 11 per cent for most of the decade of the fifties. The story is much the same with regard to several other items of traditional exports such as vegetable oils and oil seeds, and tobaccoo.[7]

Admittedly, the growth in world demand for many of these traditional products was low during the fifties; but, mainly because of the increase in the price of her exports relative to that of her competitors, India's share in the world markets for these commodities declined. Several studies have noted that increasing pressure of domestic demand, lack of attention to quality of the products exported, and a trade policy which in some cases hampered rather than promoted exports by levying export duties and export controls, contributed to the poor performance of India's exports during the fifties.[8] In sum, loss of competitiveness on the external markets rather than an external demand constraint appears to have been a major factor in India's poor export performance during the fifties. And this loss of competitiveness is to be attributed in no small measure to economic policies biased towards the home market and the export pessimism that characterized economic policy and thinking during the fifties.

Exports, however, could not be ignored for long. The capital-goods-oriented industrialization strategy of the Second Five-Year Plan had not conferred all the hoped-for benefits. Far from easing the balance of payments, the import-intensive nature of the industrialization process had imposed a strain on the balance of payments. Foreign aid could not be relied upon for ever to ease the payments position; in any case, one of the objectives of the development programmes was to relieve the country from dependence on foreign aid. The policy-makers were thus forced into the realization that increased export earnings were an imperative necessity. Promoting exports in the prevailing domestic economic climate, however, was an uphill task, for the import-substituting industrialization policies, as stated in Chapter 6, had imparted a bias against exports. Entrepreneurs had little incentive to turn to the highly competitive export markets in the presence of lucrative sheltered domestic markets. The relative profitability of producing for the domestic markets as opposed to the export markets is indicated by the estimates of 'purchasing-power-parity effective exchange rate' (PPP-EER) for imports and exports.

The effective exchange rate (EER) indicates the number of units of rupees actually paid or received for a unit of foreign exchange. This could exceed the nominal or official exchange rate at which a unit of foreign exchange is converted into rupees, if international economic transactions are subject to various forms of restrictions and incentives. If there are subsidies on exports, the EER could exceed the official rate by the extent of the subsidies. Likewise, if there are tariffs and various sorts of surcharge on imports, the EER for imports could exceed the official rate by the extent of tariffs and surcharges. The EER, adjusted for changes in international prices of traded goods relative to their domestic prices, yields the PPP-EER.

Depending on the rates of tariffs and subsidies, the PPP-EER could differ between commodities and between different sectors. In general, if the PPP-EER for imports exceeds that for exports, production of import substitutes would be relatively profitable. In other words, the number of rupees earned by producing import substitutes would exceed that which could be earning by producing for the export market, because the domestic price of import substitutes would exceed that of comparable imports by the extent of tariffs and quotas on imports.

Estimates by Bhagwati and Srinivasan indicate that the PPP-EER for imports was consistently higher than that for exports throughout the fifties and the sixties, although the differential tended to narrow after 1962.[9] The obvious reason for this differential was the import control policy pursued by the government.

The wide-ranging scheme of export subsidies instituted with the beginning of the Third Five-Year Plan in 1961 was in effect an attempt at redressing this bias against exports. It included outright cash subsidies, various sorts of tax rebate and entitlements to imports for exporters of selected commodities. Principal among these were the import-entitlement schemes under which exporters of selected commodities, mostly the so-called new manufactures including engineering goods, received import licences pro rata to the value of exports effected. As these licences fetched sizeable premiums on the open market, the value of subsidies enjoyed by the recipients of the licences could be considerable.

It is the institution of these subsidies that narrowed the differential in the EERs between exports and imports since 1962, indicating that they were an attempt at redressing the bias against exports. It should be noted that these subsidies, coupled with the continuing presence of tariffs and quotas on imports, amounted to an effective devaluation of the rupee. Further, because of the varying nature of the subsidies on exports and tariffs, and controls over imports, the country was in effect operating a system of multiple exchange rates. In other words, the EERs differed not only between imports and exports but also between the various tradeable goods.

The devaluation of the official exchange rate by 57.5 per cent in June 1966 was, in effect, an attempt at rationalizing and unifying these exchange rates. The devaluation was accompanied by the withdrawal of a number of export subsidies, and also sizeable reductions in the rates of tariffs on a number of imports. As Bhagwati and Srinivasan note, the elimination of the export subsidies and the changes in the tariff structure resulted in a net devaluation of the rupee of only 44.8 per cent, compared with the

Table 9.5 Commodity Composition of India's Exports

	1950–1	1955–6	1960–1	1965–6	1970–1	1975–6	1976–7	1977–8	1979–80
				(percentage of total exports)					
Traditional exports, of which	70.6	68.9	64.4	60.0	42.6	28.9	26.9	31.6	39.0
Tea	13.4	17.9	18.7	14.3	9.7	5.9	5.7	10.3	5.6
Jute manufactures	18.9	19.4	20.5	22.7	12.4	6.2	3.9	4.5	5.2
Cotton textiles	19.7	9.3	8.7	6.9	4.9	4.0	5.2	4.1	6.3
Non-traditional exports, of which	6.5	7.0	15.2	24.5	40.0	53.7	53.3	50.5	61.0
Iron ore	–	1.0	2.6	5.2	7.5	5.3	4.6	4.5	4.4
Silver	n.a.	n.a.	n.a.	n.a.	n.a.	4.3	3.3	1.5	8.0
Gems	n.a.	n.a.	–	1.8	2.7	3.7	5.6	10.1	–
Leather and leather manufactures	4.3	3.8	4.1	4.3	5.3	5.6	4.6	4.9	8.6
Iron and steel	0.3	n.a.	1.5	1.6	5.9	1.7	5.6	3.5	1.6
Engineering goods	0.1	n.a.	2.7	2.5	7.6	10.2	11.0	11.5	10.1
Chemicals	1.4	0.9	0.5	1.1	1.9	2.1	2.2	2.2	3.2
Clothing	–	–	0.1	0.8	2.0	5.0	6.5	6.1	7.5
Total exports ($ million)	1261.3	1278.9	1386.5	1691.8	2046.9	4672.1	5753.1	6287.1	5273.6

Data are for fiscal years beginning 1 April.
Source: *Monthly Statistics of the Foreign Trade of India* (Director General of Commercial Intelligence and Statistics, Government of India).

nominal devaluation of 57.5 per cent. Furthermore, the effective devaluation rate on the export side is estimated to have been around 27 per cent, lower than the 41.3 per cent effective devaluation on the import side. In other words, the reduction in the tariff rates were not big enough to offset the extra protection to importables resulting from the devaluation. The suspension of the export subsidies, however, was to be shortlived. Before the end of 1966 most of the subsidies were reinstituted (albeit with modifications to the import-entitlement schemes), and have continued to form an integral part of India's economic policy.[10]

What has been the impact of these export promotion measures on India's export performance? Does the new-found enthusiasm for exports since the sixties constitute a radical shift in India's economic philosophy towards outward-looking economic policies? Admittedly, India's export growth has exhibited an upward trend since the sixties. There has also been a significant change in the composition of exports, with the addition of a number of relatively fast-growing items in world trade – such as chemicals, engineering goods, clothing, handicrafts and leather manufactures – to India's list of exports (Table 9.5). Nor can it be disputed that the export subsidy schemes have been a factor of importance in sustaining the upward trend in India's exports since the sixties. They appear to have achieved this by rendering exports, as opposed to sales on the domestic market, a profitable activity in a number of new manufactures. Furthermore, the upward trend in the growth of India's exports since the sixties also serves to show that the export pessimism characterizing earlier economic policy and thinking was misplaced.

There are good grounds, however, for arguing that neither the export performance nor the policy moves have been robust enough to suggest that India has entered a new era in her development effort. The total value of exports show a remarkable acceleration since the mid-sixties, reaching an annual average compounded rate of 21 per cent over the period 1971–6 (Table 9.6). It should be noted, however, that there were a number of fortuitous factors which contributed to this acceleration. The closure of the Suez canal in 1967 improved India's competitive position in Asian and East African markets relative to her European and American competitors. Nearly 70 per cent of India's engineering goods are directed to other developing countries and another 16 per cent are

Table 9.6 Exports: Annual Average Growth Rates

	Total value of exports (Rs million)	Annual average growth rate (per cent) for 5-year period	Volume (index of 1968–69 = 100)	Annual average growth rate (per cent) for 5-year period
1951–2	7,289		58	
1952–3	5,273		65	
1953–4	5,262	−6.8	65	5.4
1954–5	5,885		68	
1955–6	6,039		75	
1956–7	6,130		71	
1957–8	5,845		77	
1958–9	5,532	0.88	70	−0.2
1959–60	6,299		75	
1960–1	6,329		70	
1961–2	6,606		74	
1962–3	6,853		79	
1963–4	7,932	4.2	89	3.7
1964–5	8,163		93	
1965–6	8,056		87	
1966–7	10,949		84	
1967–8	11,987		86	
1968–9	13,579	7.1	100	4.9
1969–70	14,133		100	
1970–1	15,352		106	
1971–2	16,080		107	
1972–3	19,708		120	
1973–4	25,230	21.0	125	6.3
1974–5	33,288		133	
1975–6	40,430		147	
1976–7	51,460		174	
1977–8	54,040		168	
1978–9	57,260	5.4	180	5.2
1979–80	64,590		199	
1980–1	66,750			

Note: For the base 1951–2 the unit value index for exports was exceptionally high at 145, and declined to 91 by 1955–6.

Sources: Estimates on the basis of data in *Basic Statistics Relating to the Indian Economy 1950–51 to 1968–69* (Planning Commission), *Report on Currency and Finance 1980–81*, vol. II (Reserve Bank of India), and *International Financial Statistics* (International Monetary Fund, various issues).

accounted for by the East European countries. One of the principal reasons for the growth of India's engineering goods exports to these countries is her bilateral trading agreements with the East European countries and with Sudan, Nigeria and Iran among the developing countries. The domestic recession during 1965–7 was also a factor in the growth of exports during the late sixties. Faced with a stagnant domestic market during the recession, firms may have turned to external markets, often selling goods below their average costs of production in an attempt to recoup as much of their fixed costs of production as possible.

The dramatic increase in the rate of growth of the total value of exports during the first half of the decade of the seventies was principally due to the growth in grant-aided exports to Bangladesh, the commodity price boom in the world markets during the early seventies and the phenomenal increase in the value of sugar and silver exports during 1972–6. India cashed in on the world shortage of sugar during the period 1972–6 by diverting large quantities of sugar from the domestic to the export markets. The total value of sugar exports increased from Rs 138 million in 1972–3 to Rs 3397 million in 1975–6, and accounted for 12 per cent of India's total exports during that year. In addition, the rupee exchange rate – which was pegged to the pound sterling during the years 1973–5 – depreciated considerably, contributing to an increase in India's total value of exports measured in rupees. As S. K. Verghese's estimates show, when the impact of these fortuitous factors and the increase in world price of exports are accounted for, the rate of growth of India's exports in real terms during the period 1971–6 turns out to be 6.6 per cent per annum as opposed to the recorded rate of growth of 21 per cent per annum in value terms.[11] The recorded annual average rate of growth of the total value of exports during the period 1975–80 was around 5.5 per cent.

Admittedly, a rate of growth in excess of 5 per cent is a distinct improvement over the earlier dismal record. Even so, India's exports have lacked the dynamism and competitive strength displayed by the newly industrializing countries (Table 9.7). Save in the case of clothing, India's export performance has lagged behind that of most other newly industrializing countries. It is a well-known fact that, for the large part, the competitive strength of the newly industrializing countries is to be attributed to the relative labour intensity of their techniques of production, and to their speciali-

Table 9.7 Growth Rates of Total and Selected Exports in the 1970s (Annual percentage growth rate of exports 1971–7 in dollar values)

	Total Manufactures SITC 5–8	Textile yarns and fabrics SITC 65	Clothing (not fur) SITC 841	Footwear SITC 851	Chemicals SITC 5	Machinery and transport equipment SITC 7
Brazil	37.9	41.3	51.2	34.6	23.9	47.8
Mexico[1]	14.4	26.4	23.6	24.8	18.9	7.4
Hong Kong	22.3	17.8	22.2	6.0	19.2	28.6
Singapore	34.9	18.0	29.2	–	30.1	42.4
South Korea	46.1	41.0	37.6	53.4	57.4	64.6
Taiwan	29.5	24.3	21.8	50.6	33.3	34.0
Greece	34.7	34.7	63.4	33.3	21.9	50.9
Portugal	12.1	9.3	13.9	22.8	5.4	19.6
Spain	26.4	21.8	21.7	18.5	29.1	27.1
Yugoslavia[1]	23.0	23.1	18.7	26.9	22.0	24.8
Argentina[1]	29.8	66.1	48.3	38.3	18.7	37.5
Israel[1]	21.9	2.7	12.2	–	26.4	36.7
India[1]	22.2	7.0	50.2	19.2	21.3	25.2
Pakistan[2]	11.5	7.7	42.1	9.0	31.3	15.6
Malaysia[1]	22.7	39.3	57.4	40.8	20.6	14.3
Philippines[1]	44.5	33.2	157.6	–	32.6	55.3

[1] Exports 1971–76
[2] Exports 1971–75
Source: C. Saunders (ed.), *The Political Economy of New and Old Industrial Countries* (London, Butterworths, 1981).

zation in the production and export of labour-intensive products. In other words, they have exploited their innate comparative advantage in these goods. In India's case, though, there appears to have been a growth in the capital intensity of exports. A comparative study of India and Taiwan by Banerji and Reidel reports that between 1955 and 1970, India's manufactured exports became 20 per cent more capital-intensive, while those of Taiwan became 16 per cent less capital-intensive.[12] It is also reported that the share of capital-intensive manufactures in the total value of India's exports of new manufactures increased from 43.7 per cent in 1970–1 to 53 per cent by 1975–6.[13] Although India possesses a diversified industrial structure, it would be an exaggeration to say that she is endowed with a comparative advantage in the exports of capital-intensive manufactures. Arguably, a proximate cause for the relatively low competitive strength of India's exports is their capital intensity.

But it should be of little surprise that the composition and factor proportions of India's exports of manufactured goods tend to be capital-intensive. For reasons discussed at length in Chapter 6, the import-substituting industrialization strategy imparted a strong bias in favour of capital-intensive methods of production and the establishment of capital-intensive industries. And the natural consequence of the export promotion measures adopted since the sixties was growth in the exports of capital-intensive goods, for it was only the already established capital-intensive industries which could take full advantage of the export subsidies.

Indeed, the export promotion measures adopted since the sixties, though they may have sustained the rate of growth of exports, appear to have done little to promote an efficient pattern of resource allocation and foreign trade. They have been, in effect, an attempt at attacking the symptoms rather than the root cause of the export problem. The root cause of the export problem is the indiscriminate import-substitution policy which the country has pursued. Symptomatic of the problem are the domestic demand pressures, lack of imported inputs, high costs of production, capital-intensity of exports, and the poor quality of products exported – all of which have constrained India's exports. Most of the export subsidy schemes such as cash grants, import-entitlement and its later variant, the import-replenishment schemes, were attempts at offsetting these problems.

Attempts at replacing the administered system of controls with a market-based policy have been short-lived, as the events during the post-1966 devaluation years illustrate. Not only were the administered system of export-subsidies reinstituted during this period but the quota régime was also stiffened. In the absence of a liberalized import régime, a policy of promoting exports through a system of bureaucratically administered subsidies, though it might prop up the growth rate of exports, is unlikely to promote an efficient and internationally competitive export sector. The combination of an import-substitution strategy grounded in physical controls on imports and a scheme of wide-ranging export subsidies is no more than a variant of the in-principle principle referred to earlier. Bhagwati and Desai's comment on the pre-1966 export promotion measures – that they were based on the belief that 'India should produce whatever it can', and India should export 'whatever it produces' – aptly sums up India's economic philosophy during the sixties and the early seventies.[14]

Since the late seventies, though, there has been a perceptible change in attitudes towards the role of foreign trade in India's development process. Significant in this context is the recognition that the earlier import-substitution policies were conflicting with export growth, that export growth could induce efficiency gains and that resource allocation should be based on lines of comparative advantage. Indicative of this change in attitudes is the following extract from the 1980 Tandom Committee Report on export strategy:

> Rapid export growth will undoubtedly help the overall rate of growth of the economy because of efficiency gains obtained from the pursuit of dynamic comparative advantage and the flexibility regarding foreign exchange availability.

Further, it is recognized that there is '. . . a case for reallocating future investment of resources from import-substitution to export promotion in a manner consistent with dynamic comparative advantage . . .' – for allocating productive resources optimally between import-substituting production and export-oriented production.[15]

It should be recognized, however, that despite this change in attitudes, there still persists a considerable gulf between intent and action. Admittedly, there has been a relaxation of the import control régime; a number of imports have been placed on the Open General Licence system; both the value and number of import licences issued have increased; and controls and restrictions have been eased. On the export front, besides the various subsidy schemes, export industries have been offered favourable treatment in the rules governing importation of technology and installation of capacity. All this, though, is still a far cry from a truly liberalized foreign trade régime, for there has been no major departure in the trade régime from a bureaucratically administered system of controls to a market-oriented policy. Quotas and licences continue to be the main instrument of import control; and with rare exceptions, the criterion of 'indigenous availability' has continued to govern the allocation of import licences.[16] The complex scheme of export subsidies continues to be administered in an *ad hoc* and selective fashion, with little heed to notions of economic efficiency and comparative advantage. Spasmodic and half-hearted attempts at relaxing the controls over imports, coupled with a cumbersome scheme of export subsidies, hardly constitutes a liberalized foreign trade régime.

Even so, there is an articulated view among some economists in India that Indian economic policy in recent years has, in fact, swung too far in favour of an outward-looking strategy and that it has not conferred the hoped-for benefits. On a more general plane, it is argued that an export-led growth strategy is neither feasible nor desirable for India.[17] It is not feasible because demand conditions in the world markets are unfavourable and supply conditions at home are not conducive to larger exportable surpluses. As Deepak Nayyar succinctly puts it, 'the problem of Indian exports is a problem of production. In the ultimate analysis, exports can increase on a sustainable basis only if there is a growth in real national income.'[18] It is not desirable because in a country of India's size, domestic markets afford ample opportunities for investment and growth and there is no need to rely on external markets.

These strictures, however, may be misplaced, arising out of misconceptions concerning the nature and intent of liberalized foreign trade régimes. A liberalized foreign trade régime does not necessarily imply an excessive bias in favour of exports. All that it implies is a removal of the bias against exports entailed by a policy of import-substitution. As Bhagwati defines it, a policy of import-substitution is one where the effect of the foreign trade régime is to make the effective exchange rate for the production of importables greater than the effective exchange rate for the production of exportables. An export promotion policy is one which eliminates this bias against exports and equates the effective exchange rate for exportables with that of the domestic production of importables.[19] In essence, all that is implied by a liberalized foreign trade régime or an export promoting strategy is that the bias against the production of exportables is removed, and resource allocation between sectors is allowed to proceed on the basis of relative costs and economic efficiency.

It should also be noted that advocacy of exports usually associated with an outward-looking strategy of development is based on empiricism and not just on theoretical grounds. It is based on the observed gains in employment, savings and growth that several of the newly industrializing countries following an export promotion strategy have achieved. It is not, however, an irrefutable generalization that exports are the panacea for the development problem.

The critics of India's recent economic policy moves, though, appear to equate an outward-looking economic strategy with indiscriminate export promotion based on an armoury of export subsidy schemes. The case of the critics of recent Indian economic policy is, in fact, largely based on the deficiency of the export subsidy schemes. Data are cited to show that such subsidies have been excessive; quite often the level of subsidies have been in inverse proportion to export performance; in many cases, subsidy-assisted exports have grown at a much slower rate than that achieved by unassisted exports; and the direct and indirect employment-creation effects of export growth have been negligible. All this merely reinforces the conclusions of earlier analysts of the subsidy schemes that they were inefficiently designed and badly implemented. But these arguments do not constitute a case against an outward-looking economic policy, for the simple reason that indiscriminate export promotion does not form an integral part of the policy.

The advocates of a liberalized foreign trade régime for India, such as Bhagwati, Desai and Srinivasan, can hardly be accused of advocating indiscriminate export promotion. In fact, they have explicitly condemned it. Their emphasis is on an efficient system of resource allocation, and the concomitant gains in productivity and growth that a liberalized foreign trade régime would confer. Export growth could result as a by-product of such a liberalized trade régime. It would not be the result of unwanted surpluses of domestic production over consumption, but of efficient inter-sectoral allocation of resources based on considerations of comparative advantage.

There have been several suggestions for the reform of India's foreign trade régime with a view to promoting an efficient system of resource allocation. One such recent suggestion is the two-stage scheme advocated by Deepak Lal.[20] In his scheme, the first stage would involve the substitution of a system of import tariffs for existing systems of administered quotas, and the second stage a phased reduction of tariffs. He also advocates suitable adjustment assistance for the industries hurt by the withdrawal of protection. In sum, such a scheme would be a move towards a market-based system from the present inefficient and cumbersomely administered system of trade policy.

The prospects for India adopting such a liberalized trade régime in the near future, however, appear to be remote. India's businessmen and entrepreneurs, long conditioned to the attractions of sheltered domestic markets and the rents to be derived from a system of import licences, are unlikely to support such a move. Nor it is likely that politicians and civil servants will easily surrender the power and benefits which a system of administered controls confers on them. The growth in protectionism in the developed industrialized countries in recent years is also not likely to ease the task of advocates of liberal trade policies to countries such as India. Indeed, the prevailing unfavourable external market conditions are an often-cited reason in support of the proposition that an outward-looking strategy is not the solution for India's economic problems. Yet the mounting import bill, accumulating debt service payments and the bleak prospects for official aid all point to the need for an efficient export sector. And an efficient export sector could only evolve from the pursuit of an economic policy which recognizes the interrelationship between import and export policies, and not from an indiscriminate export promotion policy. The intent to promote such an efficient trade policy is repeatedly affirmed in official pronouncements and reports of experts. Whether such intentions will materialize into action in the near future is hard to say.

10
Summing Up

This book has attempted to sketch the story of India's economic performance and policies over the past three decades. It is a complex story which permits few generalizations or firm conclusions. But it is not without its lessons. This concluding chapter highlights the achievements and failures of India's development effort over the past three decades and the lessons we have learned from the experience.

As frequently noted, in several respects India is unique among the developing countries. Her vast size, the heterogeneity of her regions and the diversity of her culture and social institutions set India apart from most other developing countries. The fact that, despite her size and diversity, India has held together as one country and survived as a functioning democracy is in itself a remarkable achievement. The rate of growth of national product of 3.5 per cent per annum which she has achieved over the past three decades is also commendable, for it represents a remarkable acceleration over the growth rate of 1 per cent per annum for the three decades preceding independence. Epidemic diseases and famines are also largely a thing of the past. Life expectancy at birth has gone up from thirty-three years to fifty-two years, and in recent years the country has achieved self-sufficiency in food. The diversified industrial structure she possesses and the strides she has made in the expansion of science and technology are also high on the list of India's achievements.

India, however, is not unique in achieving a relatively high rate of growth in the post-colonial period. Several other developing countries have, in fact, achieved much higher rates of growth than India. And the actual rates of growth have been generally lower than those targeted in the various Five-Year Plans (Chapter 3). It is also a matter of concern among Indian economists that the process of industrialization and growth has lost momentum since the mid-sixties, and the rate of growth of industrial output has decelerated.

Much more disconcerting, however, is the fact that despite the growth in output which the country has achieved, malnutrition, hunger and unemployment continue to be the lot of a substantial number of the population. The nature and extent of poverty and unemployment in the economy is a matter of dispute among Indian economists, but they are agreed that there has been no decisive change for the better (Chapter 2). Again, while India has an enviable record in the field of higher education, the adult literacy rate continues to be dismally low at 36 per cent.

Why is the growth rate relatively low in a country with an endowment of natural and human resources far superior to that of most other developing countries? Where have the fruits of the growth that has been achieved gone? Why the persistence of massive poverty, unemployment, and glaring disparities in incomes and levels of living in a country the objective of whose economic policy is the promotion of a socialistic pattern of society?

There are no simple answers to these questions. The continuing debate on these issues, though, has yielded a number of insights and lessons. One such lesson is that high rates of savings and investment are not necessarily the recipe for growth. For long, it was the popular belief that shortage of savings and foreign exchange were the main obstacles to growth. The intellectual lineage for this belief could be traced to the so-called post-Keynesian 'growth models'. The celebrated Harrod-Dormar growth model, for instance, although it recognizes the interrelationship between supply and demand factors, accords pride of place to the savings rate. The procedure employed in economic plans based on this model is to set out targeted rates of growth of output, estimate capital-output ratios and then calculate the required levels of savings and investment to achieve these growth rates. Obviously, the higher the savings rate, the higher will be the feasible growth rate. The later genre of the so-called supply-side-oriented neo-classical models also accord pride of place to capital accumulation and technology in the growth process. Modified versions of these models, such as the Mahalanobis model, have provided the theoretical basis for the emphasis placed on savings and investment in India's Five-Year Plans (Chapters 3 and 4).

Several academic economists, both in India and abroad, however, had all along expressed misgivings about this savings and capital accumulation-centred approach to development.[1] The turning-point in academic thinking on these issues, though, occurred in the mid-seventies, when several developing countries – including India – achieved savings rates comparable to those of the developed countries, with the savings rate in some years outstripping the investment rate in India (Chapter 4). During this period, India was also comfortably placed with regard to her stocks of foreign exchange and food. Yet the dramatic increase hoped for in the growth rate failed to materialize, and the industrial sector exhibited no signs of recovery from the stagnation that had set in during the latter half of the decade of the sixties. Frequently heard was the wistful question 'Now that the savings rate has increased, the balance of payments is healthy, the food situation is less critical, and the basic industrial structure is in place, why can Indian not attain growth rates of from 8 to 10 per cent?'[2]

Another popular theme is that there was nothing intrinsically wrong with the Mahalanobis strategy of emphasizing investment, but that where the strategy went wrong was in not paying adequate attention to the production of wage goods. In particular, agricultural development was accorded a relatively low priority; and in the production of manufactured consumer goods, resources were diverted to the production of luxury goods. Admittedly, the low growth in the supply of wage goods has been a factor of significance in the low growth performance and the disparities in income which the economy has experienced. It may be an exaggeration, though, to say that the resources devoted to the agricultural sector were inadequate (Chapter 5). The basic constraint on agricultural growth in the early years was the low level of technology at hand. And it is doubtful if, in the face of the technological constraint, additional investment would necessarily have resulted in a major increase in agricultural output. As argued in Chapter 6, the advent of the Green Revolution in the mid-sixties helped to sustain the rate of growth of agricultural output. The new high-yielding varieties do hold a promise for the future and their potential is yet to be exploited fully.

It may, however, be inconsistent to argue at one and the same time that the emphasis placed on heavy-industry-oriented investment by the Mahalanobis strategy was basically right, but that its folly lay in devoting inadequate attention to the production of wage goods. Apart from the fact that in the face of an overall resource constraint it would not have been possible to increase the production of both wage goods and investment goods, the operational mechanics of the strategy and the pattern of economic organization imparted a bias against the increased production of wage goods. Not only was the strategy oriented towards the production of capital-intensive goods, but the mechanics of the strategy also favoured the adoption of capital-intensive technologies even in lines of production where the substitution of labour for capital was feasible (Chapter 6). Needless to say, the choice of technology and of products produced, themselves contain an income distribution formula. It favours the owners of capital and skilled labour at the expense of unskilled labourers. In a mixed economy such as that of India, where the government does not have complete control over consumer expenditure, this pattern of income distribution generates a demand for luxury goods, and resources are diverted to the production of luxury goods instead of wage goods. In sum, the economy failed to generate increased production of wage goods because the chosen strategy of development had a built-in bias against the production of such goods. It deprived the poor of the purchasing power to demand wage goods by denying them employment opportunities.

The lesson to be learnt from this experience is that the only lasting solution to the problem of poverty and income disparities is to integrate the poor into the production process efficiently. This is not to say that there is no need for institutional reform designed to redistribute wealth and income in favour of the poor; but the limitations of a radical programme of redistribution should be recognized. It may be neither politically feasible nor economically efficient as a solution to the problem of poverty.

Mere redistribution of productive assets, unaccompanied by other growth-inducing factors such as infra-structural development, credit facilities and the spread of education and health, is unlikely to work the miracle of growth with distributive justice. And statistical simulation exercises have shown that income redistribution policies are likely to have only a marginal effect on the standard of living of the poorest 30 per cent of the population in India. Further, such policies are likely to be mere palliatives to the problem of poverty, effective only as long as they are constantly renewed.[3]

There is not much dispute among economists of differing ideological persuasions on the need for restructuring the economy with a view to increasing productive efficiency and generating employment opportunities, but the operational mechanics of ushering in such a policy are a hotbed of controversy.

It is the thesis of this book that a viable method of doing this would be to shift the development strategy in favour of outward-looking economic policies. Such a strategy would involve replacement of the present bureaucratic controls over trade and resource allocation with a system based on market forces and the price mechanism. As stated in Chapter 9, although such a strategy would involve a closer integration of the Indian economy with the world economy through foreign trade, it does not necessarily imply the adoption of an export-led strategy of growth. Its emphasis is on opening up the economy to forces of competition, and on resource allocation based on comparative advantage. Nor does the strategy imply that India should depart from her philosophy of planned development and the fostering of a mixed economy. It is just that the efficiency of public-sector enterprises should also be measured by considerations of profitability, cost effectiveness and their ability to withstand competition.

Nor would an outward-looking strategy of development deny the need for regulating the activities of the private sector. Indeed, as Paul Streeten notes, in South Korea, a country which has followed an outward-looking strategy of development with impressive gains in employment and growth, a strong arm of intervention has visibly guided economic policy.[4] The point to note, though, is that the visible arm in South Korea (meaning the government) has guided private enteprise and not stifled it with a panoply of bureaucratic controls such as the ones that prevail in India. Again, as Paul Streeten notes, South Korea has not eschewed import-substitution and the domestic market wholly in favour of export promotion. But here again, the domestic industries she has fostered have been on the basis of their comparative advantage. Indeed, few of the so-called neo-classical economists would take issue with import-substitution as a philosophy of development. Their criticisms are not directed at import-substitution as a strategy of development, but at the manner in which it has been implemented. It is the indiscriminate and exorbitantly high levels of protection, and the attempts at replacing the price mechanism with bureaucratic decision-making with which they take issue. The social costs and economic inefficiencies associated with these policies have been discussed at length in Chapters 6 and 9.

Economists to the left of the political spectrum would have none of this. They ascribe the growth in income disparities, unemployment and the low growth performance of the economy to the decline in public sector investment, growth in the monopoly power of big business, dependence of the economy on imported technology, the operations of foreign firms, policies of the donors of foreign aid, and the speculative activities of the private sector (Chapters 6, 7 and 9). Not surprisingly, they find little to be gained by the adoption of outward-looking policies; they associate such policies with an export-led strategy of growth and argue that such a strategy is hardly relevant in a country of India's size. Their policy prescriptions appear to revolve around a programme of asset redistribution, decentralization of decision-making power, expansion of the public sector and increased public investment in the production of wage goods.[5]

Many of the propositions of this thesis appear to be based on insufficient evidence. As argued in Chapter 7, although there is a sizeable amount of private foreign investment in the economy, it does not appear to be of a magnitude big enough to dominate the economy. To the extent that foreign firms do enjoy a monopoly rent, it appears to be a consequence of the trade and resource allocation policies pursued by the country. The evidence in support of the proposition that foreign aid has been counter-productive is also inconclusive. The growth in income disparities, monopoly power of big business and dependence of the economy on foreign technology are all largely consequences of the trade and industrialization policies which the country has pursued. The thesis, however, appears to exhibit a reluctance to acknowledge the adverse economic and social consequences of these policies. The wisdom of the policy prescription of increasing the power and share of the public sector in the economy in the face of its lacklustre performance in the past is also debatable.

In sum, there is no escape from the conclusion that the only viable solution to the problems of low growth, unemployment and poverty is to promote conditions favourable to an efficient allocation of resources and technological progress. The mechanics of such a policy would involve the pursuit of a liberalized foreign trade régime and emphasis on market forces. Whether or not India's economic policy would radically change course in this direction, or would muddle through as in the past with *ad hoc* changes in policy, is hard to say. It is as much a political issue as an economic one.

This book has covered a wide terrain, but has by no means exhausted it. An endless list of topics, including inter-regional disparities, education and education policy, issues concerning monetary and fiscal policies, rural credit and marketing of agricultural products, and issues on the impact of the oil crisis and energy problems in India, have been omitted or glossed over, not because these issues are unimportant but because of limitations of space and the author's lack of comparative advantage in these areas. The issues that have been discussed, though, should convince the student of development economics of the complex nature of the development problem, especially in India with its vast size and its heterogeneity of regions, cultures and social institutions.

Notes and References

1 *Introduction*

1. Quoted in J. N. Bhagwati and P. Desai, *India: Planning for Industrialisation* (London, Oxford University Press, 1970), p. 14.
2. Countries with per capita incomes below $410 are classified as low-income countries by the World Bank.
3. See Chapter 2 for a detailed discussion of the extent of poverty in India.
4. J. S. Uppal, 'The Unemployment Problem', in J. S. Uppal (ed.), *India's Economic Problems, An Analytical Approach* (New Delhi, Tata-McGraw Hill, 1983).
5. *Draft Sixth Five Year Plan* (Planning Commission, Government of India, New Delhi, 1977), p. 82.
6. J. S. Uppal, 'Regional Inequalities and Economic Development', in J. S. Uppal, *op. cit.*
7. For an extensive discussion of India's economic performance during the period 1920–47, see A. Heston, 'National Income', in Dharma Kumar (ed.), *The Cambridge Economic History of India* (London, Cambridge University Press, 1983).
8. Amartya Sen, 'How Is India Doing', *Mainstream* 26 January 1983.
9. J. N. Bhagwati, *India In the International Economy* (Hyderabad, Institute of Public Enterprise, 1973), p. 1.
10. This view is forcefully argued in P. R. Bramhananda and C. N. Vakil, *Planning For an Expanding Economy* (Bombay, Voula, 1958).
11. Pramit Chaudhuri, *The Indian Economy; Poverty and Development* (London, Crosby, Lackwood and Staples, 1978), p. 255.
12. For an exposition of this view see Amartya Sen, *Poverty and Famines; An Essay on Entitlement and Deprivation* (London, Oxford University Press, 1981).
13. P. K. Bardhan, 'The Pattern of Income Distribution in India', in T. N. Srinivasan and P. K. Bardhan (eds), *Poverty and Income Distribution in India* (Calcutta, Calcutta Statistical Publishing Society, 1974).
    R. Cassen, *India: Population, Economy, Society* (London, Macmillan, 1978).
    B. S. Minhas, 'Rural Poverty, Land Distribution and Development

Strategy', *Indian Economic Review* (April 1970).
V. M. Dandekar and N. Rath: 'Poverty in India', *Economic and Political Weekly* vol. VI, nos 1 and 2 (January 1971).

14. T. W. Schultz, *Transforming Traditional Agriculture* (New Haven, Yale University Press, 1964).
15. F. Frankel, *India's Green Revolution, Economic Gains and Political Costs* (New Jersey, Princeton University Press, 1971).
P. K. Bardhan, 'Green Revolution and Agricultural Labourers', *Economic and Political Weekly* (special number, June 1970).
A. Mitra, *Terms of Trade and Class Relations* (London, Frank Cass, 1977).
A. M. Khusro, *Economics of Land Reform and Farm Size in India* (New Delhi, Macmillan, 1973).
16. J. N. Bhagwati and P. Desai, *op.cit.*; J. N. Bhagwati and T. N. Srinivasan, *Foreign Trade Regimes and Economic Development: India* (London, Macmillan, 1976).
17. Notable amongst studies on India's export performance are Man Mohan Singh, *India's Export Trends* (Oxford, Clarendon Press, 1964); D. Nayyar, *India's Exports and Export Policies in the 1960s* (London, Cambridge University Press, 1976); M. Wolfe, *India's Exports* (London, Oxford University Press, 1982; see also J. N. Bhagwati and P. Desai, *op. cit.*, chs 18, 19 and 20.
18. A concise review of the debate on foreign aid is found in J. N. Bhagwati and P. Desai, *op. cit.*, ch. 10.
19. A pioneering study on the role of foreign private investment and technology in the Indian economy is by M. Kidron, *Foreign Investments in India* (London, Oxford University Press, 1965).
20. For a succinct review of India's planning techniques see J. N. Bhagwati and S. Chakravarthy, 'Contributions to Indian Economic Analysis', *American Economic Review* (supplement, September 1970); also K. N. Raj, 'Growth Models and Indian Planning', *Indian Economic Review* vol. v, no. 3 (1961).
21. T. N. Srinivasan and P. K. Bardhan (eds), *Poverty and Income Distribution in India*, *op. cit.*
22. Ved Mehta, *The New India* (Harmondsworth, Penguin, 1978), p. 24.

2 *The Teeming Millions and Their Livelihood*

1. This estimate refers to the year 1964–5 cited in Gary S. Fields, *Poverty, Inequality and Development* (London, Cambridge University Press, 1980), p. 204.
2. R. Cassen, *op.cit.*

3. S. P. Jain, 'Some aspects of mortality', in Ashish Bose (ed.), *Population in India's Development: 1947–2000* (Delhi, Vikas Publishing House, 1974), p. 320.
4. H. J. Habbakuk, *Population Growth and Economic Development Since 1750* (Leicester University Press, 1972), pp. 84–5.
5. *Sixth Five Year Plan*, *op.cit.*, p. 19.
6. H. J. Habbakuk, *op.cit.*, ch. 3.
7. P. T. Bauer, *Equality, the Third World and Economic Delusion* (London, Weidenfeld and Nicolson, 1981), pp. 59–61.
8. R. Cassen, *op.cit.*, ch. 2.
9. S. Enke, 'The Economics of Slowing Population Growth', *Economic Journal* 76 (March 1966).
10. See W. C. Robinson, 'Population Control and Development Strategy', in Ian Livingstone (ed.), *Development Economics and Policy, Readings* (London, Allen and Unwin, 1981), pp. 51–8.
11. *Sixth Five Year Plan*, *op.cit.*, p. 21.
12. *People*, vol. 5, no. 3 (1978), pp. 36–7.
13. Gary S. Fields, *op.cit.*, p. 185.
14. P. Visaria and L. Visaria, 'Indian Population Scene after 1981 Census: A Perspective', *Economic and Political Weekly* (special number, November 1981), p. 1742.
15. See H. J. Habbakuk, *op.cit.*, ch. 2, p. 33.
16. Ester Boserup, *Conditions of Agricultural Growth: The Economics of Agrarian Change Under Population Pressure* (London, Allen and Unwin, 1965).
17. J. W. Mellor, *The New Economics of Growth: A Strategy for India and the Developing World* (Ithaca, Cornell University Press, 1976), ch. 3.
18. J. W. Mellor, *op.cit.*
19. Rati Ram and T. W. Schultz, 'Some Economic Implications of Increases in Life Span with Special Reference to India', in C. H. Hanumantha Rao and P. C. Joshi (eds), *Reflections on Economic Development and Social Change* (London, Martin Robertson, 1979).
20. *Sixth Five Year Plan*, *op.cit.*, pp. 365–6.
21. K. L. Gupta, 'Dependency rates and Savings Rates: Comment' *American Economic Review* (June 1971).
22. R. Cassen, *op.cit.*, p. 227.
23. For a summary of these studies see Gary S. Fields, *Poverty, Inequality and Development*, *op.cit.*, pp. 201–9.
24. P. K. Bardhan, 'The Pattern of Income Distribution In India: A Review', in T. N. Srinivasan and P. K. Bardhan (eds), *Poverty and Income Distribution In India*, *op.cit.*
25. B. S. Minhas, *Planning and the Poor* (Delhi, S. Chand and Co., 1974).
26. V. M. Dandekar and N. Rath, 'Poverty In India', *op.cit.*
27. *Sixth Five Year Plan*, *op.cit.*, p. 7.

28 S. Sukhatme, 'Assessment of Adequacy of Diets at Different Income Levels', *Economic and Political Weekly* (special number, August 1978). See also T. N. Srinivasan, 'Malnutrition; some measurement and policy issues', *Journal of Development Economics* 8 (1981).
29. Cited in R. Sinha, P. Pearson, G. Kadekodi and M. Gregory, *Income Distribution, Growth and Basic Needs in India* (London, Croom Helm, 1979).
30. For an exposition of this view see Amantya Sen, *Poverty and Famines: An Essay on Entitlement and Deprivation, op. cit.*.
31. R. Sinha *et al.*, *op.cit.*
32. *Sixth Five Year Plan*, *op.cit.*, p. 8.
33. See Chapter 5 for an extended discussion of land reform policies in India.
34. Raj Krishna, 'Unemployment In India', *Economic and Political Weekly* 3 March 1973.
35. *Ibid*, p. 475.
36. *Sixth Five Year Plan*, *op.cit.*, p. 205.

3 *Growth Performance*

1. See articles in C. R. Rao (ed.), *Data Base on the Indian Economy* (Calcutta, Statistical Publishing Society, 1972).
2. Simple annual average based on the movements in the Wholesale Price Index. This may be something of an underestimate as the prices of several commodities are valued at the controlled prices rather than 'true' prices.
3. See *World Development Report* (Washington D.C., World Bank, 1982).
4. W. Malenbaum, 'Modern Economic Growth in India and China: The Comparison Revisited: 1950–1980', *Economic Development and Cultural Change* (October 1982).
5. S. L. Shetty, 'Structural Retrogression in the Indian Economy since the Mid-Sixties', *Economic and Political Weekly* (annual number, February 1978).
6. S. Kuznets, *Modern Economic Growth; Rate, Structure and Spread* (New Delhi, Oxford and IBH Publishing Company, 1972).
7. J. N. Sinha, '1981 Census, Economic Data: A Note', *Economic and Political Weekly* 6 February 1982.
8. P. Chaudhuri, *The Indian Economy, Poverty and Development*, *op.cit.*, p. 46.
9. C. Rangarajan, 'Industrial Growth: Another Look', *Economic and Political Weekly* (annual number, 1982), p. 591.
10. M. A. Zaidi and S. K. Mukhopadhyay, 'Economic Development, Structural Change and Employment Potential', in Frances Stewart

(ed.), *Employment Income Distribution and Development* (London, Frank Cass, 1975). See also C. Rangarajan, *op.cit.*

11. For a detailed review of the growth performance of agriculture see Chapter 5.
12. P. Chaudhuri, *op. cit.*, p. 56.
13. C. Rangarajan, *op. cit.*

4 *Savings and Investment in the Indian Economy*

1. For a succinct discussion of the Mahalanobis model see J. N. Bhagwati and S. Chakravarthy, 'Contributions to Indian Economic Analysis; A Survey', *op. cit.*
2. J. N. Bhagwati and P. Desai, *India; Planning for Industrialization*, *op. cit.*, p. 118.
3. *Ibid*, p. 69.
4. *Sixth Five Year Plan, op. cit.*
5. For detailed estimates of savings and investment from 1950–1 to 1976–7 see V. K. R. V. Rao, 'Savings, Capital Formation and National Income' *Economic and Political Weekly* 31 May 1980), pp. 965–77. Rao's estimates of savings and investment, based on the data in the Central Statistical Organisation's white papers on national accounts are somewhat higher than that reported in other government publications.
6. *Ibid*, p. 968.
7. For a summary of the econometric evidence and sample survey studies see I. Z. Bhatty and M. J. R. Sarma, 'Savings behaviour in India and Implications for Policy', in C. Wadhva (ed.), *Some Problems in Indian Economic Policy* (New Delhi, Tata-McGraw Hill, 1977).
8. Raj Krishna and G. S. Ray Chaudhuri, 'Trends In Rural Savings and Capital Formation In India, 1950–51 to 1973–74', *Economic Development and Cultural Change* vol. 30, no. 2 (January 1982).
9. Ashok Mitra, *Terms of Trade and Class Relations*, *op. cit.* and Francine Frankel, *India's Green Revolution: Economic Gains and Political Costs*, *op. cit.*
10. Raj Krishna and Ray Chaudhuri, *op. cit.*
11. Data on savings in physical assets have been recently revised upwards by the Central Statistical Organisation. It should be noted that data on savings in general are subject to a high degree of error and the several estimates available often differ widely from each other. For a critical evaluation of these estimates see Ashok Rudra, 'Savings, Investment and Consumption', in C. R. Rao (ed.), *Data Base on the Indian Economy*, *op. cit.*

12. V. A. Avadhani, 'Asset Preferences of the Middle Class', *Economic and Political Weekly* (8 June 1968), pp. 873–6.
13. *Basic Statistics Relating to the Indian Economy: 1950–51 to 1978–79* (Central Statistical Organisation, Government of India, New Delhi, 1980), p. 114.
14. J. N. Bhagwati and T. N. Srinivasan, *Foreign Trade Regimes and Economic Development: India, op. cit.*, pp. 235–8.
15. Ashok Mitra, *op. cit.*
16. The Direct Taxes Enquiry Committee of the Government of India has estimated that tax-evaded income was Rs 8,110 million in 1961–2, Rs 12,160 million in 1965–6 and Rs 14,000 million in 1968–9: *Direct Taxes Enquiry Committee, Final Report* (Government of India, New Delhi, 1972).
17. See Chapter 3.
18. Poonam Gupta and Sanjeev Gupta, 'Estimates of the Unreported Economy in India', *Economic and Political Weekly* (January 1982).
19. J. Sandersara, 'Estimates of the Unreported Economy in India', *Economic and Political Weekly* (20 March 1982).
20. Quoted in Dilip Hiro, *Inside India Today* (London, Routledge and Kegan Paul, 1976), p. 42.
21. B. S. Cheema, 'Capital Formation In India', in J. S. Uppal (ed.), *India's Economic Problems* (New Delhi, Tata-McGraw Hill, 1978), p. 243.
22. B. M. Bhatia, 'Food Distribution', *The Statesman* 21 May 1982.
23. For an exposition of the debate on inflationary financing in Latin America see Olivera De Campos, 'Economic Development and Inflation with special reference to Latin America', in *Development Plans and Programmes* (Paris, OECD Development Centre, 1964).
24. H. G. Johnson, *Economic Policies towards Less Developed Countries* (New York, Allen and Unwin, 1968), p. 76.
25. *Sixth Five Year Plan, op. cit.*, p. 1.
26. V. K. R. V. Rao, *op. cit.*
27. Asit Banerjee, 'Productivity Growth and Factor Substitution in Indian Manufacturing', *Indian Economic Review* New Series, no. 1 (1971).
28. J. Sandesara, 'Industrial Growth in India – Performance and Prospects', *Indian Economic Journal* vol. 30, no. 22.
29. Estimates cited in R. Ranga Rajan, 'Industrial Stagnation in India: Afterthoughts', *op. cit.*
30. R. Rajan, *op. cit.*
31. S. Chakravarthy, 'On the question of Home Market and Prospects for Indian Growth', *Economic and Political Weekly* (special number, August 1979), pp. 1229–40.

5 The Agricultural Sector

1. *First Five Year Plan* (Planning Commission, Government of India).
2. For a discussion of this point see P. Chaudhuri, *The Indian Economy op. cit*, pp. 114–6.
3. *Sixth Five Year Plan*, *op. cit.*, p. 97.
4. G. Blynn, *Agricultural Trends in India 1891–1947. Output, Availability and Productivity* (Philadelphia, University of Pennsylvania Press, 1966), pp. 94–7.
5. J. Mellor, *The New Economics of Growth; A Strategy for India and the Developing World* (Ithaca, Cornell University Press, 1976), pp. 43–4.
6. T. N. Srinivasan, 'Trends in Agriculture in India, 1949–50 to 1977–78' *Economic and Political Weekly* (annual number, August 1979).
7. *Ibid*, p. 1286.
8. A. Rudra, 'Organisation of Agriculture for Rural Development: The Indian Case', *Cambridge Journal of Economics* vol. 2 (1978), p. 394.
9. Data from National Sample Survey, 16 Round cited in A. M. Khusro, *Economics of Land Reform and Farm Size in India* (Madras, Macmillan, 1973).
10. *Sixth Five Year Plan*, *op. cit.*, p. 8.
11. A. M. Khusro, *Economics of Land Reform and Farm Size in India*, *op. cit.*, p. 22.
12. *Ibid*, p. 26.
13. For a discussion of this issue see G. O. Jaynes, 'Production and Distribution in Agrarian Economics', *Oxford Economic Papers* no. 2 (July 1982).
14. For a survey of the evidence on this issue see S. S. Bhalla, 'Farm Size, Productivity and Technical Change in Indian Agriculture', in R. Albert Berry and William R. Cline, *Agrarian Structure and Productivity in Developing Countries* (Baltimore, John Hopkins Press LTW, 1979), pp. 141–93.
15. A. M. Khusro, *Economics of Land Reform*, *op. cit.*, chs 4–8.
16. For a critique of the proposition see J. N. Bhagwati and S. Chakravarthi, *op. cit.* For statistical evidence in support for the proposition see S. S. Bhalla, *op. cit.*
17. A. M. Khusro, *Economics of Land Reform*, *op. cit.*, ch. 13.
18. Data cited in A. M. Khusro, *op. cit.*
19. See M. L. Dantawala, 'Small Farmers Not Small Farms', *Indian Journal of Agricultural Economics* (July–September 1959).
20. For a detailed discussion of the policy debates on these issues during the fifties see F. R. Frankel, *India's Political Economy 1947–1977, the Gradual Revolution* (New Jersey, Princeton University Press, 1978).
21. For a succinct summary see J. S. Uppal, 'Agrarian Structure and Land Reform in India', in J. S. Uppal (ed.), *op. cit.*

22. P. K. Bardhan, 'Country Experience; India', in H. B. Chenery *et al.* (eds), *Redistribution with Growth* (London, Oxford University Press, 1974), p. 256.
23. D. Gale Johnson, *World Agriculture in Disarray* (For the Trade Policy Research Centre London, Macmillan, 1973), p. 17.
24. T. W. Schultz, *Transforming Traditional Agriculture*, *op. cit.*
25. *Ibid*, p. 29.
26. Raj Krishna, 'Agricultural Price Policy and Economic Development', in H. M. Southworth and B. F. Johnston (eds), *Agricultural Development and Economic Development* (Ithaca, Cornell University Press, 1967). This article provides a summary of the statistical studies on the response of acreage to prices in developing countries, including India.
27. Another widely debated issue in this context relates to the response of marketed surplus of food grains to price movements. The issue under debate is whether or not farmers, who are both producers and consumers of food, increase their own consumption of food and market a lower proportion of a given output, following an increase in the relative price of food grains. The general conclusion on this issue appears to be that while the own consumption of food on the part of farmers does increase following a rise in the relative price of food, the positive supply elasticity of food with respect to prices outweighs the consumption effect, resulting in a positive response of marketed surplus with respect to price. For a detailed discussion of this issue, see T. N. Krishnan, 'The Marketed Supply of Food Grains', in Pramit Chandhuri (ed.), *Readings in Indian Agricultural Development* (London, Allen and Unwin, 1977).
28. F. R. Frankel, *op. cit.*, p. 277.
29. Quoted in F. R. Frankel, *op. cit.*, p. 277.
30. Estimated from data reported in the *Annual Economic Survey 1981–82* (Government of India).
31. A. Mitra, *Terms of Trade and Class Conflict*, *op. cit.*
32. Estimates for the period since 1974 suggest that the terms of trade may have moved against agriculture and in favour of industry. See A. K. Kahlon and D. S. Tyagi, 'Inter-sectoral Terms of Trade', *Economic and Political Weekly* (17 December 1980).
33. *Economic Survey 1981–82*, *op. cit.*, p. 85.
34. *Ibid*, p. 33.
35. This estimate for 1971, was based on the assumptions that imports of food would be negligible, growth of population would be around 2.5 per cent per annum and the rate of growth of food output would be 3 per cent per annum. These assumptions appear to have held good since 1971. See Raj Krishna, 'Government Operations in Food Grains', in C. Wadva (ed.), *Some Problems of Indian Economic Policy* (New Delhi, Tata-McGraw Hill, 1977).

36. See Raj Krishna, 'Agricultural Pricing Policy and Economic Development', *op. cit.*.
37. M. Prahaladachar, 'Income Distribution Effects of the Green Revolution in India; A Review of the Empirical Evidence', *World Development* vol. 11 (November 1983), p. 939.
38. C. T. Kurien, *Dynamics of Rural Transformation, A Study of Tamil Nadu, 1950–1975* (New Delhi, Orient Longman, 1981).
39. See F. R. Frankel, *India's Green Revolution*, *op. cit.* For a concise review of most of the case-studies on the issue see Prahaladachar, *op. cit.*
40. For a succinct review of these case-studies see Prahaladachar, *op. cit.*
41. Bhalla's study cited in Prahaladachar, *op. cit.*.
42. S. S. Johl, 'Gains of the Green Revolution; How they have been shared in the Punjab', *Journal of Development Studies* (April 1975). See also Prahaladachar, *op. cit.*, for a summary of other case-studies on this issue.
43. T. J. Byres, 'The New Technology, Class Formation and Class Action in the Indian Countryside', *Journal of Peasant Studies* vol. 8, no. 4 (July 1981), pp. 415–17.
44. C. H. Hanumantha Rao, 'Employment Implications of the Green Revolution and Tractorisation; A Case Study of the Punjab' in Nurul Islam (ed.), *Agricultural Policy in Developing Countries* (London, Macmillan, 1974).
45. For a succinct discussion of the studies on tractorisation and employment see A. K. Sen, *Employment, Technology and Development* (Oxford, Clarendon Press, 1975), pp. 154–65.
46. D. Lal, 'Agricultural Growth, Real Wages, and the Rural Poor in India', *Economic and Political Weekly* (Review of Agriculture, June 1976).
47. W. Ladjinsky, 'Green Revolution in Bihar: The Kosi Area', *Economic and Political Weekly* (27 September 1969).

6 *The Manufacturing Sector*

1. R. B. Sutcliffe, *Industry and Underdevelopment* (London, Addison-Wesley Publishing Company, 1971), p. 17.
2. Padma Desai, 'Alternative Measures of Import Substitution', *Oxford Economic Papers* (November 1969).
3. H. B. Chenery and L. Taylor's estimates cited in R. B. Sutcliffe, *op. cit.*, p. 44.
4. Quoted in F. Frankel, *India's Political Economy, 1947–77, the Gradual Revolution*, *op. cit.*, p. 117.
5. J. N. Bhagwati and P. Desai, *op. cit.*, p. 157.

6. *Sixth Five Year Plan*, *op. cit.*, p. 187.
7. The dramatic increase in the rate of growth of manufacturing output in 1976 was the result of a bumper harvest in 1976 and the Emergency Régime regulations, which prohibited strikes and industrial disputes and also stepped up public investment.
8. J. N. Bhagwati and Desai, *India: Planning for Industrialisation*, *op. cit.*, and J. N. Bhagwati and T. N. Srinivasan, *Foreign Trade Regimes and Economic Development: India*, *op. cit.*
9. Bhagwati and Srinivasan, *op. cit.*, pp. 179–81.
10. *Ibid.*
11. Asit Banerjee, 'Productivity Growth and Factor Substitution in Indian Manufacturing', *op. cit.*
12. Raj Krishna and Mehta, 'Productivity Trends in Large Scale Industries', *Economic and Political Weekly* (October 1968).
13. For a discussion of these methods of estimating total factor productivity see Murray Brown, *On the Theory and Measurement of Technological Change* (Cambridge University Press, 1968).
14. Asit Banerjee, *op. cit.*
15. See Randev Banerji and James Riedel, 'Industrial Employment Expansion under Alternative Trade Strategies', *Journal of Development Economics* 7 (1980), pp. 567–77.
16. D. Lall, *Prices for Planning* (London, Heinemann, 1980), p. 27–45.
17. A. Krueger, 'The Political Economy of the Rent Seeking Society', *American Economic Review* (June 1974), pp. 293–4.
18. See J. N. Bhagwati and P. Desai, *op. cit.*, ch. 9, for a succinct discussion of the productive efficiency of public enterprises in India.
19. Bhagwati and Desai, *op. cit.*
20. Yair Aharoni, *Markets, Planning and Development, The Public and Private Sectors in Economic Development* (Cambridge Massachusetts, Ballinger Publishing Company, 1977), p. 273.
21. J. N. Bhagwati and P. Desai, *op. cit.*, p. 164, summarizes the findings of H. K. Paranjape's report on the *Flight of Technical Personnel in Public Undertakings* (Indian Institute of Public Administraiton, New Delhi, 1964).
22. Estimates of employment growth reported in S. L. Shetty, *Structural Retrogression in the Indian Economy*, *op. cit.*
23. J. W. Mellor, *op. cit.*, p. 116.
24. R. Banerji and J. Reidal, *op. cit.* p. 567–77.
25. J. W. Mellor, *op. cit.*, ch. XI.
26. *Sixth Five Year Plan*, *op. cit.*, p. 187.
27. P. N. Dhar, 'Some observations on small-scale enterprise development', in C. H. Hanumantha Rao and P. C. Joshi (eds), *Reflections on Economic Development and Social Change* (Oxford, Martin Robertson, 1979), pp. 178–9.

28. *Ibid.*
29. *Ibid*, p. 173.
30. *Sixth Five Year Plan*, *op. cit.*, p. 188.
31. See J. C. Sandersara, 'Scale and Technology in Indian Industry', *Bulletin of Oxford University Institute of Economics and Statistics* (August 1966).
32. Nirmala Banerjee, 'Is small beautiful', in Amiya Baggchi and Nirmala Banergee (eds), *Change and Choice in Indian Industry* (Calcutta, K. P. Baggchi and Co., 1981), pp. 277–96.
33. V. N. Balasubramanyam, *The South Indian Entrepreneur*, mimeograph (1976).
34. Based on interview responses in V. N. Balasubramanyam, *ibid.*
35. J. N. Bhagwati and P. Desai, *op. cit.*, p. 302.
36. T. N. Srinivasan and N. S. Narayana, 'Economic Performance Since the Third Plan and its Implications for Policy', *Economic and Political Weekly* (annual number, February 1977), pp. 225–39.
37. Deepak Nayyar, 'Industrial Development in India: Growth or Stagnation', in Baggchi and Nirmala Banerjee (eds), *op. cit.*, pp. 91–117.
38. P. Patnaik, 'An explanatory hypothesis on the Indian industrial stagnation', in Baggchi and Banerjee (eds), *op. cit.*, pp. 66–89.
39. Ashok V. Desai, 'Factors underlying the slow growth of Indian industry' *Economic and Political Weekly* (annual number, March 1981), pp. 381–92.
40. S. Mundle, 'Growth, Disparity and Capital Reorganization in Indian Economy', *Economic and Political Weekly* (annual number, March 1981), pp. 393–408.
41. Deepak Nayyar, *op. cit.*, p. 99.
42. For a detailed discussion of these policies, see J. N. Bhagwati and T. N. Srinivasan, *op. cit.*; also Chapter 9 of this book.
43. A. Maddison, *Class Structure and Economic Growth* (London, Allen and Unwin, 1971), pp. 89–90.

7 *Private Foreign Investment and Technology*

1. N. K. Chandra, 'Western Imperialism and India Today', *Economic and Political Weekly* (February 1973).
2. National Council of Applied Economic Research, *Foreign Technology and Investment: A Study of their Role in India's Industrialisation* (New Delhi, 1971).
3. For a discussion of India's official policy towards private foreign investment and technology see V. N. Balasubramanyam, *International Transfer of Technology to India* (New York, Praeger, 1973).

4. *Development Cooperation*, 1979 Review (Paris, OECD Secretariat).
5. S. Lal and S. Mohammad, 'Multinationals in Indian Big Business', *Journal of Development Economics* no. 13 (1983), p. 144.
6. Estimated from data in *Statistical Outline of India* (Department of Economics and Statistics, Tata Services Ltd, Bombay, 1976), tables 97 and 93.
7. Vijay L. Kelkar, 'The Impact of Private Foreign Investment in India, 1964–72; An Economic Analysis' in C. Wadhva (ed.), *Some Problems of India's Economic Policy*, *op. cit.*, p. 735.
8. C. P. Kindleberger, *American Business Abroad* (New Haven, Yale University Press, 1969).
9. Vijay L. Kelkar, *op. cit.*, p. 737.
10. Vijay L. Kelkar, *op. cit.*
11. J. P. Agarwal, 'Productivity of Foreign and Domestic Firms in Indian Industries', *Weltwirtschaffliches Archiv* (Band 115, Heft 1) (1979).
12. Deepak Lal, *Appraising Foreign Investment in Developing Countries* (London, Heinemann, 1975).
13. *Ibid*, pp. 94–144.
14. P. Streeten, 'New Approaches to Private Overseas Investment', in P. Ady (ed.), *Private Foreign Investment and the Development World* (New York, Praeger, 1971), p. 250.
15. For a detailed discussion of these arguments see V. N. Balasubramanyam and A. I. MacBean, *Meeting the Third World Challenge* (London, Macmillan, 1976), ch. 8.
16. Howard Pack, 'The Substitution of Labour for Capital in Kenyan Manufacturing', *Economic Journal* (March 1976), pp. 45–58; also William Courtney and M. Leipziger, 'Multinational Corporations in LDCs, The Choice of Technology', *Bulletin of the Oxford University Institute of Economics and Statistics* (November 1974), pp. 297–304.
17. J. P. Agarwal, 'Factor Proportions in Foreign and Domestic Firms in Indian Manufacturing', *Economic Journal* (September 1976), pp. 589–664.
18. J. P. Agarwal, 'Productivity of Foreign and Domestic Firms in Indian Industries', *op. cit.*
19. S. Morley and G. Smith, 'Limited Search and the Technology Choices of Multinational Firms in Brazil', *Quarterly Journal of Economics* (May 1977), pp. 263–87.
20. For a succinct discussion of the problems associated with the pricing of technologies see Farok J. Contractor, *International Technology Licensing; Compensation, Costs and Negotiation* (Massachusetts, Lexington Books, D. C. Heath and Company, 1981).
21. V. N. Balasubramanyam, *op. cit.*, ch. 5.
22. V. N. Balasubramanyam, *op. cit.*, p. 83.
23. V. N. Balasubramanyam, *op. cit.*, ch. 6.

24. Reserve Bank of India, *Foreign Collaboration in Indian Industry: Second Survey Report 1974* (Bombay 1974).
25. R. Vernon, *Storm Over the Multinationals; the Real Issues* (Cambridge Massachusetts, Harvard University Press, 1977), pp. 160–1.
26. V. N. Balasubramanyam, *op. cit.*, ch. 5.

8 *Foreign Aid in India's Development Process*

1. For an exposition of this view see Teresa Hayter, *Aid as Imperialism* (Harmondsworth, Pelican, 1971).
2. Keith Griffin, 'Foreign Capital Domestic Savings and Economic Development', *Bulletin, Oxford University Institute of Economics and Statistics* (May 1970).
3. See P. T. Bauer, *Dissent on Development* (London, Weidenfeld and Nicolson, 1971).
4. B. R. Shenoy, *Indian Economic Policy* (Bombay, Popular Porakashan, 1968).
5. C. P. Bhambri, *World Bank and India* (New Delhi, Vikas Publishing Houses, 1980), p. 3.
6. *Ibid*, p. 128.
7. R. Sau, 'Economic Crisis and Economic Theory', *Economic and Political Weekly* (annual number, 1982), p. 585.
8. *Sixth Five Year Plan*, *op. cit.*, p. 6.
9. Estimated from data in *Development Co-operation*, Development Assistance Committee Report (Paris, OECD, 1980).
10. For comprehensive estimates for the years 1961–4 see J. N. Bhagwati, *Amount and Sharing of Aid* (Washington D.C., Overseas Development Council, 1970).
11. *Ibid*, pp. 52 and 68.
12. R. Cassen, *India, Population, Economy and Society op. cit.*, p. 332.
13. J. N. Bhagwati, *The Economics of Underdeveloped Countries* (New York, McGraw-Hill, 1966), p. 218.
14. Even in the case of grants the amount of real resources transferred may fall short of the nominal amounts of the grants, both because of increases in the price level in the donor countries, and through the practice of 'aid-tying'.
15. *Development Co-operation*, *op. cit.*, p. 241.
16. M. Lipton and J. Firn, *The Erosion of a Relationship: India and Britain since 1960* (London, Oxford University Press, 1975).
17. For a comprehensive discussion of the methods and costs of tied aid, see J. N. Bhagwati, 'The Tying of Aid' in J. N. Bhagwati and R. S. Eckaus (eds), *Foreign Aid* (Harmondsworth, Penguin, 1970).

18. In this context it is of significance, as Bhagwati and Desai argue, that India's import-licensing system which has often specified both the source and the commodities to be imported may have contributed to *de facto* double-tying of aid: J. N. Bhagwati and P. Desai, *India, Planning For Industrialisation*, *op. cit.*, p. 203.
19. Bhagwati and Desai, *op. cit.* p. 201.
20. See Bhagwati, *Amount and Sharing of Aid*, *op. cit.*
21. Estimated from data in Report on Currency and Finance (Reserve Bank of India, Bombay, various issues).
22. *Sixth Five Year Plan*, *op. cit.*
23. Pramit Chaudhuri, *The Indian Economy*, *op. cit.*, p. 106.
24. *Ibid*, p. 107.
25. Isher J. Ahluwalia, 'An Analysis of Price and Output Behaviour in the Indian Economy', *Journal of Development Economics* (1979), pp. 363–90.
26. For a succinct review of these studies, see J. N. Bhagwati and S. Chakvarty, 'Contributions to Indian Economic Analysis: A Survey', *American Economic Review* (September 1969).

9 *Foreign Trade*

1. M. Lipton and J. Firn, *The Erosion of a Relationship: India and Britain since 1960, op. cit.*, p. 219.
2. For a detailed exposition of India's import control régime see J. N. Bhagwati and T. N. Srinivasan, *Foreign Trade Regimes and Economic Development: India*, *op. cit.*
3. For a summary of the critique of the comparative cost doctrine see H. B. Chenery, 'Comparative Advantage and Development Policy', *American Economic Review* (March 1961).
4. J. N. Bhagwati and V. K. Ramaswamy, 'Domestic Distortions Tariffs and the Theory of Optimum Subsidy', *Journal of Political Economy* (February 1963).
5. R. Nurkse, *Patterns of Trade and Development* (Wicksell Lectures, Amquist and Wicksell, Stockholm, 1959).
6. R. Prebisch, 'The Role of Commercial Policies in Underdeveloped Countries', *American Economic Review* (Papers and Proceedings) (May 1959); H. Singer, 'The Distribution of Gains between Investing and Borrowing Countries', *American Economic Review* (Papers and Proceedings) (May 1950).
7. For a succinct discussion of India's export performance during the fifties see J. N. Bhagwati and P. Desai, *India: Planning for Industrialisation*, *op. cit.*, ch. 18.
8. J. N. Bhagwati and P. Desai, *op. cit.*

9. J. N. Bhagwati and T. N. Srinivasan, *Foreign Trade Regimes and Economic Development: India*, *op. cit.*, p. 46–9.
10. For a detailed analysis of the June 1966 devaluation and the export subsidy schemes see J. N. Bhagwati and T. N. Srinivasan, *op. cit.*
11. S. K. Verghese, 'Export Assistance Policy and Export Performance of India in the Seventies', *Economic and Political Weekly* (annual number, February 1978), pp. 245–76.
12. R. Banerji and J. Reidel, 'Industrial Employment Expansion under Alternative Trade Strategies; case of India and Taiwan, 1950–1970', *op. cit.*
13. Sumitra Chishti, 'Exports and Employment in India', *Economic and Political Weekly* (17 October 1981), pp. 1710–14.
14. J. N. Bhagwati and P. Desai, *op. cit.*, p. 466.
15. Quoted in Sunanda Sen, 'From Import Substitution to Export Promotion; Policy Planning in India's Foreign Trade Sector', *Economic and Political Weekly* (annual number, 1982), p. 631.
16. See for instance the summary of import-export policy for 1981–2 in *Report on Currency and Finance 1980–81* (Reserve Bank of India, Bombay), p. 290–3.
17. See articles by Sunanda Sen, *op. cit.*; Deepak Nayyar, 'India's Balance of Payments', *Economic and Political Weekly* (annual number, April 1982), and Sumitra Chisti, *op. cit.*
18. Deepak Nayyar, *India's Exports and Export Policies in the Sixties* (Cambridge University Press, 1976), p. 376.
19. J. N. Bhagwati, *Anatomy and Consequences of Exchange Control Regimes* (New York, National Bureau of Economic Research, 1978), ch. 8.
20. Deepak Lal, *Prices for Planning, Towards the Reform of Indian Planning*, *op. cit.*, ch. 8.

10 *Summing Up*

1. See Alec Cairncross, *Factors in Economic Development*, *op. cit.*; and for a discussion of this view in the Indian context, P. R. Brahmananda and C. N. Vakil, *Planning for an Expanding Economy* (Vora, Bombay, 1965).
2. See for instance Helen Hughes, 'Pessimism and a way out', in C. Saunders (ed.), *The Political Economy of New and Old Industrial Countries* (London, Butterworth, 1981), p. 105.
3. R. Sinha, P. Pearson, G. Kadekodi and M. Gregory, *Income Distribution, Growth and Basic Needs in India* (London, Croom Helm, 1979).
4. P. Streeten, 'Trade as the Engine, Handmaiden, Brake or Offspring of Growth', *The World Economy* (December 1982), p. 416.

5. For one of the very few cogent expositions of the Left-oriented views on Indian economic performance and policy see Amiya K. Bagchi, 'Reinforcing and offsetting constraints in Indian industry', in A. Baggchi and N. Banerjee (eds), *Change and Choice in Indian Industry*, *op. cit.*, pp. 23–62.

Selected Bibliography

Set out below is a selected bibliography relating to various aspects of the Indian economy. It is in no sense a comprehensive list. Having been prepared for general readers as well as students, it is confined to books, monographs, and volumes of collected essays; journal articles, of which there are legion, have been cited, where relevant, in the Notes and References. In addition to books specifically on India, general books on economic development incorporating India's development experience as a case-study have also been cited.

General

P. T. Bauer, *Indian Economic Policy and Development* (London, George Allen and Unwin, 1961): a critique of India's industrialization-oriented development strategy, concentrating on the Second Five-Year Plan.

J. N. Bhagwati, *The Economics of Underdeveloped Countries* (London, Weidenfeld and Nicolson, 1966): a general introduction to problems of underdevelopment with several references to India's experience.

J. N. Bhagwati and S. Chakravarthy, *Contributions to Indian Economic Analysis: A Survey* (New Delhi, Lalvani Publishing Company, 1972). Originally published as a supplement to the *American Economic Review*, this monograph provides a succinct analysis of the theoretical framework of India's first three Five-Year Plans, and a lucid review of the writings by Indian economists on agriculture and foreign trade aspects of the Indian economy.

Pramit Chaudhuri, *The Indian Economy: Poverty and Development* (London, Crosby Lockwood Staples, 1978). Provides a survey of India's economic problems and performance from the fifties to the early seventies. The emphasis of the book is on the structure and measurement of poverty in India. Also of interest to the student are the chapters on agriculture and the role of the State.

Francine Frankel, *India's Political Economy, 1947–1977, The Gradual Revolution* (New Jersey, Princeton University Press, 1978): a detailed annotated account of the evolution of India's economic policy. An invaluable guide to the study of the role of institutional factors in the development process and the interrelationship between economic and political development strategies.

John P. Lewis, *Quiet Crisis in India* (New York, Doubleday and Company Inc., 1964). Provides an analysis of planning strategy and plan implementation, including a review of the Third Five-Year Plan document. Worth reading for its defence of India's heavy-industry-oriented strategy, the analysis of problems of agriculture and exports, and the stake of the United States in India's development.

A. I. MacBean and V. N. Balasubramanyam, *Meeting the Third World Challenge* (London, Macmillan, for the Trade Policy Research Centre, 1978). Provides a review of the major issues relating to industrialization, trade, aid and foreign private investment in the developing countries. The chapters on the roles of the State and industrialization draw heavily on India's experience.

A. Maddison, *Class Structure and Economic Growth: India and Pakistan Since the Moghuls* (London, George Allen and Unwin, 1971): a concise and highly readable discussion of the relationship between social structure and economic performance in India and Pakistan. Especially interesting are the chapters on 'Moghul economy and society', emphasizing the institutional constraints which prevented the economy from making optimal use of its resources, and 'Social Impact of India's Socialist Pattern', which discusses the failure of Indian economic policy to achieve the stated objectives during the first fifteen years of planning.

W. Malenbaum, *Prospects for Indian Development* (London, George Allen and Unwin Ltd, 1962). Provides a scholarly analysis of the structure of the Indian economy and economic performance during the first decade of economic planning.

Gunnar Myrdal, *Asian Drama: An Enquiry into the Poverty of Nations* (New York, Pantheon, 1968): a massively detailed study of the economic, social and political conditions, attitudes and institutions in eleven Asian countries including India. This two-thousand-page book in three volumes is a daunting prospect for the student, but it would be rewarding to read selectively on such issues as corruption – its causes and effects – problems of labour utilization, and population and population policy.

Collected Essays

Pramit Chaudhuri (ed.), *Aspects of Indian Economic Development* (London, George Allen and Unwin, 1971): a collection of ten previously published essays principally on agriculture, aid and human resources. Noteworthy are the editor's introductory essay on India's economic objectives, achievements and constraints, Robert Cassen's essay on population control, and Amartya Sen's essay on crisis in Indian education.

C. H. Hanumantha Rao and P. C. Joshi (eds), *Reflections on Economic Development and Social Change*, essays in honour of V. K. R. V. Rao (Oxford, Martin Robertson, 1979): a collection of twenty-four essays by economists and sociologists on various aspects of economic development and social change, including issues relating to the role of economic theory in the analysis of development problems. Of particular interest to students of the Indian economy are P. N. Dhar's essay on 'Small-scale Enterprise

Development', C. H. Hanumantha Rao's essay on 'Factor Endowments, Technology and Farm Employment', and Rati Ram and T. W. Schultz's essay on 'Some Economic Implications of Increases in Life Span with Special Reference to India'.

J. S. Uppal (ed.), *India's Economic Problems: An Analytical Approach* (New Delhi, Tata-McGraw Hill, 1983): a collection of essays written by Indian economists residing abroad on various aspects of the Indian economy, such as structural change, problems of agricultural development, inflation and economic growth, and taxation and economic development.

C. Wadhava (ed.), *Some Problems of India's Economic Policy* (New Delhi, Tata-McGraw Hill, 1977): a collection of forty-two essays – mostly previously published – on various aspects of the Indian economy. This volume includes a number of celebrated but not easily accessible essays, such as K. N. Raj's essay on 'Growth Models and Indian Planning' and essays by Raj Krishna, M. L. Danlawala and V. M. Dandekar on various aspects of India's agricultural sector.

Population, Poverty and Employment

R. H. Cassen, *India: Population, Economy, Society* (London, Macmillan, 1978). Provides a lucid discussion of the interrelationship between population growth and development. Especially valuable to the student are the discussion on the rate of return to investment in children, and the analysis of various aspects of population policy. This book also provides a cogent summary of the literature on poverty and unemployment in India.

H. B. Chenery *et al.*, *Redistribution with Growth* (London, Oxford University Press, for the World Bank and the Institute of Development Studies Sussex, 1974). This book consists of thirteen essays on various aspects of growth and inequality in developing countries, including issues relating to the concept and measurement of inequality and policies directed at promoting growth with redistribution. The annex to the book, on country experience, includes a case-study of India by Pranab Bardhan.

V. M. Dandekar and N. Rath, *Poverty in India* (Poona, Indian School of Political Economy, 1971). Originally published in the pages of the *Economic and Political Weekly*, this monograph represents one of the first attempts at estimating the extent of poverty in India. It is also well worth reading for its advocacy of increased employment opportunities, as opposed to land redistribution policies, as a solution to the problem of poverty.

G. S. Fields, *Poverty, Inequality and Development* (Cambridge, Cambridge University Press, 1980). Analyses the relationship between different patterns of growth and inequality. Provides a concise discussion of the concepts and measurement of inequality and development, and also includes a review of the empirical estimates of inequality and poverty in India and other developing countries.

A. K. Sen, *Employment, Technology and Development* (Oxford, Clarendon Press, 1965). This monograph discusses the general issue of technological choice as a part of economic policy in developing countries. It is invaluable to the student of development economics for its concise discussion of the concepts of employment, surplus labour and disguised unemployment. Also included are four lengthy appendices on various aspects of unemployment in India, including a study of tractorization in Indian agriculture.

A. K. Sen, *Poverty and Famines: An Essay on Entitlement and Deprivation* (Oxford, Clarendon Press, 1982): a lucid presentation of the view that it is not a decline in the availability of food but lack of purchasing power that is the major cause of starvation and poverty.

T. N. Srinivasan and P. K. Bardhan (eds), *Poverty and Income Distribution In India* (Calcutta, Statistical Publishing Society, 1974): a collection of essays by eminent Indian economists on methodological, empirical and policy issues relating to poverty and income distribution. Notable are the essays by P. K. Bardhan on the pattern of income distribution in India, A. Vaidyanathan's essay on inequalities in living standards in India, and T. N. Srinivasan's survey of policy aspects.

Agriculture

K. Bharadwaj, *Production Conditions in Indian Agriculture* (Cambridge, Cambridge University Press, 1974). This monograph is an empirical analysis of the factors accounting for the observed inverse relationship between farm size and productivity. It is a notable example of scholarly empirical analysis of a widely debated issue.

Pramit Chaudhuri, *Readings in Indian Agricultural Development* (London, George Allen and Unwin, 1972): a collection of ten essays with an empirical slant on Indian agriculture. Of particular interest to the student are R. Thamarajakshi's essay on intersectoral terms of trade, S. Mehra's essay on surplus labour in Indian agriculture, and T. N. Krishnan's essay on the marketed surplus in food grains.

Francine Frankel, *India's Green Revolution: Economic Gains and Political Costs* (New Jersey, Princeton University Press, 1971). Analyses the impact of the Green Revolution on growth and equity in Indian agriculture. The four case-studies in the book provide interesting reading. This study is well known for its conclusion that although the Green Revolution has improved incomes and yields it has widened income disparities in Indian agriculture.

A. M. Khusro (ed.), *Readings in Agricultural Development* (Bombay, Allied Publishers, 1968): a book of readings on various aspects of Indian agriculture. It is useful as a work of reference, and includes such classic articles as 'Farm Supply Responses in India and Pakistan: A Case Study of the Punjab' by Raj Krishna and 'Returns to Scale in Indian Agriculture' by A. M. Khusro.

A. M. Khusro, *Economics of Land Reform and Farm Size in India* (Madras, Macmillan Studies, 1973): a pioneering study of the problems of farm size and tenurial conditions in Indian agriculture. Notable for its application of the tools of economic theory to an analysis of the case for land reform, and the analysis of optimum size of farms in India.

Louis J. Walinsky (ed.), *Agrarian Reform as Unfinished Business*; selected papers of Wolf Ladejinsky (London, Oxford University Press, 1977): a collection of more than sixty articles by Ladejinsky on various aspects of agricultural development. Of interest to the student of the Indian economy are the articles on land reform and the Green Revolution.

J. W. Mellor, *The New Economics of Growth: A Strategy for India and the Developing World* (Ithaca, Cornell University Press, 1976). Provides a discussion of the problems and performance of India's agricultural sector, and outlines a strategy for growth centred on technological change in agriculture and rural development. The effects of the proposed strategy on employment and growth is illustrated in the context of a simulation model. It is also worth reading for its succinct review of India's industrialization experience and the commentary on foreign aid.

Industrialization and Foreign Trade

Amiya Bagchi and Nirmala Banerji (eds), *Change and Choice in Indian Industry* (Calcutta, J. P. Bagchi and Company, 1981): a collection of fifteen essays on various aspects of India's industrialization. This book is invaluable to students attempting to get a perspective on current policy debates in India.

J. N. Bhagwati and P. Desai, *India, Planning for Industrialisation* (London, Oxford University Press, 1970): a lucid and well-documented critique of India's industrialization and trade policies in the two decades since 1947. The main thesis of the book is that Indian planning was excessively detailed and was characterized by an extravagant display of bureaucratic controls and restrictions which had no economic rationale. The book provides valuable lessons on how neglect of basic economic cost considerations can bring the best-laid plans to grief.

J. N. Bhagwati and T. N. Srinivasan, *Foreign Trade Regimes and Economic Development: India* (Delhi, Macmillan, 1976): an incisive analysis of the impact of India's foreign-trade and exchange-rate policies on growth, innovation, savings and investment. The major conclusion of the book is that the interventionist foreign-trade régime of India in conjunction with domestic licensing policies led to economic inefficiencies and impaired the performance of the economy. Of particular interest to students of development economics is the analysis and estimation of purchasing-power-parity effective exchange rates for imports and exports, and domestic resource costs for various Indian industry groups.

Manmohan Singh, *India's Export Trends and Prospects for Self-Contained Growth* (Oxford, Clarendon Press, 1964). Provides a comprehensive account of the performance of India's exports, commodity by commodity, during the decade of the fifties.

Deepak Nayyar, *India's Exports and Export Policies in the 1960s* (Cambridge, Cambridge University Press, 1976). Provides a detailed account of India's export performance and policies during the decade of the sixties. One of the principal conclusions of the book is that India's export performance is likely to be determined by economic growth rather than the other way round.

Martin Wolf, *India's Exports* (London, Oxford University Press, 1982): a critical review of India's export performance and policies up to the end of the decade of the 1970s. One of the main conclusions of the book is that India's overall trade and development policies, rather than the external economic environment, have been a major constraint on the growth of Indian exports.

Index

Index

For Product Safety Concerns and Information please contact our EU representative GPSR@taylorandfrancis.com Taylor & Francis Verlag GmbH, Kaufingerstraße 24, 80331 München, Germany

Batch number: 10726013

Printed by Printforce, the Netherlands